Reinforcement Learning

From Basics to Expert Proficiency

Contents

1 Introduction to Reinforcement Learning **11**

1.1 What is Reinforcement Learning? 11

1.2 History and Evolution of Reinforcement Learning 13

1.3 Key Concepts and Terminology 17

1.4 Differences Between Supervised, Unsupervised, and Reinforcement Learning 20

1.5 Elements of a Reinforcement Learning System 23

1.6 The Reinforcement Learning Problem 25

1.7 Exploration vs. Exploitation 28

1.8 Case Studies and Real-World Applications 30

1.9 Tools and Libraries for Reinforcement Learning 35

1.10 Challenges and Future Directions in Reinforcement Learning 38

2 Markov Decision Processes **43**

2.1 Introduction to Markov Decision Processes 43

2.2 Components of MDPs: States, Actions, and Rewards . 46

2.3 The Markov Property 48

2.4 Transition Probabilities and Transition Matrices 51

2.5 Policies: Deterministic and Stochastic 53

2.6 Value Functions and Bellman Equations 55

2.7 Optimality and Solution Methods for MDPs 58

2.8 Discount Factor and Horizon 60
2.9 Solving MDPs Using Dynamic Programming 63
2.10 MDPs in Continuous Spaces 66
2.11 Applications and Examples of MDPs 69

3 Dynamic Programming **73**
3.1 Introduction to Dynamic Programming 73
3.2 Principles of Optimality 76
3.3 Value Iteration 79
3.4 Policy Iteration 82
3.5 Asynchronous Dynamic Programming 84
3.6 Efficiency and Convergence of Dynamic Programming . 87
3.7 Generalized Policy Iteration 89
3.8 Comparing Value and Policy Iteration 91
3.9 Dealing with Infinite State and Action Spaces 94
3.10 Approximate Dynamic Programming 97
3.11 Applications and Examples of Dynamic Programming . 99

4 Monte Carlo Methods **103**
4.1 Introduction to Monte Carlo Methods 103
4.2 Monte Carlo Prediction 106
4.3 Monte Carlo Control 109
4.4 First-Visit vs. Every-Visit Monte Carlo 112
4.5 Exploring Starts 114
4.6 Importance Sampling 116
4.7 Off-Policy Prediction Using Importance Sampling 119
4.8 Monte Carlo with Function Approximation 122
4.9 Batch Monte Carlo Methods 125
4.10 Applications and Examples of Monte Carlo Methods . . 128

5 Temporal-Difference Learning **133**

5.1 Introduction to Temporal-Difference Learning 133
5.2 TD Prediction 136
5.3 TD Control 138
5.4 Q-learning 140
5.5 SARSA 142
5.6 n-step Bootstrapping 145
5.7 Eligibility Traces 147
5.8 Comparing TD, Monte Carlo, and Dynamic Programming 149
5.9 TD with Function Approximation 152
5.10 Off-policy TD Learning 154
5.11 Applications and Examples of TD Learning 157

6 Function Approximation 161

6.1 Introduction to Function Approximation 161
6.2 Linear Function Approximation 163
6.3 Non-linear Function Approximation 167
6.4 Gradient Descent Methods 170
6.5 Incremental Methods and Stochastic Gradient Descent 173
6.6 The Bias-Variance Trade-off 176
6.7 Training and Evaluating Approximators 178
6.8 Function Approximation in Value Prediction 182
6.9 Function Approximation in Control 184
6.10 Tile Coding and Coarse Coding 187
6.11 Applications and Case Studies of Function Approximation 190

7 Policy Gradient Methods 195

7.1 Introduction to Policy Gradient Methods 195
7.2 Concept of Policy Gradient 197
7.3 REINFORCE Algorithm 199
7.4 Variance Reduction Techniques 202

7.5 Actor-Critic Methods 205

7.6 Advantage Actor-Critic (A2C) and Asynchronous A2C (A3C) 207

7.7 Natural Gradient 209

7.8 Deterministic Policy Gradients (DPG) 211

7.9 Trust Region Policy Optimization (TRPO) 213

7.10 Proximal Policy Optimization (PPO) 216

7.11 Applications and Examples of Policy Gradient Methods 218

8 Deep Reinforcement Learning 223

8.1 Introduction to Deep Reinforcement Learning 223

8.2 Deep Q-Networks (DQN) 226

8.3 Improvements on DQN: Double DQN, Dueling DQN, and Prioritized Experience Replay 230

8.4 Deep Deterministic Policy Gradient (DDPG) 234

8.5 Twin Delayed DDPG (TD3) 236

8.6 Soft Actor-Critic (SAC) 238

8.7 Combining Convolutional Neural Networks with RL . . . 242

8.8 Combining Recurrent Neural Networks with RL 245

8.9 Model-Based Deep Reinforcement Learning 248

8.10 Exploration Strategies in Deep RL 251

8.11 Applications and Case Studies of Deep Reinforcement Learning 254

9 Hierarchical Reinforcement Learning 257

9.1 Introduction to Hierarchical Reinforcement Learning . . 257

9.2 Motivation and Benefits of Hierarchical RL 260

9.3 Temporal Abstraction and Options Framework 262

9.4 Semi-Markov Decision Processes (SMDPs) 264

9.5 Learning and Planning with Options 267

9.6 Hierarchical DQN 270

9.7 Feudal Reinforcement Learning 273
9.8 Subgoal Discovery and Identification 276
9.9 Hierarchical Actor-Critic Methods 280
9.10 Applications and Case Studies of Hierarchical Reinforcement Learning 282
9.11 Challenges and Future Directions in Hierarchical RL . . 285

10 Applications of Reinforcement Learning 289
10.1 Introduction to Applications of Reinforcement Learning . 289
10.2 Reinforcement Learning in Robotics 292
10.3 Reinforcement Learning for Game Playing 295
10.4 Recommendation Systems 298
10.5 Finance and Trading 301
10.6 Healthcare and Medicine 304
10.7 Autonomous Vehicles 307
10.8 Energy Management 309
10.9 Natural Language Processing and Dialog Systems . . . 312
10.10 Industrial Automation 316
10.11 Future Trends and Innovations in RL Applications 319

Introduction

Reinforcement Learning (RL) stands as one of the most dynamic areas in machine learning, bringing numerous possibilities to tackle decision-making problems where agents learn to make a series of decisions by interacting with the environment. The goal is to maximize cumulative reward, with strategies that have found applications in various domains, from robotics to finance.

The origins of Reinforcement Learning can be traced back to the fields of psychology and neuroscience, hinting at the processes by which animals, including humans, learn from interactions. Throughout its history, advancements in computational power and theoretical understanding have crystallized into the sophisticated algorithms used today.

In RL, key concepts and terminology form the foundation of understanding. The agent, environment, states, actions, rewards, policy, value function, and model are central elements. These terms refer to the components involved in decision-making processes and guide the development of RL algorithms.

One must distinguish Reinforcement Learning from other paradigms in machine learning. Unlike supervised learning, where the model learns from a provided set of example inputs and outputs, RL learns from the consequences of actions in an environment. Unsupervised learning, on the other hand, deals with finding patterns and structure in data without explicit feedback. RL's uniqueness lies in its focus on sequential decision making through interaction.

The elements of an RL system include the policy, which defines the agent's behavior, the reward signal as the goal to achieve, the value function providing an expectation of future rewards, and the model, which mimics the behavior of the environment. Together, these components create the architecture upon which RL algorithms are constructed.

The RL problem can be framed as a Markov Decision Process (MDP), providing a mathematical foundation for defining states, actions, rewards, and state transitions. The agent's goal is to discover a policy that maximizes the long-term return, a process that involves balancing exploration (trying new actions) and exploitation (leveraging known actions).

Real-world applications of RL are vast and varied. From learning policies for playing games such as Go and Chess, managing investments in finance, optimizing recommendations in e-commerce, to controlling robots and autonomous vehicles, the potential of RL continues to expand.

Tools and libraries such as TensorFlow, PyTorch, OpenAI Gym, and others provide practitioners with resources to develop and experiment with RL algorithms. These resources facilitate the practical implementation and testing of theoretical concepts, bringing research advancements closer to real-world applications.

Despite the significant progress made, challenges remain. Issues such as sample inefficiency, the trade-off between exploration and exploitation, and the difficulty of reward design, as well as the generalization to unseen states and tasks, continue to drive research in this field. Additionally, ethical considerations, particularly around the deployment of autonomous systems, require ongoing attention.

Reinforcement Learning promises substantial advancements and applications across various domains. This book is designed to guide readers through the essential subjects of RL, from the basics to expert proficiency, offering comprehensive insights into core concepts and methodologies. By the end of this journey, readers will be equipped with the necessary knowledge and tools to apply RL to complex decision-making problems.

Chapter 1

Introduction to Reinforcement Learning

Reinforcement Learning (RL) is a branch of machine learning focused on training agents to make sequential decisions by interacting with an environment to maximize cumulative reward. This chapter explores the key concepts and terminology in RL, differentiates it from supervised and unsupervised learning, and outlines the components of an RL system. Additionally, the chapter addresses the fundamental RL problem, highlights real-world applications, discusses available tools and libraries, and examines the current challenges and future directions in the field.

1.1 What is Reinforcement Learning?

Reinforcement Learning (RL) is an area of machine learning concerned with how agents ought to take actions in an environment to maximize some notion of cumulative reward. Unlike supervised learning, where the learning process is guided by a dataset of input-output pairs, RL deals with agents that must learn from the consequences of their actions, guided by the feedback received from the environment.

The basic premise of RL involves an agent that interacts with an environment E. The agent can take various actions A, observe the state S of the environment resulting from those actions, and receive rewards

R that indicate the value of those actions with respect to an objective. Formally, this can be represented as a tuple (S, A, P, R), where:

- S denotes the set of all possible states of the environment.
- A denotes the set of all possible actions the agent can take.
- P is the state transition probability, $P(s'|s, a)$, representing the probability of transitioning to state s' from state s after taking action a.
- R denotes the reward function $R(s, a, s')$, representing the immediate reward received after transitioning from state s to state s' due to action a.

The goal of the RL agent is to learn a policy π, which is a mapping from states to actions, $\pi : S \rightarrow A$, that maximizes some cumulative reward over time. This cumulative reward is often termed as the *return* and is typically defined as the sum of discounted future rewards:

$$G_t = \sum_{k=0}^{\infty} \gamma^k R_{t+k+1}$$

where γ ($0 \leq \gamma \leq 1$) is the discount factor that reduces the value of rewards received in the future, emphasizing the importance of immediate rewards over distant ones.

A key distinction in Reinforcement Learning is whether the environment is modeled explicitly (model-based) or implicitly (model-free). In model-based RL, the agent builds an explicit model of P and R to understand the environment fully and uses this model to plan its actions. Conversely, in model-free RL, the agent directly learns the policy π or the value functions associated with the states and actions, broadly falling into methods like Q-learning and policy gradient methods.

The agent's learning process can be described as follows:

1. **Initialization:** The agent starts with an initial policy π and initializes the value functions.
2. **Interaction:** At each time step, the agent observes the current state s_t and selects an action a_t based on its policy π. The environment responds to this action by transitioning to a new state s_{t+1} and provides a reward r_t.

3. **Update:** The agent updates its policy π and value functions based on the received reward and the new state s_{t+1}. This involves altering the policy or value functions to improve future actions.

4. **Iteration:** Steps 2 and 3 are repeated until a termination condition is met, which could be reaching a certain number of time steps, episodes, or convergence of policy or value functions.

To understand RL in concrete terms, consider a classic example: an RL agent learning to play a game like chess. The states S may represent different board configurations, actions A are possible moves, the state transition probability P denotes the resulting board configuration after a move, and the reward R may be defined such that winning the game yields a positive reward, losing yields a negative reward, and intermediate moves may yield smaller rewards reflecting good or bad positional play.

A critical aspect of Reinforcement Learning is the balance between *exploration* and *exploitation*. Exploration involves trying out new actions to discover their effects and improve the understanding of the environment. Exploitation, on the other hand, involves selecting the best-known action to maximize reward based on current knowledge. Balancing these two aspects is fundamental to the RL agent's success and is often handled under strategies like ϵ-greedy policies, where with probability ϵ, the agent explores randomly, and with probability $1 - \epsilon$, it exploits the best-known action.

The versatility of Reinforcement Learning allows it to be applied in a wide array of domains, from robotics, where agents learn to perform tasks, to finance, where they optimize trading strategies, and to games, where they master complex strategies. The continuous interaction between the agent and the environment, coupled with the objective of cumulative reward maximization, sets RL apart as a powerful paradigm within the broader spectrum of machine learning.

1.2 History and Evolution of Reinforcement Learning

The origins of reinforcement learning (RL) can be traced back to the early 20th century and the fields of psychology and control theory.

While control theory focused on optimizing system behaviors given a set of constraints, psychological theories on animal learning provided the groundwork by studying how behaviors could be shaped by rewards and punishments. These roots eventually merged to form the foundation of RL as we know it today.

The early 1900s saw the introduction of *classical conditioning* by Ivan Pavlov and *operant conditioning* by B.F. Skinner. Pavlov's experiments demonstrated that behaviors could be conditioned through repeated associations between a neutral stimulus and an unconditioned stimulus. On the other hand, Skinner's work introduced the concept of reinforcement—positive reinforcement (rewards) and negative reinforcement (punishments)—as mechanisms for encouraging or discouraging behaviors. These ideas were fundamental in shaping the concept that actions could be influenced by their consequences, a core principle in RL.

In the mid-20th century, the field of cybernetics, introduced by Norbert Wiener, established connections between feedback mechanisms in biological and computational systems. Although cybernetics primarily influenced control theory, the idea of feedback loops and goal-directed behavior further hinted at the possibility of machines capable of learning behaviors through interactions with their environment.

The formalization of RL as an area of study commenced in the 1950s and 1960s with the development of dynamic programming. Richard Bellman's work in *dynamic programming* laid the theoretical groundwork for many RL algorithms. Bellman introduced concepts such as the *Bellman equation*, which expresses the relationship between the value of a state and the values of subsequent states. This principle became the backbone for later developments like *value iteration* and *policy iteration* methods.

It was in the 1980s that RL began to emerge as a distinct area within artificial intelligence (AI) and machine learning. Researchers like Sutton and Barto made significant strides in formalizing RL concepts and algorithms. They introduced the *temporal-difference learning* (TD Learning) method, which combined ideas from dynamic programming and Monte Carlo methods. TD Learning estimates the value of a policy based on an observed reward and the estimated value of the subsequent state, thus enabling efficient learning from raw experience.

```
def td_learning(env, episodes, alpha, gamma):
    state_values = defaultdict(float)
    for episode in range(episodes):
        state = env.reset()
```

```
        done = False
        while not done:
            next_state, reward, done = env.step()
            best_next_value = state_values[next_state]
            state_values[state] += alpha * (reward + gamma * best_next_value -
                state_values[state])
            state = next_state
    return state_values
```

During the same period, Q-learning was introduced by Watkins. Q-learning is an off-policy RL algorithm that aims to learn the action-value function, which estimates the expected utility of taking a given action in a given state and following the optimal policy thereafter. Notably, Q-learning can find an optimal policy without requiring a model of the environment, making it a model-free approach.

```
def q_learning(env, episodes, alpha, gamma, epsilon):
    q_table = defaultdict(lambda: np.zeros(env.action_space.n))
    for episode in range(episodes):
        state = env.reset()
        done = False
        while not done:
            if np.random.rand() < epsilon:
                action = env.action_space.sample()
            else:
                action = np.argmax(q_table[state])
            next_state, reward, done = env.step(action)
            best_next_action = np.argmax(q_table[next_state])
            q_table[state][action] += alpha * (reward + gamma * q_table[next_state][
                best_next_action] - q_table[state][action])
            state = next_state
    return q_table
```

The 1990s marked significant progress in the application and refinement of RL algorithms. Techniques such as *SARSA* (State-Action-Reward-State-Action) were introduced, providing the basis for on-policy learning. Moreover, researchers began exploring the integration of RL with function approximation methods like neural networks, addressing scalability issues in state and action spaces.

```
def sarsa(env, episodes, alpha, gamma, epsilon):
    q_table = defaultdict(lambda: np.zeros(env.action_space.n))
    for episode in range(episodes):
        state = env.reset()
        if np.random.rand() < epsilon:
            action = env.action_space.sample()
        else:
            action = np.argmax(q_table[state])
        done = False
        while not done:
            next_state, reward, done = env.step(action)
            if np.random.rand() < epsilon:
                next_action = env.action_space.sample()
            else:
                next_action = np.argmax(q_table[next_state])
            q_table[state][action] += alpha * (reward + gamma * q_table[next_state][
```

```
            next_action] - q_table[state][action])
        state, action = next_state, next_action
    return q_table
```

With the advent of deep learning in the 2010s, RL experienced a resurgence. The integration of deep neural networks with RL, known as *Deep Reinforcement Learning* (DRL), enabled agents to handle high-dimensional state and action spaces. One landmark of this integration is the *Deep Q-Network* (DQN) introduced by Mnih et al., where a deep neural network is used to approximate the Q-value function.

```
import torch
import torch.nn as nn
import torch.optim as optim
import numpy as np

class DQN(nn.Module):
    def __init__(self, input_dim, output_dim):
        super(DQN, self).__init__()
        self.fc1 = nn.Linear(input_dim, 128)
        self.fc2 = nn.Linear(128, 128)
        self.fc3 = nn.Linear(128, output_dim)

    def forward(self, x):
        x = torch.relu(self.fc1(x))
        x = torch.relu(self.fc2(x))
        x = self.fc3(x)
        return x

def optimize_model(policy_net, target_net, memory, optimizer, gamma, batch_size):
    if len(memory) < batch_size:
        return
    transitions = memory.sample(batch_size)
    batch = Transition(*zip(*transitions))
    state_batch = torch.cat(batch.state)
    action_batch = torch.cat(batch.action)
    reward_batch = torch.cat(batch.reward)
    non_final_mask = torch.tensor(tuple(map(lambda s: s is not None, batch.
        next_state)))

    non_final_next_states = torch.cat([s for s in batch.next_state if s is not None])
    state_action_values = policy_net(state_batch).gather(1, action_batch)
    next_state_values = torch.zeros(batch_size)
    next_state_values[non_final_mask] = target_net(non_final_next_states).max(1)
        [0].detach()
    expected_state_action_values = (next_state_values * gamma) + reward_batch
    loss = nn.SmoothL1Loss()(state_action_values, expected_state_action_values.
        unsqueeze(1))

    optimizer.zero_grad()
    loss.backward()
    optimizer.step()
```

The progression from simple, rule-based learning methods to sophisticated, neural network-based approaches has dramatically expanded the applicability of RL across various domains, from game-playing (e.g., AlphaGo) to robotics and autonomous systems. Today, RL continues to evolve, incorporating advancements in computational power, algorithmic theory, and interdisciplinary research, poised to tackle increasingly complex problems.

1.3 Key Concepts and Terminology

Reinforcement learning (RL) is a domain that encompasses a variety of concepts and terminologies which are fundamental to understanding how agents learn to make decisions. These terms form the basis of the theory and practical implementation of RL algorithms. This section elucidates the core concepts and terminologies, linking them coherently to facilitate comprehension for readers with varying levels of expertise.

- **Agent**: The agent is the learner or decision-maker in reinforcement learning. It interacts with the environment by taking actions and receiving feedback in the form of rewards or penalties.
- **Environment**: This represents everything outside the agent. It is the external system with which the agent interacts. The environment provides observations and rewards to the agent in response to the actions taken by the agent.
- **Action (A)**: Actions are the choices available to the agent. At any given time, the agent can choose an action from a set of possible actions, denoted as A. The set of actions could be discrete or continuous.
- **State (S)**: The state is a description of the current situation of the environment. States encapsulate all relevant information needed for decision-making. The set of all possible states is denoted by S.
- **Reward (R)**: The reward is the feedback signal received by the agent in response to an action it has taken. Rewards can be immediate (after a single action) or delayed (accumulated over a sequence of actions). The goal of the agent is to maximize the cumulative reward over time.
- **Policy (π)**: A policy defines the agent's behavior at any given time. It is a mapping from states to actions. Policies can be deterministic or stochastic. A deterministic policy strictly defines a specific action for each state, while a stochastic policy provides a probability distribution over actions for each state.

- **Value Function (V)**: The value function estimates the expected cumulative reward that can be obtained from a given state, following a particular policy. The state-value function $V(s)$ represents the value of being in state s.

$$V^{\pi}(s) = \mathbb{E}^{\pi}[R_t + \gamma R_{t+1} + \gamma^2 R_{t+2} + \ldots \mid S_t = s]$$

- **Action-Value Function (Q)**: Also known as Q-function, it estimates the expected cumulative reward of taking a particular action in a given state, following a specific policy. The action-value function $Q(s, a)$ represents the value of taking action a in state s.

$$Q^{\pi}(s, a) = \mathbb{E}^{\pi}[R_t + \gamma R_{t+1} + \gamma^2 R_{t+2} + \ldots \mid S_t = s, A_t = a]$$

- **Discount Factor (γ)**: The discount factor is a value between 0 and 1 that represents the degree to which future rewards are considered in the present value. A discount factor close to 1 indicates that future rewards are highly valued, whereas a factor close to 0 implies that immediate rewards are prioritized.

- **Episode**: An episode is a sequence of states, actions, and rewards that ends in a terminal state. In many RL problems, interactions are divided into episodes, each beginning from an initial state and proceeding until a terminal state is reached.

- **Exploration vs. Exploitation**: This is a fundamental trade-off in reinforcement learning. Exploration refers to the agent's actions to discover more about the environment, while exploitation denotes using known information to maximize rewards. Balancing exploration and exploitation is crucial for effective learning.

- **Markov Decision Process (MDP)**: MDP is a mathematical framework used to describe an environment in RL. It includes a tuple (S, A, P, R, γ):
  - **S**: A finite set of states.
  - **A**: A finite set of actions.
  - **P**: State transition probabilities $P(s' \mid s, a)$ which describe the probability of moving to state s' from state s given action a.

- **R**: Reward function $R(s, a, s')$ which represents the immediate reward received after transitioning from state s to state s' due to action a.
- γ: Discount factor.

- **Example of MDP Transition**:

```
P = {
    ('s1', 'a1', 's1'): 0.2,
    ('s1', 'a1', 's2'): 0.8,
    ...
}
```

- **Bellman Equation**: A central element in dynamic programming and RL, the Bellman equation expresses the relationship between the value of a state and the values of subsequent states. For a policy π, the Bellman equation for the value function is:

$$V^{\pi}(s) = \sum_{a \in A} \pi(a \mid s) \sum_{s' \in S} P(s' \mid s, a) \left[R(s, a, s') + \gamma V^{\pi}(s')\right]$$

Similarly, the Bellman equation for the Q-function is:

$$Q^{\pi}(s, a) = \sum_{s' \in S} P(s' \mid s, a) \left[R(s, a, s') + \gamma \sum_{a' \in A} \pi(a' \mid s') Q^{\pi}(s', a')\right]$$

- **Model-Free vs. Model-Based RL**: In model-free RL, the agent learns to make decisions without a model of the environment. Popular algorithms include Q-learning and SARSA. In model-based RL, the agent builds a model of the environment's dynamics, which is used to simulate and evaluate potential actions.

- **Temporal Difference Learning (TD)**: An approach that combines the ideas of Monte Carlo methods and dynamic programming. TD methods, such as TD(0), learn directly from raw experience without a model of the environment's dynamics.

```
TD Target = R_{t+1} + \gamma V(S_{t+1})
TD Error = TD Target - V(S_t)
V(S_t) = V(S_t) + \alpha * TD Error
```

- **Q-Learning**: An off-policy algorithm that aims to learn the optimal action-value function $Q^*(s, a)$ independent of the policy being followed. The update rule is given by:

$$Q(s,a) \leftarrow Q(s,a) + \alpha \left(R + \gamma \max_{a'} Q(s',a') - Q(s,a) \right)$$

- **SARSA (State-Action-Reward-State-Action)**: An on-policy algorithm where the update rule is conditioned on the action taken by the current policy.

$$Q(s,a) \leftarrow Q(s,a) + \alpha \left(R + \gamma Q(s',a') - Q(s,a) \right)$$

```
# Example Q-Learning Update in Python
Q[state, action] = Q[state, action] + alpha * (reward + gamma * np.max(Q[
    next_state, :]) - Q[state, action])
```

Through mastery of these foundational concepts and terminologies, one gains the essential tools required to delve deeper into the field of reinforcement learning. These elements construct the building blocks upon which more complex theories and applications can be built.

1.4 Differences Between Supervised, Unsupervised, and Reinforcement Learning

Supervised Learning (SL), Unsupervised Learning (UL), and Reinforcement Learning (RL) are the three principal paradigms in machine learning. Each distinguishes itself by the nature of the learning task, the type of feedback or data available, and the ultimate learning objective. A detailed examination elucidates these distinctions.

In supervised learning, the training process is directed by a labeled dataset, i.e., a set comprising input-output pairs. The primary goal is to learn a mapping from inputs to outputs, often framed as a function approximation problem. The algorithms are trained using examples of input-output tuples, and the learning process is guided by minimizing the difference between the predicted and actual outputs, typically through loss functions. For instance, let (x_i, y_i) be a sample from the training set, where x_i denotes the input features and y_i represents the corresponding label. The objective is to learn a function $f : X \to Y$ that accurately maps inputs $x \in X$ to labels $y \in Y$.

The most common applications of supervised learning include classification tasks, such as image recognition or email spam filtering, where the outputs are categorical labels, and regression tasks like predicting house prices, where the outputs are continuous values. The learning process involves algorithms such as Support Vector Machines (SVM), Decision Trees, and Neural Networks.

```
from sklearn.model_selection import train_test_split
from sklearn.datasets import load_iris
from sklearn.tree import DecisionTreeClassifier

# Load dataset
iris = load_iris()
X, y = iris.data, iris.target

# Split the data
X_train, X_test, y_train, y_test = train_test_split(X, y, test_size=0.2,
    random_state=42)

# Initialize and train the classifier
clf = DecisionTreeClassifier()
clf.fit(X_train, y_train)

# Make predictions
predictions = clf.predict(X_test)
```

Unsupervised learning differs fundamentally from supervised learning in the nature of the training data, which lacks labeled outputs. Instead, the objective is to uncover the underlying data structure. The algorithms aim to infer patterns, groupings, or statistical properties from the input data alone. Common tasks involve clustering and dimensionality reduction.

Clustering, as exemplified by k-means and hierarchical clustering, involves partitioning the dataset into groups, or clusters, of similar data points. Dimensionality reduction techniques, such as Principal Component Analysis (PCA), transform data into a lower-dimensional form while preserving essential characteristics.

A practical use case involves clustering customers based on purchasing habits to enable targeted marketing. This process is unsupervised because it does not require pre-labeled categories or groups; instead, the algorithm identifies the inherent customer segments in the data.

```
from sklearn.cluster import KMeans
from sklearn.datasets import load_digits
import matplotlib.pyplot as plt

# Load digits dataset
digits = load_digits()
X = digits.data

# Initialize and fit the KMeans model
kmeans = KMeans(n_clusters=10, random_state=42)
kmeans.fit(X)
```

```
# Plot the cluster centers
fig, axes = plt.subplots(2, 5, figsize=(8, 6))
centers = kmeans.cluster_centers_.reshape(10, 8, 8) % reshape to 8x8 images

for ax, center in zip(axes.ravel(), centers):
    ax.imshow(center, cmap=plt.cm.binary)
    ax.axis('off')
plt.show()
```

Reinforcement Learning diverges markedly from both supervised and unsupervised learning paradigms. Here, the focus is on agents that learn to make a sequence of decisions by interacting with an environment. The agent receives feedback in the form of rewards or punishments based on the actions taken, aiming to maximize cumulative rewards over time. RL problems are often modeled as Markov Decision Processes (MDPs) characterized by states (s), actions (a), rewards (r), and transitions (P).

The learning objective involves developing a policy (π), which dictates the action an agent should take when in a particular state. RL leverages value functions and policy optimization algorithms, such as Q-learning and Policy Gradients, to iteratively improve the decision-making policy. Unlike SL or UL, which use static datasets, RL's feedback loop (agent-environment interaction) is dynamic and sequential.

A prototypical example of RL is training an agent to play a game, such as the classic case of DeepMind's DQN algorithm that excels at Atari games. The agent begins with no knowledge of the game's rules and must learn from experience to improve its strategy, often encountering and overcoming the exploration-exploitation trade-off.

```
import gym

# Initialize environment
env = gym.make('CartPole-v1')

# Initial observations
observation = env.reset()
for _ in range(1000):
    env.render()
    action = env.action_space.sample() # Your agent here (this takes random actions)
    observation, reward, done, info = env.step(action)
    if done:
        observation = env.reset()
env.close()
```

The differentiation among these paradigms hinges on the form and usage of data, the learning objectives, and the feedback mechanism. Supervised learning relies on labeled datasets to map inputs to outputs, unsupervised learning elucidates hidden patterns from unlabeled data, and reinforcement learning focuses on sequential decision-making to maximize cumulative rewards through interactive feedback from the environment. Understanding these differences aids in selecting the appropriate approach for various machine learning tasks and applications.

1.5 Elements of a Reinforcement Learning System

In a Reinforcement Learning (RL) system, several key components function cohesively to enable an agent to learn from its environment and optimize its decision-making process. Understanding these elements is fundamental to both grasping the intricacies of RL and applying it effectively.

Agent: The agent represents the learner or decision-maker that interacts with the environment. It's responsible for taking actions based on a policy, which determines its behavior at any given time. The ultimate goal of the agent is to maximize cumulative reward over time.

Environment: The environment is everything the agent interacts with. It comprises all possible states and actions that define the context in which the agent operates. The environment responds to the agent's actions and provides feedback in the form of rewards and new states.

State (S): A state represents a specific situation or configuration of the environment. It encapsulates all relevant information that the agent needs to make informed decisions. State transitions occur as a result of the agent's actions, leading to new states.

Action (A): An action is a decision taken by the agent that influences the state of the environment. The set of all possible actions is known as the action space. Actions can be deterministic or stochastic, depending on how they affect the outcome.

Reward (R): The reward is a scalar feedback signal the agent receives from the environment after taking an action. It quantifies the immediate benefit of the action in the given state. The agent's objective is to maximize the cumulative sum of rewards, known as the return.

Policy (π): A policy is a strategy used by the agent to determine the next action based on the current state. A policy can be deterministic, represented as $\pi(s) = a$, where s is the state and a is the action, or stochastic, described by $\pi(a \mid s)$, which gives the probability of taking action a in state s.

Value Function: The value function provides an estimate of the expected return from a state or a state-action pair, under a particular policy. There are two primary types of values functions:

- **State Value Function ($V(s)$):** Represents the expected return starting from state s and following policy π thereafter.
- **Action Value Function ($Q(s,a)$):** Represents the expected return starting from state s, taking action a, and following policy π thereafter.

The formal definitions are:

$$V^\pi(s) = \mathbb{E}_\pi\left[\sum_{t=0}^{\infty} \gamma^t R_{t+1} \mid S_t = s\right]$$
$$Q^\pi(s,a) = \mathbb{E}_\pi\left[\sum_{t=0}^{\infty} \gamma^t R_{t+1} \mid S_t = s, A_t = a\right]$$

where γ is the discount factor, ensuring the sum of returns converges.

Model of the Environment: Models are used to simulate the behavior of the environment. They include:

- **Transition Model (T):** Predicts the next state given the current state and action; mathematically represented as $T(s' \mid s, a)$.
- **Reward Model (R):** Estimates the reward for a particular state-action pair; represented as $R(s,a)$.

A model-based RL utilizes these models to plan and predict future states and rewards, whereas model-free RL does without them, learning directly from interactions with the environment.

Return (G_t): The return is the total accumulated reward that the agent aims to maximize. For episodic tasks, where the interaction breaks into episodes, the return is:

$$G_t = R_{t+1} + \gamma R_{t+2} + \gamma^2 R_{t+3} + \cdots + \gamma^{T-t-1} R_T$$

For continuing tasks, it is:

$$G_t = \sum_{k=0}^{\infty} \gamma^k R_{t+k+1}$$

Discount Factor (γ): The discount factor lies in the range $0 \leq \gamma \leq 1$ and affects how future rewards are valued compared to immediate rewards. A value close to 1 indicates a preference for distant rewards, whereas a value close to 0 emphasizes immediate rewards.

Considering the combined function of these elements, the RL system operates under the following protocol: The agent observes the current state S_t, selects an action A_t based on its policy π, observes the reward R_{t+1} and the next state S_{t+1} as per the environment dynamics, and then updates its policy. This leads to an iterative process of learning whereby the agent ideally improves its decision-making policy over time.

In practical terms, the interaction between these components can be illustrated with a simple example. Consider the classic grid world problem, where an agent is situated on a grid and must navigate to a goal position:

```
# Agent's position
S_t = (2, 3)
# Agent performs an action, move right
A_t = 'RIGHT'
# Environment response
R_{t+1} = -1 (e.g., penalty for each move)
S_{t+1} = (2, 4)
```

The agent's objective is to develop a policy that directs it to the goal position while minimizing penalties. This involves iteratively evaluating and improving its actions based on the rewards received and the value of states encountered. The interplay of these elements forms the crux of reinforcement learning, enabling the agent to strive toward optimality in varied environments.

1.6 The Reinforcement Learning Problem

The reinforcement learning problem is fundamentally concerned with enabling an agent to make a sequence of decisions in an environment with the objective of maximizing cumulative reward over time. This problem encompasses several key components, including states, actions, rewards, policies, and value functions, each of which plays a crucial role in the agent's learning and decision-making process.

A reinforcement learning problem can be formally represented by a Markov Decision Process (MDP). An MDP is defined by a tuple (S, A, P, R, γ), where:

- S represents the set of all possible states in the environment.
- A is the set of all possible actions that the agent can take.
- $P : S \times A \times S \to [0, 1]$ is the state transition probability function, $P(s'|s, a)$, which defines the probability of transitioning from state s to state s' under action a.
- $R : S \times A \to \mathbb{R}$ is the reward function, $R(s, a)$, which provides the immediate reward received after taking action a in state s.
- $\gamma \in [0, 1]$ is the discount factor that represents the importance of future rewards compared to immediate rewards.

The agent's objective is to learn a policy $\pi : S \to A$ that maximizes the expected cumulative reward, also known as the return. The return is defined as the sum of discounted rewards obtained over time, given by:

$$G_t = \sum_{k=0}^{\infty} \gamma^k R(S_{t+k}, A_{t+k}),$$

where G_t is the return at time step t, S_{t+k} and A_{t+k} represent the states and actions at time step $t + k$ respectively, and $\gamma \in [0, 1]$ is the aforementioned discount factor.

A central concept in reinforcement learning is the value function, which is used to estimate the expected return from a given state. There are two primary types of value functions:

- The state-value function $V^\pi(s)$ gives the expected return starting from state s and following policy π:

$$V^\pi(s) = \mathbb{E}_\pi[G_t|S_t = s].$$

- The action-value function $Q^\pi(s, a)$ gives the expected return starting from state s, taking action a, and thereafter following policy π:

$$Q^\pi(s, a) = \mathbb{E}_\pi[G_t|S_t = s, A_t = a].$$

Reinforcement learning methods can be broadly classified into three categories based on how they approach the learning problem: model-based methods, model-free methods, and policy gradient methods.

Model-based methods involve explicitly learning a model of the environment's dynamics, i.e., the state transition probabilities and the reward function. Once the model is learned, planning algorithms such as dynamic programming can be used to derive an optimal policy. A classic example is the Dyna-Q algorithm, which integrates planning, acting, and learning by maintaining and updating a model of the environment.

Model-free methods do not attempt to learn the environment's model. Instead, they directly learn a policy or value function. Popular model-free methods include:

- **Monte Carlo methods** involve learning from complete episodes by averaging sample returns. For example, suppose we want to estimate $V^\pi(s)$. Monte Carlo methods will simulate episodes starting from state s under policy π and use the average of observed returns to update the value function.

- **Temporal Difference (TD) methods** combine ideas from Monte Carlo methods and dynamic programming. They update value functions based on the difference between predicted and actual rewards, known as the temporal difference error. A well-known TD method is Q-learning. Q-learning updates the action-value function $Q(s,a)$ using the TD error:

$$Q(s,a) \leftarrow Q(s,a) + \alpha \left(R(s,a) + \gamma \max_{a'} Q(s',a') - Q(s,a) \right),$$

  where α is the learning rate, and s' is the state resulting from taking action a in state s.

Policy gradient methods directly optimize the policy by adjusting its parameters in the direction that increases expected reward. These methods use gradient ascent on the expected reward to find the optimal policy. The policy gradient theorem provides the foundation for these methods, with a representative algorithm being the REINFORCE algorithm. It updates the policy parameters θ by:

$$\theta \leftarrow \theta + \alpha \nabla_\theta \log \pi_\theta(A_t|S_t) G_t,$$

where α is the learning rate.

The reinforcement learning problem involves balancing the trade-off between exploration and exploitation. Exploration refers to trying out new actions to discover potentially better rewards, while exploitation involves selecting actions known to yield high rewards based on current knowledge.

Solving the reinforcement learning problem requires the agent to interact with the environment, gather experience, and iteratively improve its policy. Determining the right balance between exploration and exploitation, adapting to dynamic environments, and scaling to complex tasks remain active research areas within this field.

1.7 Exploration vs. Exploitation

In Reinforcement Learning (RL), the dilemma of exploration versus exploitation is a fundamental challenge that an agent faces while interacting with an environment. This dilemma involves choosing between two opposing strategies: exploitation, where the agent leverages its current knowledge to maximize immediate reward, and exploration, where the agent tries new actions to discover potentially higher rewards in the future. The balance between these strategies is essential for efficient learning and achieving optimal long-term performance.

Exploitation refers to the strategy where the agent consistently chooses actions that it believes will yield the highest reward based on its existing knowledge. This approach is grounded in the principle of maximizing the expected return at each step. Exploitation is crucial because it allows the agent to utilize learned information effectively, thereby capitalizing on opportunities that present themselves.

Exploration, on the other hand, involves taking actions that may not necessarily lead to immediate high rewards but hold the promise of discovering more advantageous strategies or state-action pairs. Exploration is vital for the agent to gain comprehensive knowledge of the environment, which can subsequently inform more effective exploitation.

To illustrate this concept more concretely, consider the classic *multi-armed bandit problem*, where an agent must choose between multiple slot machines (referred to as "arms" of the bandit), each with an unknown payout distribution. The agent must decide whether to keep playing the arm that has given the best rewards so far (exploitation) or to try other arms in search of potentially better payouts (exploration). The trade-off between exploration and exploitation can be formulated mathematically and approached using various strategies.

One commonly used strategy to address the exploration-exploitation trade-off is the **ϵ-greedy** policy. In this approach, the agent largely follows an exploitation strategy but occasionally explores with a probability ϵ. For instance, if ϵ is set to 0.1, the agent exploits 90% of the time and explores 10% of the time. This balance allows the agent to gather new information while still leveraging its existing knowledge to gain rewards. Below is a basic implementation of the ϵ-greedy strategy in Python:

```
import random
import numpy as np

class EpsilonGreedyAgent:
    def __init__(self, n_actions, epsilon=0.1):
        self.n_actions = n_actions
        self.epsilon = epsilon
        self.q_values = np.zeros(n_actions) # Initialize Q-values for all actions

    def select_action(self):
        if random.random() < self.epsilon:
            return random.randint(0, self.n_actions - 1) # Exploration
        else:
            return np.argmax(self.q_values) # Exploitation

    def update_q_values(self, action, reward, alpha=0.1):
        self.q_values[action] += alpha * (reward - self.q_values[action])

# Example usage
agent = EpsilonGreedyAgent(n_actions=10)
action = agent.select_action()
# Assume reward received
reward = 1.0
agent.update_q_values(action, reward)
```

Another effective strategy is the **Upper Confidence Bound (UCB)** algorithm. The UCB approach balances exploration and exploitation by considering not only the expected reward of actions but also the uncertainty or variance in the reward estimates. This method ensures that actions with higher uncertainty are explored more frequently while still prioritizing actions with historically higher rewards. The UCB selection formula can be given by:

$$a_t = \arg\max_a \left(Q(a) + c\sqrt{\frac{\ln t}{N(a)}} \right)$$

where $Q(a)$ is the estimated reward of action a, c is a constant determining the degree of exploration, t is the total number of steps taken, and $N(a)$ is the number of times action a has been chosen. Below is a Python implementation of the UCB algorithm:

```
import numpy as np

class UCB1Agent:
    def __init__(self, n_actions, c=2):
        self.n_actions = n_actions
        self.c = c
        self.q_values = np.zeros(n_actions)
        self.action_counts = np.zeros(n_actions) # Count of action selections
        self.total_steps = 0
```

```
    def select_action(self):
        self.total_steps += 1
        ucb_values = self.q_values + self.c * np.sqrt(np.log(self.total_steps) / (self.
            action_counts + 1))
        return np.argmax(ucb_values)

    def update_q_values(self, action, reward, alpha=0.1):
        self.action_counts[action] += 1
        self.q_values[action] += alpha * (reward - self.q_values[action])

# Example usage
agent = UCB1Agent(n_actions=10)
action = agent.select_action()
# Assume reward received
reward = 1.0
agent.update_q_values(action, reward)
```

Thompson Sampling is another sophisticated method for managing the exploration-exploitation trade-off. It frames the problem in a Bayesian context, where the agent maintains a probability distribution over the reward of each action and samples from these distributions to make decisions. This allows actions with higher uncertainty to be chosen more frequently, thus facilitating exploration while benefiting from exploitation.

The challenge of balancing exploration and exploitation is not exclusive to simple scenarios like the multi-armed bandit problem but extends to more complex RL environments involving sequential decision-making. Effective strategies often dynamically adjust the exploration rate based on the agent's accumulated experience, ensuring both adequate exploration and efficient exploitation.

Understanding and implementing the exploration versus exploitation balance is crucial in designing effective RL algorithms. Proper management of this trade-off enables agents to learn more efficiently and achieve more optimal policies in various environments.

1.8 Case Studies and Real-World Applications

Reinforcement Learning (RL) has made significant inroads into various domains, demonstrating its practical utility and theoretical strength. This section explores several case studies and real-world applications that illustrate the effectiveness of RL in solving complex problems, optimizing processes, and driving innovation across different fields. By understanding these applications, readers can appreciate the versatility and impact of RL in our modern world.

- **Game Playing**

RL gained widespread attention through its success in game playing, particularly with the development of algorithms that outperform human experts. One prominent example is *AlphaGo*, a program developed by DeepMind to play the ancient Chinese board game of Go. AlphaGo utilized a combination of supervised learning from human expert games and RL through self-play. The program employed deep neural networks to evaluate board positions and select moves, ultimately defeating the world champion Go player.

Another noteworthy example is *OpenAI Five*, an RL-based system developed to play the complex multiplayer online battle game *Dota 2*. The system trained on thousands of GPUs over several months, learning strategies and tactics through self-play. OpenAI Five demonstrated its proficiency by defeating professional *Dota 2* players in exhibition matches, showcasing the strength of RL in strategic decision-making and teamwork coordination.

- **Robotics and Control**

Robotic systems benefit significantly from RL, particularly in tasks requiring precise control and adaptability. One remarkable application is the use of RL in robotic manipulation. For instance, OpenAI developed a model that enables a robotic hand to solve a Rubik's Cube. By using a technique called *automatic domain randomization*, the system trained in a variety of simulated environments, enhancing its robustness to real-world variances, such as lighting changes and sensor noise.

In autonomous vehicle control, RL has been used to optimize driving policies. NVIDIA implemented an RL-based approach to teach an autonomous car to drive in a simulated environment. The system, trained through trial and error, learned to control the vehicle's steering, acceleration, and braking effectively. The transition from simulation to real-world driving observed promising results as the RL model transferred its learned behavior to actual roads.

- **Healthcare**

RL has vast potential in healthcare, particularly in personalized medicine and treatment planning. A notable application is in optimizing treatment strategies for chronic diseases. Researchers have employed RL to devise individualized insulin dosing policies for patients with diabetes. By training RL agents on patient data, these systems can recommend insulin doses that maintain blood glucose levels within a target range, improving patient outcomes.

Another application involves *sepsis management*, where RL algorithms are used to recommend treatment protocols for septic patients. By analyzing historical patient data, RL-based systems can predict the most effective interventions, such as the optimal timing and dosage of medications. These systems are poised to support clinicians in making informed decisions, ultimately enhancing patient care and survival rates.

- **Finance**

In the finance sector, RL is leveraged to develop algorithms for portfolio management, trading strategies, and risk assessment. RL-based portfolio management systems can dynamically adjust asset allocations to maximize returns while managing risk exposure. For example, the *Markowitz portfolio optimization model* can be enhanced using RL to adapt to changing market conditions and investor preferences.

High-frequency trading (HFT) is another domain where RL excels. HFT strategies rely on rapid decision-making to capitalize on market opportunities. By employing RL, trading algorithms learn to execute orders efficiently, manage trade execution risks, and respond to market fluctuations. These systems continuously adapt their strategies to evolving market dynamics, aiming for higher profitability and reduced execution costs.

- **Energy Management**

RL's ability to optimize decision-making is particularly valuable in energy management, where it is used to enhance the efficiency of energy systems. In *smart grid* applications, RL algorithms manage the distribution of electricity to balance supply and demand. These systems can adjust power generation and consumption dynamically to minimize costs and maintain grid stability.

Building energy management is another area benefiting from RL, where algorithms optimize heating, ventilation, and air conditioning (HVAC) systems. For instance, Google's DeepMind applied RL to reduce energy consumption at its data centers. The RL system learned to adjust cooling and airflow controls, achieving a significant reduction in energy usage while maintaining optimal operating conditions.

- **Natural Language Processing**

Reinforcement Learning also contributes to advancements in natural language processing (NLP), particularly in tasks that involve interactive dialog systems and language generation. Chatbots and virtual assistants, such as Amazon's Alexa and Google's Assistant, utilize RL to improve their conversational capabilities. By interactively learning from user interactions, these systems refine their responses, leading to more natural and contextually appropriate conversations.

In machine translation, RL has been used to refine translation models for better accuracy and fluency. By evaluating the quality of translations based on human feedback or predefined metrics, RL algorithms can adjust model parameters and improve translation performance over time.

- **Example Implementation: Training an RL Agent for Grid-World**

Below is an implementation of a simple RL agent trained using Q-Learning to navigate a GridWorld environment. The agent aims to maximize its cumulative reward by reaching the goal state while avoiding obstacles.

```
import numpy as np
import gym
import matplotlib.pyplot as plt

# Define the GridWorld environment
class GridWorld(gym.Env):
  def __init__(self, grid_size=(4, 4), goal=(3, 3)):
    self.grid_size = grid_size
    self.goal = goal
    self.state = (0, 0)
    self.action_space = gym.spaces.Discrete(4) # 4 actions (left, right, up, down)
    self.observation_space = gym.spaces.Tuple(
      [gym.spaces.Discrete(size) for size in self.grid_size]
    )

  def reset(self):
    self.state = (0, 0)
    return self.state

  def step(self, action):
    x, y = self.state
    if action == 0: # left
```

```
            y = max(0, y - 1)
        elif action == 1: # right
            y = min(self.grid_size[1] - 1, y + 1)
        elif action == 2: # up
            x = max(0, x - 1)
        elif action == 3: # down
            x = min(self.grid_size[0] - 1, x + 1)

        self.state = (x, y)
        if self.state == self.goal:
            return self.state, 1, True, {}
        else:
            return self.state, -0.01, False, {}

env = GridWorld()

# Q-Learning Agent
q_table = np.zeros(env.grid_size + (env.action_space.n,))
alpha = 0.1
gamma = 0.99
epsilon = 0.1
episodes = 1000

for episode in range(episodes):
  state = env.reset()
  done = False
  while not done:
    if np.random.uniform(0, 1) < epsilon:
      action = env.action_space.sample() # Explore action space
    else:
      action = np.argmax(q_table[state]) # Exploit learned values

    next_state, reward, done, info = env.step(action)
    old_value = q_table[state + (action,)]
    next_max = np.max(q_table[next_state])

    new_value = (1 - alpha) * old_value + alpha * (reward + gamma * next_max)
    q_table[state + (action,)] = new_value

    state = next_state

# Visualizing the Q-Table
plt.imshow(np.max(q_table, axis=2))
plt.colorbar()
plt.title("State-Action Values (Max)")
plt.show()

# Testing the trained agent
state = env.reset()
done = False
grid_path = [state]

while not done:
  action = np.argmax(q_table[state])
  state, reward, done, info = env.step(action)
  grid_path.append(state)

print("Path taken by the trained agent:")
print(grid_path)
```

```
Path taken by the trained agent:
[(0, 0), (1, 0), (2, 0), (3, 0), (3, 1), (3, 2), (3, 3)]
```

The above code illustrates a practical example of an RL agent learning to navigate a GridWorld environment. Through iterative training, the agent improves its policy to maximize cumulative rewards, demonstrating key RL concepts such as exploration, exploitation, and value iteration.

1.9 Tools and Libraries for Reinforcement Learning

The field of Reinforcement Learning (RL) has seen a significant boost with the development of numerous tools and libraries that facilitate the design, implementation, and evaluation of RL algorithms. These tools are crucial for both researchers and practitioners, providing robust environments and pre-built algorithms that accelerate development cycles. This section delves into some of the most widely adopted tools and libraries in RL, highlighting their unique features and use cases.

OpenAI Gym

OpenAI Gym is one of the most popular environments for developing and comparing reinforcement learning algorithms. It consists of a diverse collection of standardized environments, which allows consistent benchmarking of RL agents. OpenAI Gym facilitates the creation, training, and assessment of RL models by providing a simple, user-friendly interface. The consistency of environments helps ensure comparability and reproducibility across different research works.

```
import gym

# Create the 'CartPole' environment
env = gym.make('CartPole-v1')

# Initialize the environment
state = env.reset()

done = False
while not done:
    # Render the environment
    env.render()

    # Random action selection
    action = env.action_space.sample()

    # Apply action to the environment
    state, reward, done, info = env.step(action)

env.close()
```

TensorFlow Agents (TF-Agents)

TF-Agents is a library under TensorFlow that focuses on RL research and specifically the development of RL algorithms. It provides a flexible and scalable framework for building RL models. TF-Agents support both policy-based and value-based methods, and it includes state-of-the-art algorithms such as DQN, PPO, and SAC.

```
import tensorflow as tf
import tensorflow_agents as tfa

# Create the environment
env = tf_py_environment.TFPyEnvironment(suite_gym.load('CartPole-v0'))

# Define the DQN agent
q_net = tfa.networks.q_network.QNetwork(
    env.observation_spec(),
    env.action_spec(),
    fc_layer_params=(100,))

# Define the optimizer
optimizer = tf.compat.v1.train.AdamOptimizer(learning_rate=1e-3)

# Define the DQN agent using the QNetwork and optimizer
train_step_counter = tf.compat.v2.Variable(0)
agent = tfa.agents.dqn.dqn_agent.DqnAgent(
    env.time_step_spec(),
    env.action_spec(),
    q_network=q_net,
    optimizer=optimizer,
    td_errors_loss_fn=tfa.common.element_wise_squared_loss,
    train_step_counter=train_step_counter)

agent.initialize()
```

PyTorch RL Libraries (Stable-Baselines3, RLlib)

Several libraries built on PyTorch provide RL functionalities. Among these, Stable-Baselines3 and RLlib are noteworthy. Stable-Baselines3 offers a simple interface with various pre-trained RL algorithms, making it easy to deploy and test RL models. RLlib, on the other hand, is part of the Ray framework and is designed for large-scale reinforcement learning applications. It supports distributed training and hyperparameter tuning.

```
from stable_baselines3 import PPO
from stable_baselines3.common.envs import DummyVecEnv

# Create the environment
env = DummyVecEnv([lambda: gym.make('CartPole-v1')])

# Initialize the PPO agent
model = PPO('MlpPolicy', env, verbose=1)

# Train the agent
model.learn(total_timesteps=10000)
```

```
# Save the trained model
model.save("ppo_cartpole")

# Load the trained model
model = PPO.load("ppo_cartpole")

# Test the trained agent
obs = env.reset()
done = False
while not done:
    action, _states = model.predict(obs)
    obs, rewards, done, info = env.step(action)
    env.render()
env.close()
```

Unity ML-Agents

Unity's ML-Agents toolkit links reinforcement learning with the Unity game engine, enabling the creation of highly sophisticated and customizable training environments. Unity ML-Agents support using environments designed specifically with Unity, allowing for highly complex and three-dimensional training spaces.

```
from mlagents_envs.environment import UnityEnvironment

# Load the Unity environment
env = UnityEnvironment(file_name="path_to_unity_environment")

# Start interacting with the environment
env.reset()

# Get behavior names
behavior_names = env.behavior_specs.keys()
behavior_name = list(behavior_names)[0]

# Get behavior specification
spec = env.behavior_specs[behavior_name]

# Set the actions
actions = np.random.randn(spec.action_spec.continuous_size) * 0.1

# Execute actions and receive observations
env.set_actions(behavior_name, actions)
env.step()
```

Comparison and Selection Criteria

Each of these tools and libraries has unique advantages that make them better suited for particular applications. OpenAI Gym's simplicity and standardization make it ideal for initial prototyping and education. TF-Agents and Stable-Baselines3, with their extensive collection of algorithms, are well-suited for applied research and experimentation. RLlib excels in scalability and distributed training, making it suitable for large scale RL applications. Unity ML-Agents stands out for tasks requiring rich environments with complex, 3D interactions.

Selecting an appropriate tool depends on the specific requirements of the RL project, including the complexity of the environment, the need for scalable training, the familiarity of the algorithms, and the ease of integration into existing workflows. By leveraging these tools, researchers and practitioners can significantly accelerate their RL development process while maintaining a high standard of experiment reproducibility and model performance.

1.10 Challenges and Future Directions in Reinforcement Learning

Reinforcement Learning (RL) has demonstrated significant potential in various domains, from gaming to robotics to healthcare. Despite these advancements, substantial challenges remain that must be addressed to realize its full potential. This section delves into these challenges and explores promising avenues for future research and development.

Scalability and Sample Efficiency: One of the foremost challenges in RL is scalability. Many RL algorithms require an extensive number of interactions with the environment to converge to an optimal policy. This high sample complexity is particularly problematic in real-world applications where data collection is costly or time-consuming. Approaches like experience replay, model-based RL, and transfer learning have been proposed to improve sample efficiency, but the problem remains far from solved.

```
import numpy as np
from collections import deque
import random

class ReplayBuffer:
    def __init__(self, buffer_size):
        self.buffer = deque(maxlen=buffer_size)

    def add(self, experience):
        self.buffer.append(experience)

    def sample(self, batch_size):
        return random.sample(self.buffer, batch_size)

# Initialize Replay Buffer
replay_buffer = ReplayBuffer(buffer_size=10000)

# Add experience
replay_buffer.add((state, action, reward, next_state, done))
```

```
# Sample a mini-batch
batch = replay_buffer.sample(batch_size=64)
```

Exploration vs. Exploitation: Balancing exploration (trying new actions) and exploitation (using known actions to maximize reward) is a fundamental challenge in RL. Classic approaches like ϵ-greedy and more sophisticated techniques such as Upper Confidence Bound (UCB) and Thompson Sampling provide various strategies to address this balance, but each has its trade-offs. Moreover, in high-dimensional state-action spaces, effective exploration remains an open research problem.

Generalization and Transfer Learning: Most RL algorithms are designed to solve specific tasks in specific environments. However, a more general intelligent system should be able to apply knowledge from one task to another, a process known as transfer learning. While some advances have been made using meta-learning and multi-task RL, achieving robust generalization across diverse tasks and environments remains a significant hurdle.

Reward Design: Defining an appropriate reward function is crucial because it drives the learning process. Poorly designed rewards can lead to suboptimal or even harmful policies. Automating reward design or learning reward structures from data is a promising research direction. Techniques such as inverse reinforcement learning (IRL) aim to infer reward functions from expert demonstrations, although this approach introduces its own complexities and challenges.

Safety and Ethical Considerations: As RL algorithms are increasingly applied in real-world scenarios, ensuring the safety and ethical behavior of these systems is crucial. This entails developing algorithms that can handle uncertainty, avoid harmful behaviors, and operate within ethical boundaries. Safety-focused approaches like Constrained Markov Decision Processes (CMDPs) and robust RL are active research areas aimed at addressing these issues.

```
from robust_rl_framework import RobustAlgorithm

env = RobustEnvironment()
algorithm = RobustAlgorithm(env)

# Train the robust algorithm
algorithm.train(num_episodes=1000)

# Evaluate the performance
performance = algorithm.evaluate()
```

```
print(performance)
```

Interpretability and Transparency: The black-box nature of many RL models, especially deep RL, poses challenges for interpretability. Stakeholders often require understandable rationales for the decisions made by RL agents. Efforts in this area include developing models that are inherently interpretable or employing methods to explain the decision-making process post hoc. This also includes visualizing policies and value functions effectively.

Computational Resources: Training RL models, especially those based on deep learning, demands significant computational resources. This includes not only processing power but also memory and storage capabilities. Distributed RL methods, hardware acceleration (e.g., GPUs and TPUs), and more efficient algorithms are being explored to mitigate these computational challenges.

Future Directions: The field of RL is rapidly evolving, and several forward-looking areas offer exciting prospects:

- **Hierarchical RL**: Developing hierarchical structures where complex tasks are broken down into simpler sub-tasks can improve learning efficiency. This approach mimics human problem-solving and has the potential to enhance scalability and generalization.
- **Multi-Agent RL (MARL)**: Many real-world problems involve multiple interacting agents. MARL focuses on these scenarios and seeks to develop agents that can cooperate, compete, and coexist effectively. Coordination, communication, and learning in these multi-agent settings remain active areas of research.
- **Continual Learning**: Enabling RL agents to learn continually from a stream of data, adapting to new information without forgetting previously learned tasks, is essential for long-term deployment in dynamic environments. Techniques like model consolidation and memory systems are being explored to address catastrophic forgetting.
- **Incorporating Human Feedback**: Leveraging human input during the training process can facilitate more robust and aligned learning. This includes interactive learning approaches, where

human feedback helps shape the RL agent's behavior in real-time.

- **Quantum Reinforcement Learning**: As quantum computing advances, the integration of quantum algorithms with RL presents a promising frontier. Quantum RL could potentially offer computational advantages for solving complex, high-dimensional problems.

Each of these directions not only promises to overcome current limitations but also aims to expand the applicability and robustness of RL in solving increasingly complex and meaningful problems.

Chapter 2

Markov Decision Processes

Markov Decision Processes (MDPs) provide the mathematical framework underpinning Reinforcement Learning. This chapter delves into the components of MDPs, including states, actions, rewards, and transition probabilities, and explains the Markov property. It covers policies, both deterministic and stochastic, value functions, Bellman equations, and methods for achieving optimality. Additionally, it addresses the discount factor, horizon, dynamic programming solutions, and applications in continuous spaces, offering practical examples and insights for solving MDPs.

2.1 Introduction to Markov Decision Processes

In the development and study of reinforcement learning, Markov Decision Processes (MDPs) provide a foundational mathematical framework that models decision-making situations where outcomes are partly random and partly under the control of a decision-maker. An MDP is defined by a tuple (S, A, P, R, γ) where:

- S is a finite set of states.

- A is a finite set of actions.
- P is the state transition probability function $P : S \times A \times S \to [0, 1]$.
- R is the reward function $R : S \times A \to \mathbb{R}$.
- γ is the discount factor $0 \leq \gamma \leq 1$.

The essence of MDPs lies in their ability to model environments in which an agent interacts by taking actions that affect future states. The key components and characteristics of an MDP are discussed to lay the foundation for deeper exploration.

A state $s \in S$ represents a configuration of the system at a particular time. The total set of states S encompasses all possible configurations the system can have. Actions $a \in A$ are the choices available to an agent at any given state. The transition probability function $P(s'|s, a)$ denotes the probability that the agent will transition to state s' when action a is taken in state s. The reward function $R(s, a)$ provides a scalar value that indicates the immediate gain or cost of performing action a in state s.

The discount factor γ, typically in the range $[0, 1]$, determines the present value of future rewards, ensuring that the sum of rewards over an infinite horizon remains finite. When γ is close to 1, future rewards are considered nearly as important as immediate rewards. Conversely, when γ is close to 0, the agent prioritizes immediate rewards over future gains.

To illustrate the structure of MDPs, consider the following Python example demonstrating a simple grid-world environment. The grid-world is composed of a 3x3 grid where an agent can move up, down, left, or right. Each action moves the agent to an adjacent cell, with certain cells providing rewards and others being terminal states. The following code initializes such an environment:

```
import numpy as np

class GridworldEnv:
    def __init__(self, grid_size=(3, 3), start_state=(0, 0), terminal_states=[(2, 2)]):
        self.grid_size = grid_size
        self.start_state = start_state
        self.terminal_states = terminal_states
        self.state = start_state

        self.action_space = ['UP', 'DOWN', 'LEFT', 'RIGHT']
        self.action_effects = {
            'UP': (-1, 0),
            'DOWN': (1, 0),
            'LEFT': (0, -1),
```

```
        'RIGHT': (0, 1)
    }

def step(self, action):
    if action in self.action_space:
        effect = self.action_effects[action]
        new_state = (self.state[0] + effect[0], self.state[1] + effect[1])

        if 0 <= new_state[0] < self.grid_size[0] and 0 <= new_state[1] < self.
            grid_size[1]:
            self.state = new_state

        if self.state in self.terminal_states:
            reward = 1
            done = True
        else:
            reward = -0.1
            done = False

        return self.state, reward, done
    else:
        raise ValueError("Invalid action provided")
```

The above Python environment specifies states as grid positions, actions as movements in a specified direction, and rewards based on reaching terminal states. The agent aims to navigate the grid to maximize cumulative rewards.

Executing the following steps in the grid-world would yield the sequence of states and rewards:

```
env = GridworldEnv()

print("Initial State:", env.state)

actions = ['DOWN', 'DOWN', 'RIGHT', 'RIGHT']
for action in actions:
    new_state, reward, done = env.step(action)
    print("Action:", action, "| New State:", new_state, "| Reward:", reward, "| Done:",
        done)
    if done:
        break
```

```
Initial State: (0, 0)
Action: DOWN | New State: (1, 0) | Reward: -0.1 | Done: False
Action: DOWN | New State: (2, 0) | Reward: -0.1 | Done: False
Action: RIGHT | New State: (2, 1) | Reward: -0.1 | Done: False
Action: RIGHT | New State: (2, 2) | Reward: 1 | Done: True
```

Through this progressive execution, the agent transitions from the initial state $(0, 0)$ to the terminal state $(2, 2)$, accruing incremental penalties and a final positive reward upon reaching the terminal state.

MDPs assume the Markov property, where the probability of transitioning to any state s' from state s depends only on s and action a, and not on any prior states or actions. This memoryless property allows MDPs to be efficiently tackled with various algorithmic strategies.

Understanding MDPs and their properties is critical for designing and implementing reinforcement learning algorithms, which seek to find optimal policies that maximize expected cumulative reward. This section outlines the framework and sets the stage for more sophisticated methods of solving MDPs discussed in subsequent sections.

2.2 Components of MDPs: States, Actions, and Rewards

A Markov Decision Process (MDP) is characterized by several key components: states, actions, and rewards. Understanding these components is crucial for mastering the framework of MDPs and, by extension, reinforcement learning. These elements define the environment in which an agent operates and the objectives it seeks to achieve through its interactions.

The **state** represents a specific configuration of the environment at a given time. Denoted as $s \in S$, where S is the set of all possible states, the state encapsulates all relevant information required for decision-making. States are assumed to provide sufficient information to make optimal decisions without needing to reference prior states, encapsulating the Markov property. Formally, a state at time t, s_t, contains all necessary information such that the future states depend only on the current state and action, and not on prior states or actions.

An **action**, represented as $a \in A$ where A is the set of all possible actions, is a decision or move taken by an agent from a given state. The set of actions available in state s is denoted by $A(s)$. Actions influence the transition between states, and the choice of action profoundly affects the ensuing reward and subsequent states based on the underlying transition dynamics of the MDP.

```
// Example structure for state and action in a C-like pseudocode
struct State {
    int position_x;
    int position_y;
    int velocity;
    // Add other relevant state variables
};

enum Action { UP, DOWN, LEFT, RIGHT, // Depending on the actions possible
    in the environment
};
```

The **reward**, indicated as $R(s,a)$, is a scalar feedback signal received after taking an action a in state s. The reward quantifies the immediate benefit or cost associated with the state-action pair, guiding the agent towards the objective, often involving maximization of cumulative reward over time. Mathematically, the reward function $R : S \times A \to \mathbb{R}$ assigns a real number reward to each state-action pair. Rewards can be deterministic or stochastic, depending on the nature of the environment.

Transition probabilities, which we will address more thoroughly in subsequent sections, define the dynamics of moving from one state to another given a particular action. Transition probabilities $P(s'|s,a)$ denote the probability of transitioning to state s' from state s after taking action a.

The illustration of these components can be refined through a practical example. Consider a gridworld environment where an agent navigates a matrix grid to reach a goal state:

- States (S) represent the agent's position on the grid, described as (x,y) coordinates.
- Actions (A) include moving up, down, left, or right.
- Rewards (R) might assign +1 for reaching the goal, -1 for hitting an obstacle, and 0 for all other transitions.

We can visualize a part of the environment's dynamics in pseudocode as follows:

```
class GridWorldMDP:
    def __init__(self, width, height):
        self.width = width
        self.height = height
        self.goal_state = (width - 1, height - 1)

    def is_goal_state(self, state):
        return state == self.goal_state

    def get_actions(self, state):
        actions = ["UP", "DOWN", "LEFT", "RIGHT"]
        return actions # Assume all actions are available in this simple example

    def get_reward(self, state, action):
        if self.is_goal_state(state):
            return 1 # Reward for reaching the goal
        elif state in self._obstacles():
            return -1 # Penalty for hitting an obstacle
        else:
            return 0 # Neutral reward for other transitions
```

```
    def _obstacles(self):
        return [(1, 1), (2, 3)] # Example coordinates of obstacles
```

The reward function R and the set of actions A are critical in shaping the agent's behavior. In easy-to-understand environments like gridworld, these concepts can be simplified, but in more complex environments the definitions and structures grow to accommodate richer dynamics and interactions.

Each of these components—states, actions, and rewards—play an integral role in defining the MDP's framework for decision-making and policy optimization. Formulating clear representations and accurately defining these components is essential in applying MDP concepts effectively.

2.3 The Markov Property

The Markov property is a fundamental characteristic of Markov Decision Processes (MDPs) and is pivotal for the simplification and tractability of these models. It asserts that the future state depends solely on the present state and action and is independent of the past states and actions. Formally, the Markov property can be expressed as:

$$P(S_{t+1} = s' \mid S_t = s, A_t = a) = P(S_{t+1} = s' \mid S_t = s, A_t = a,$$
$$S_{t-1} = s_{t-1}, A_{t-1} = a_{t-1}, \ldots, S_0 = s_0, A_0 = a_0)$$

Here, S_t denotes the state at time t and A_t denotes the action taken at time t. The equation states that the probability of transitioning to a state s' (at time $t+1$) depends only on the current state s and action a, not on any previous states or actions. This property significantly reduces the complexity of modeling and solving MDPs, as it allows the formulation of transition dynamics and policies without considering the entire trajectory history.

Implications of the Markov Property

By adhering to the Markov property, we assume that the state representation S_t is sufficiently comprehensive, encapsulating all relevant information about the history needed for decision-making. This ensures that past actions and states are effectively rendered irrelevant once the current state is known. This perspective is crucial for the following reasons:

- **Simplified Computation**: The Markov property simplifies computational requirements since decisions only depend on the current state. This leads to more efficient algorithms.
- **Modeling Flexibility**: It allows the use of recursive definitions, such as the Bellman equations, which underpin dynamic programming approaches used to solve MDPs.
- **Reduced State Space Complexity**: Instead of considering a potentially vast number of historical combinations, we only need to consider state-action pairs at each decision step.

Verifying the Markov Property

Ensuring that a given process adheres to the Markov property typically involves verifying that future states depend solely on the current state and action. Consider a process where this is not immediately clear, for example, if state S_t includes redundant components that contain historical information. One might need to redefine or refine the state representation to isolate the truly relevant components.

```
import numpy as np

# Define a transition function based on the Markov property
def transition_function(state, action):
    transition_matrix = {
        ('s1', 'a1'): 's2',
        ('s1', 'a2'): 's3',
        ('s2', 'a1'): 's3',
        ('s2', 'a2'): 's1',
    }
    return transition_matrix.get((state, action), None)

# Example to verify transition independence from historical states
current_state = 's1'
action = 'a1'
next_state = transition_function(current_state, action)
print(f"Next state from ({current_state}, {action}): {next_state}")
```

The above code snippet demonstrates a simple transition function in Python, illustrating the state transition based on the current state and action only. This exemplifies the Markov property in practice.

The Role of Memoryless Property in MDP

The Markov property is often referred to as the memoryless property because the system's behavior at any given time depends only on its current state, not on the sequence of events that preceded it. This is formally encapsulated in the definition of a memoryless random process or a Markov process. The significance is particularly evident in reinforcement learning, where learning algorithms rely on the assumption that future rewards and transitions are conditioned on the current state-action pair. This assumption allows the use of efficient learning algorithms like Q-learning, SARSA, and REINFORCE.

Relationship with Bellman Equations

The Bellman equations are foundational to solving MDPs and directly leverage the Markov property. The Bellman equation for the state-value function $V(s)$ in a finite MDP is:

$$V(s) = \mathbb{E}[R_{t+1} + \gamma V(S_{t+1}) \mid S_t = s]$$

Here, the expectation $\mathbb{E}$ is taken over all possible next states S_{t+1} and rewards R_{t+1}, conditioned only on the current state $S_t = s$. The Markov property ensures that this expression is valid.

Similarly, the Bellman equation for the action-value function $Q(s, a)$ is:

$$Q(s, a) = \mathbb{E}[R_{t+1} + \gamma \max_{a'} Q(S_{t+1}, a') \mid S_t = s, A_t = a]$$

In both cases, the future rewards and states are conditioned solely on the current state and action, underscoring the utilization of the Markov property.

Practical Considerations

When designing systems or models that are intended to exhibit Markovian behavior, it is crucial to ensure that the state representation is comprehensive enough to capture all relevant information. In practical applications, this might involve feature engineering or state abstraction techniques to encode the state accurately.

For example, in a robotics application where an agent navigates a maze, the state might need to include the robot's position and orientation but might exclude detailed historical paths traversed. Ensuring that the state space captures all pertinent dynamics is essential for the applicability of MDP solutions and the validity of the Markov property.

The Markov property provides a cornerstone for the theoretical foundation and practical implementation of MDPs, enabling a robust framework for sequential decision-making and reinforcement learning.

2.4 Transition Probabilities and Transition Matrices

A Markov Decision Process (MDP) is fundamentally characterized by its transition dynamics, which describe the probabilistic outcomes of taking actions in various states. The concept of transition probabilities and corresponding transition matrices lies at the heart of these dynamics.

Transition Probabilities $P(s'|s,a)$ represent the likelihood of transitioning from state s to state s' under action a. Formally, for any states $s \in S$ and $s' \in S$, and action $a \in A$:

$$P(s'|s,a) = \text{Pr}(S_{t+1} = s' \mid S_t = s, A_t = a)$$

where S_t is the state at time t and A_t is the action taken at time t. These probabilities must satisfy the properties of a probability distribution:

- Non-negativity: $P(s'|s,a) \geq 0$ for all $s, s' \in S$ and $a \in A$.
- Normalization: $\sum_{s' \in S} P(s'|s,a) = 1$ for all $s \in S$ and $a \in A$.

In practice, these probabilities can be presented in various forms. One common method involves using a **transition matrix**, denoted as P^a for each action $a \in A$. Each matrix P^a has dimensions $|S| \times |S|$ and encapsulates the transition probabilities when action a is taken:

$$P^a = \begin{pmatrix} P(s_1 \mid s_1, a) & P(s_2 \mid s_1, a) & \cdots & P(s_n \mid s_1, a) \\ P(s_1 \mid s_2, a) & P(s_2 \mid s_2, a) & \cdots & P(s_n \mid s_2, a) \\ \vdots & \vdots & \ddots & \vdots \\ P(s_1 \mid s_n, a) & P(s_2 \mid s_n, a) & \cdots & P(s_n \mid s_n, a) \end{pmatrix}$$

Representing Transition Matrices in Code

In computational settings, transition matrices can be represented and utilized effectively. Below is an example of how to define and manipulate transition matrices using Python and NumPy.

```
import numpy as np

# States and actions
states = ['s1', 's2', 's3']
actions = ['a1', 'a2']

# Transition matrix for action 'a1'
```

```
P_a1 = np.array([[0.8, 0.1, 0.1],
                 [0.2, 0.7, 0.1],
                 [0.1, 0.2, 0.7]])

# Transition matrix for action 'a2'
P_a2 = np.array([[0.9, 0.075, 0.025],
                 [0.15, 0.8, 0.05],
                 [0.05, 0.1, 0.85]])

# Sample transition matrix lookup function
def get_transition_probability(P, s, s_prime):
    return P[s, s_prime]

# Example usage
s, s_prime = 0, 1 # Indexes corresponding to 's1' -> 's2'
action = 'a1'
P = P_a1 if action == 'a1' else P_a2
probability = get_transition_probability(P, s, s_prime)
print(f"Transition probability P(s'='s{s_prime + 1}'|s='s{s + 1}', a='{action}') = {
    probability}")
```

```
Transition probability P(s'='s2'|s='s1', a='a1') = 0.1
```

Properties and Implications

Understanding transition probabilities and matrices is critically important for analyzing the behavior of an MDP. They are integral to both theoretical analysis and practical implementation. Several important properties arise from transition matrices:

- **Ergodicity**: A transition matrix is ergodic if there is a positive probability of moving from any state to any other state in a finite number of steps.
- **Reversibility**: If the transition process is reversible, it can be analyzed using techniques from reversible Markov chains, which simplifies certain computations.
- **Stationarity**: The transition probabilities are time-invariant, meaning that they do not change over time.

These properties influence algorithms for finding optimal policies and value functions in MDPs.

Estimating Transition Probabilities

In practical scenarios, transition probabilities may not always be known a priori. They can be estimated using data or experience. Let $N(s, a)$ be the number of times action a was taken in state s, and $N(s, a, s')$ be the number of times the system moved to state s' after taking action a in state s. Then, the estimated transition probability $\hat{P}(s'|s, a)$ can be computed as:

$$\hat{P}(s'|s,a) = \frac{N(s,a,s')}{N(s,a)}$$

Below is an example to illustrate the estimation process.

```
# Example data
state_action_transitions = {
    ('s1', 'a1'): {'s1': 8, 's2': 1, 's3': 1},
    ('s2', 'a1'): {'s1': 2, 's2': 7, 's3': 1},
    ('s3', 'a1'): {'s1': 1, 's2': 2, 's3': 7}
}

def estimate_transition_probability(transitions, s, a, s_prime):
    N_sa = sum(transitions[(s, a)].values())
    N_sas_prime = transitions[(s, a)].get(s_prime, 0)
    return N_sas_prime / N_sa

# Example usage
s, a, s_prime = 's1', 'a1', 's2'
estimated_prob = estimate_transition_probability(state_action_transitions, s, a,
    s_prime)
print(f"Estimated transition probability P(s'='{s_prime}'|s='{s}', a='{a}') = {
    estimated_prob}")
```

```
Estimated transition probability P(s'='s2'|s='s1', a='a1') = 0.1
```

Transition probabilities and transition matrices are pivotal components of MDPs and form the basis for dynamic optimization and control strategies. They encapsulate the essence of uncertainty and probabilistic decision-making inherent to reinforcement learning frameworks. Understanding and manipulating these constructs enables the design and analysis of algorithms that seek to maximize accumulated rewards in probabilistic environments.

2.5 Policies: Deterministic and Stochastic

A *policy* in the context of a Markov Decision Process (MDP) is a strategy or a set of rules that defines the actions to be taken at each state in order to maximize some notion of cumulative reward over time. Policies can be broadly classified into two categories: deterministic and stochastic.

A **deterministic policy**, denoted as $\pi(s)$, maps each state $s \in S$ (where S is the set of all states) to a specific action $a \in A$ (where A is the set of all actions). Formally, a deterministic policy is a function $\pi : S \to A$. If the MDP is in state s under a deterministic policy π, the action $\pi(s)$ is taken with certainty. This means that:

$$a_t = \pi(s_t) \quad \forall t \geq 0$$

which implies that the action a_t taken at time t when the system is in state s_t is determined exclusively by the policy π.

A **stochastic policy**, on the other hand, defines a probability distribution over actions for each state. Given a state $s \in S$, a stochastic policy $\pi(a|s)$ defines the probability of taking action a when the system is in state s. Formally, a stochastic policy is a function $\pi : S \times A \to [0, 1]$, where:

$$\sum_{a \in A} \pi(a|s) = 1 \quad \forall s \in S$$

This implies that the policy $\pi(a|s)$ gives the probability of selecting action a when in state s.

The distinction between deterministic and stochastic policies is essential, especially when dealing with environments that have inherent stochasticity or when approximation methods are employed. Deterministic policies are often simpler to implement and understand, but stochastic policies provide the flexibility of exploration, which can be crucial in avoiding local optima and ensuring optimal performance in complex environments.

To gain an understanding of how policies function, consider the following pseudocode for executing a deterministic policy in a simple MDP:

```
def execute_deterministic_policy(policy, environment, num_steps):
    state = environment.initial_state()
    total_reward = 0
    for step in range(num_steps):
        action = policy(state)
        next_state, reward = environment.step(state, action)
        total_reward += reward
        state = next_state
        if environment.is_terminal(state):
            break
    return total_reward
```

The above pseudocode outlines the process of executing a deterministic policy. The 'policy' function takes a state and returns an action. The 'environment' provides the initial state and a method to perform actions and retrieve the next state along with the received reward. The loop iterates through the specified number of steps or until a terminal state is reached.

In the case of a stochastic policy, the action selection involves sampling from a probability distribution. This can be demonstrated as follows:

```
import numpy as np

def execute_stochastic_policy(policy, environment, num_steps):
    state = environment.initial_state()
```

```
    total_reward = 0
    for step in range(num_steps):
        action_probabilities = policy(state)
        action = np.random.choice(len(action_probabilities), p=action_probabilities)
        next_state, reward = environment.step(state, action)
        total_reward += reward
        state = next_state
        if environment.is_terminal(state):
            break
    return total_reward
```

Here, execute_stochastic_policy utilizes the np.random.choice function to sample an action based on the probability distribution provided by the policy function, which returns an array of action probabilities for the current state.

For small MDPs, it is feasible to evaluate policies exhaustively, but for larger state spaces, it becomes computationally intractable. In such cases, policy evaluation techniques like policy iteration and value iteration, which will be discussed later in this book, are employed to determine the optimal policy. Deterministic and stochastic policies play a crucial role in various Reinforcement Learning algorithms. Consider, for instance, Q-learning, which seeks to learn an optimal deterministic policy. On the other hand, algorithms such as REINFORCE (a policy-gradient method) inherently work with stochastic policies.

Thus, understanding the differences and applications of both deterministic and stochastic policies is fundamental to the study and practical implementation of MDPs in the realm of Reinforcement Learning.

2.6 Value Functions and Bellman Equations

The value function is a central concept in the context of Markov Decision Processes (MDPs) and reinforcement learning. It quantitatively captures the expected long-term benefit of being in a particular state and taking certain actions. This section will explore the mathematical formulation and significance of value functions and elucidate the Bellman equations that provide a foundation for evaluating and optimizing these functions.

An agent's objective in an MDP is to maximize some notion of cumulative reward. To formalize this, we define two key types of value functions: the state-value function, $V(s)$, and the action-value function, $Q(s, a)$.

The state-value function, $V(s)$, for a policy π is defined as:

$$V^{\pi}(s) = \mathbb{E}_{\pi}\left[\sum_{t=0}^{\infty} \gamma^t R_{t+1} \mid S_0 = s\right]$$

where R_{t+1} is the reward received at time $t+1$, S_0 is the initial state, γ is the discount factor capturing the present value of future rewards, and $\mathbb{E}_{\pi}[\cdot]$ denotes the expectation given that the agent follows policy π.

The action-value function, $Q(s, a)$, for a policy π is defined as:

$$Q^{\pi}(s, a) = \mathbb{E}_{\pi}\left[\sum_{t=0}^{\infty} \gamma^t R_{t+1} \mid S_0 = s, A_0 = a\right]$$

Here, $A_0 = a$ indicates that the action a is taken from state s initially.

These value functions encapsulate two principal aspects:

- **Prediction:** Given a policy π, what is the expected return? This is provided by $V^{\pi}(s)$ and $Q^{\pi}(s, a)$.
- **Control:** What is the optimal policy π^* that maximizes the expected return? This is achieved by finding the optimal value functions $V^*(s)$ and $Q^*(s, a)$.

Through the optimal value functions, we can derive the optimal policy. Now, we introduce the Bellman equations, which are recursive relationships used to compute these value functions.

The Bellman equation for the state-value function is given by:

$$V^{\pi}(s) = \mathbb{E}_{\pi}\left[R_{t+1} + \gamma V^{\pi}(S_{t+1}) \mid S_t = s\right]$$

This equation states that the value of state s under policy π is the expected reward plus the discounted value of the next state, following the same policy.

To expand further, using the law of total expectation, we can decompose this into:

$$V^{\pi}(s) = \sum_{a \in \mathcal{A}} \pi(a \mid s) \sum_{s' \in \mathcal{S}} P(s' \mid s, a)\left[R(s, a, s') + \gamma V^{\pi}(s')\right]$$

where $\mathcal{S}$ and $\mathcal{A}$ are the state and action spaces respectively, $P(s' \mid s, a)$ represents the transition probability from state s to state s' given action a, and $R(s, a, s')$ is the reward associated with transition (s, a, s').

The Bellman equation for the action-value function, analogous to the state-value function, is:

$$Q^{\pi}(s,a) = \mathbb{E}_{\pi}\left[R_{t+1} + \gamma Q^{\pi}(S_{t+1}, A_{t+1}) \mid S_t = s, A_t = a\right]$$

By expanding the total expectation, we have:

$$Q^{\pi}(s,a) = \sum_{s' \in \mathcal{S}} P(s' \mid s,a)\left[R(s,a,s') + \gamma \sum_{a' \in \mathcal{A}} \pi(a' \mid s') Q^{\pi}(s',a')\right]$$

For control purposes, we seek the optimal value functions. The Bellman optimality equation for the state-value function is:

$$V^*(s) = \max_{a \in \mathcal{A}} \sum_{s' \in \mathcal{S}} P(s' \mid s,a)\left[R(s,a,s') + \gamma V^*(s')\right]$$

The optimal state-value function $V^*(s)$ represents the maximum expected return achievable from state s.

Similarly, the Bellman optimality equation for the action-value function is:

$$Q^*(s,a) = \sum_{s' \in \mathcal{S}} P(s' \mid s,a)\left[R(s,a,s') + \gamma \max_{a' \in \mathcal{A}} Q^*(s',a')\right]$$

Here, $Q^*(s,a)$ represents the maximum expected return starting from state s, taking action a, and thereafter following the optimal policy.

Solving these equations typically involves iterative methods such as value iteration or policy iteration, which iteratively refine estimates of the value functions until they converge to the optimal functions.

Algorithm 1 presents the pseudocode for value iteration, which directly computes the optimal state-value function V^*.

```
# Value Iteration Algorithm
def value_iteration(P, R, gamma, theta):
    V = np.zeros(num_states)
    while True:
        delta = 0
        for s in range(num_states):
            v = V[s]
            V[s] = max([sum([P[s, a, s'] * (R[s, a, s'] + gamma * V[s'])
                        for s' in range(num_states)]) for a in range(num_actions)])
            delta = max(delta, abs(v - V[s]))
        if delta < theta:
            break
    return V # optimal state-value function
```

Here, P and R are the transition probability and reward matrices, γ is the discount factor, and θ is a small threshold for determining convergence. The algorithm initializes the value function V to zeros, updates it based on the Bellman optimality equation, and iterates until the value function converges within the given threshold.

Evaluating value functions and solving Bellman equations provide a rigorous mechanism for determining optimal policies in MDPs, laying the groundwork for more advanced topics in reinforcement learning.

2.7 Optimality and Solution Methods for MDPs

In this section, we delve into the intricate subject of optimality within the context of Markov Decision Processes (MDPs) and explore various methods to achieve it. The goal is to find a policy that maximizes the expected cumulative reward, and understanding the concept of optimality is critical for reinforcing learning agents.

An optimal policy π^* is a policy that produces the highest value for every state in the MDP. Formally, for any state $s \in S$,

$$V^*(s) = \max_{\pi} V^{\pi}(s)$$

where $V^{\pi}(s)$ is the value function for the policy π. The value function $V(s)$ provides the expected return starting from state s and following a particular policy π. Another critical component is the action-value function $Q^{\pi}(s, a)$, which is the expected return starting from state s, taking action a, and following policy π thereafter.

To describe the optimality, the Bellman optimality equation serves as a foundational tool. For the state-value function, it is given by:

$$V^*(s) = \max_{a \in A} \left[R(s, a) + \gamma \sum_{s'} P(s'|s, a) V^*(s') \right]$$

Similarly, the Bellman optimality equation for the action-value function is:

$$Q^*(s, a) = R(s, a) + \gamma \sum_{s'} P(s'|s, a) \max_{a'} Q^*(s', a')$$

The equations above imply that the value of a state under an optimal policy equals the expected return starting from that state, taking the best action, and thereafter following the optimal policy.

Several methods exist to solve MDPs and find these optimal policies, among which are Dynamic Programming (DP), Monte Carlo Methods, and Temporal Difference (TD) Learning. Here, we will focus on prominent dynamic programming approaches: Value Iteration and Policy Iteration.

Value Iteration:

Value Iteration starts with an initial guess of the value function $V(s)$ and iteratively refines it using the Bellman optimality equation. The key idea is to update the value of each state by considering the maximum expected return obtainable from any action at each step. The algorithm is as follows:

```
Initialize V(s), for all s in S, arbitrarily except that V(terminal) = 0
Repeat:Δ
  = 0
  For each s in S:
    v = V(s)
    V(s) = max_a ΣP(s'|s,a) [R(s,a,s') + V(s')]Δ
      = maxΔ(, |v - V(s)|)
Until Δ< (a small positive number)
```

This process continues until the change Δ in the value function $V(s)$ is smaller than a predefined threshold θ, indicating convergence.

Policy Iteration:

Policy Iteration involves two main steps: policy evaluation and policy improvement. It starts with an arbitrary policy and iteratively improves it. The steps are as follows:

- **Policy Evaluation:** Calculate the value function $V^{\pi}(s)$ for the current policy π. This step typically involves solving a system of linear equations:

$$V^{\pi}(s) = \sum_{a \in A} \pi(a|s) \left[R(s,a) + \gamma \sum_{s'} P(s'|s,a) V^{\pi}(s') \right]$$

- **Policy Improvement:** Improve the policy by acting greedily with respect to the value function obtained:

$$\pi'(s) = \arg\max_{a \in A} \left[R(s,a) + \gamma \sum_{s'} P(s'|s,a) V^{\pi}(s') \right]$$

```
Initialize (s) arbitrarily
Repeat:
  Policy Evaluation:
    Repeat:
      = 0
```

```
        For each s in S:
            v = V(s)
            V(s) = ΣP(s'|s ,(s)) [R(s ,(s)) +  V(s')]
             = max (, |v -  V(s)|)
    Until  <
Policy Improvement:
    policy-stable = true
    For each s in S:
        old-action =  (s)
        (s) = argmax_a ΣP(s'|s,a) [R(s,a) +  V(s')]
        If old-action !=  (s), then policy-stable = false
Until policy-stable
```

Both value iteration and policy iteration are guaranteed to converge to the optimal policy for a given MDP, provided sufficient computation is allowed. Practical implementations utilize these algorithms' underlying principles, optimizing iteratively to approach or achieve an optimal policy in the given state space. Accurate implementation and understanding of these methods underpin the development of advanced reinforcement learning systems.

2.8 Discount Factor and Horizon

The discount factor and horizon are pivotal concepts in the study of Markov Decision Processes (MDPs). These constructs help manage future rewards and delineate the planning span for decision-making processes. Understanding these concepts requires a thorough exploration of their definitions, implications, and applications in solving MDPs.

The *discount factor*, typically denoted by γ (where $0 \leq \gamma \leq 1$), quantifies the importance of future rewards relative to immediate rewards. It ensures that rewards received in the future are worth less than immediate rewards, thereby preventing unrealistic scenarios where long-term benefits are infinitely valued. The choice of γ profoundly influences the agent's behavior, with lower values favoring short-term gains and higher values valuing future rewards more substantially.

For any reward R_t received at time step t, the discounted reward can be represented as $\gamma^t R_t$. The total discounted reward, also known as the *return*, is defined as:

$$G_t = \sum_{k=0}^{\infty} \gamma^k R_{t+k}$$

where G_t denotes the return starting from time step t. This formulation sums the infinite series of future rewards, each weighted by a power of the discount factor γ.

When $\gamma = 0$, the agent solely prioritizes immediate rewards, effectively ignoring all future rewards:

$$G_t = R_t$$

Conversely, when $\gamma = 1$, the agent considers future rewards at par with immediate rewards, often leading to computational and practical challenges, as this implies an infinite horizon without devaluation:

$$G_t = \sum_{k=0}^{\infty} R_{t+k}$$

Typically, $0 < \gamma < 1$ strikes a balance between immediate and distant rewards, ensuring convergence in most reinforcement learning algorithms.

The notion of *horizon* refers to the temporal extent over which the agent's planning spans. The horizon can be categorized as either *finite* (episodic tasks) or *infinite* (continuing tasks):

- **Finite Horizon**: In tasks with a definitive endpoint, the planning horizon is finite. For example, consider an episode of length T. The return in this case is:

$$G_t = \sum_{k=0}^{T-t} \gamma^k R_{t+k}$$

  Here, the agent computes the sum of rewards only up to the terminal state, re-evaluating strategies at each episode's conclusion.

- **Infinite Horizon**: In ongoing tasks where there is no natural termination point, the horizon is infinite. The agent must consider a potentially unending sequence of rewards:

$$G_t = \sum_{k=0}^{\infty} \gamma^k R_{t+k}$$

  This often necessitates policies and value functions that stabilize over time through discounted sums.

Finite horizon problems lend themselves to dynamic programming solutions such as finite-time value iteration, whereas infinite horizon problems are typically addressed using steady-state assumptions, leveraging algorithms like policy iteration and Q-learning.

The choice of γ and the nature of the horizon influences the computation of the value function $V(s)$ and the state-action value function $Q(s, a)$. These functions are cornerstones in the formulation and solution of MDPs. For a given policy π, the value function captures the expected return by starting in state s:

$$V^{\pi}(s) = \mathbb{E}_{\pi}\left[\sum_{k=0}^{\infty} \gamma^k R_{t+k} \mid S_t = s\right]$$

and the state-action value function indicates the expected return for taking action a in state s under policy π:

$$Q^{\pi}(s, a) = \mathbb{E}_{\pi}\left[\sum_{k=0}^{\infty} \gamma^k R_{t+k} \mid S_t = s, A_t = a\right]$$

Consider the following Python snippet demonstrating the calculation of discounted rewards for a simple reward sequence:

```
def discounted_rewards(rewards, gamma):
    discounted = []
    for t in range(len(rewards)):
        G_t = sum([gamma**k * rewards[t + k] for k in range(len(rewards) - t)])
        discounted.append(G_t)
    return discounted

rewards = [1, 1, 1, 1]
gamma = 0.9
print(discounted_rewards(rewards, gamma))
```

The expected output for this code with $\gamma = 0.9$ and a reward sequence of $[1, 1, 1, 1]$ would be:

```
[3.439, 2.71, 1.9, 1.0]
```

Each value in the output sequence represents the discounted sum of future rewards from the respective time step, illustrating the concept of compounded discounting.

The choice of the discount factor and the nature of the planning horizon must be aligned with the specific problem context and the intended behavior of the reinforcement learning agent. By adjusting these parameters, the agent can be finely tuned to strike a balance between exploration of future possibilities and exploitation of immediate gains, facilitating efficient and effective decision-making in the scope of MDPs.

2.9 Solving MDPs Using Dynamic Programming

Dynamic programming (DP) algorithms play a crucial role in solving Markov Decision Processes (MDPs) by leveraging the inherent structure of these problems. Specifically, DP methods break down the problem into smaller subproblems and solve them recursively. This section explores the fundamental dynamic programming techniques used to solve MDPs: Policy Evaluation, Policy Iteration, and Value Iteration.

At the heart of dynamic programming methods for MDPs lies Bellman's principle of optimality, which asserts that an optimal policy has the property that, regardless of the initial state and initial decision, the remaining decisions must constitute an optimal policy concerning the state resulting from the first decision.

A common assumption for the following algorithms is the presence of finite state and action spaces, denoted as $\mathcal{S}$ and $\mathcal{A}$, respectively. We also consider a stationary policy $\pi : \mathcal{S} \to \mathcal{A}$ and a reward function $R : \mathcal{S} \times \mathcal{A} \to \mathbb{R}$. Lastly, the state transition probability $P(s'|s,a)$ governs the dynamics of the system, representing the probability of transiting to state s' given state s and action a.

Policy Evaluation

Policy evaluation entails computing the state-value function $v_\pi(s)$ for a given policy π. This function represents the expected return when starting in state s and following policy π thereafter. Formally, the state-value function satisfies the Bellman expectation equation:

$$v_\pi(s) = \sum_{a \in \mathcal{A}} \pi(a|s) \sum_{s' \in \mathcal{S}} P(s'|s,a)[R(s,a) + \gamma v_\pi(s')],$$

where $\gamma \in [0,1)$ is the discount factor.

The iterative policy evaluation algorithm updates the value function estimate $v_k(s)$ at each iteration k by:

$$v_{k+1}(s) = \sum_{a \in \mathcal{A}} \pi(a|s) \sum_{s' \in \mathcal{S}} P(s'|s,a)[R(s,a) + \gamma v_k(s')],$$

until the value function converges.

Here is a Python pseudocode implementation of Policy Evaluation using the Bellman expectation equation:

```
def policy_evaluation(policy, env, gamma=0.99, theta=1e-6):
    value_function = np.zeros(env.num_states)
    while True:
        delta = 0
        for state in range(env.num_states):
            new_value = 0
            for action in range(env.num_actions):
                for next_state in range(env.num_states):
                    prob = env.P[state][action][next_state]
                    reward = env.R[state][action][next_state]
                    new_value += policy[state, action] * prob * (reward + gamma *
                        value_function[next_state])
            delta = max(delta, np.abs(new_value - value_function[state]))
            value_function[state] = new_value
        if delta < theta:
            break
    return value_function
```

Policy Iteration

Policy iteration is an algorithm that seeks to find the optimal policy by iterating through two steps: policy evaluation and policy improvement. The idea is that if one has the correct value function for a policy, one can then improve the policy by acting greedily with respect to that value function.

The policy iteration algorithm alternates between:

- Policy Evaluation: Compute $v_\pi(s)$ for the current policy π.
- Policy Improvement: Update the policy π by selecting actions that maximize the expected return:

$$\pi'(s) = \arg\max_{a \in \mathcal{A}} \sum_{s' \in \mathcal{S}} P(s'|s,a)[R(s,a) + \gamma v_\pi(s')].$$

This process is repeated until the policy stabilizes, i.e., when policy improvement yields no changes in the policy.

The pseudocode for Policy Iteration is as follows:

```
def policy_iteration(env, gamma=0.99, theta=1e-6):
    policy = np.ones([env.num_states, env.num_actions]) / env.num_actions #
        Initialize a random policy
    value_function = np.zeros(env.num_states)

    while True:
        value_function = policy_evaluation(policy, env, gamma, theta)
        policy_stable = True
        for state in range(env.num_states):
            old_action = np.argmax(policy[state])
            action_values = np.zeros(env.num_actions)
            for action in range(env.num_actions):
                for next_state in range(env.num_states):
```

```
                prob = env.P[state][action][next_state]
                reward = env.R[state][action][next_state]
                action_values[action] += prob * (reward + gamma * value_function[
                    next_state])
            best_action = np.argmax(action_values)
            policy[state] = np.eye(env.num_actions)[best_action]
            if old_action != best_action:
                policy_stable = False
        if policy_stable:
            break
    return policy, value_function
```

Value Iteration

Value iteration simplifies the policy iteration process by combining policy evaluation and improvement in a single sweep through the state space. The algorithm directly updates the state-value function using the Bellman optimality equation:

$$v_{k+1}(s) = \max_{a \in \mathcal{A}} \sum_{s' \in \mathcal{S}} P(s'|s,a)[R(s,a) + \gamma v_k(s')],$$

At convergence, the value iteration algorithm yields the optimal state-value function v_*, from which the optimal policy π_* can be derived as:

$$\pi_*(s) = \arg\max_{a \in \mathcal{A}} \sum_{s' \in \mathcal{S}} P(s'|s,a)[R(s,a) + \gamma v_*(s')].$$

The pseudocode for Value Iteration is as follows:

```
def value_iteration(env, gamma=0.99, theta=1e-6):
    value_function = np.zeros(env.num_states)
    while True:
        delta = 0
        for state in range(env.num_states):
            best_action_value = float('-inf')
            for action in range(env.num_actions):
                action_value = 0
                for next_state in range(env.num_states):
                    prob = env.P[state][action][next_state]
                    reward = env.R[state][action][next_state]
                    action_value += prob * (reward + gamma * value_function[
                        next_state])
                best_action_value = max(best_action_value, action_value)
            delta = max(delta, abs(best_action_value - value_function[state]))
            value_function[state] = best_action_value
        if delta < theta:
            break

    policy = np.zeros([env.num_states, env.num_actions])
    for state in range(env.num_states):
        action_values = np.zeros(env.num_actions)
        for action in range(env.num_actions):
            for next_state in range(env.num_states):
```

```
            prob = env.P[state][action][next_state]
            reward = env.R[state][action][next_state]
            action_values[action] += prob * (reward + gamma * value_function[
                next_state])
        best_action = np.argmax(action_values)
        policy[state] = np.eye(env.num_actions)[best_action]

    return policy, value_function
```

These dynamic programming algorithms—Policy Evaluation, Policy Iteration, and Value Iteration—offer foundational methods for finding optimal strategies in MDPs. They exploit the recursive structure of MDPs and provide a framework for solving finite-state and finite-action decision problems efficiently.

2.10 MDPs in Continuous Spaces

In practical scenarios, it is often the case that the state and action spaces are continuous rather than discrete. Continuous state and action spaces introduce additional complexities in the formulation and solutions of Markov Decision Processes (MDPs). This section explores the theoretical foundations and computational approaches for handling MDPs in continuous spaces.

In the context of continuous spaces, the state space S and the action space A are typically subsets of $\mathbb{R}^n$. This continuous nature demands that we extend our discrete representations of the transition probabilities, policies, and value functions.

State Transition Dynamics

For MDPs with continuous state spaces, the transition dynamics are often described by a probability density function $p(s' \mid s, a)$, which represents the probability density of transitioning from state s to state s' when action a is taken. Mathematically, this can be represented as:

$$\int_{S'} p(s' \mid s, a)\, ds' = 1 \quad \forall s \in S, a \in A, S' \subset S$$

Here, $\int_{S'} p(s' \mid s, a)\, ds'$ gives the cumulative probability of transitioning from state s to any state within the subset S' in the state space.

Continuous Policies

When dealing with continuous action spaces, policies can no longer be described using simple discrete mappings. Instead, we employ deterministic and stochastic policies in the following manner:

- **Deterministic Policy:** A deterministic policy π in continuous spaces maps each state s to a specific action a, such that $\pi(s) = a$.
- **Stochastic Policy:** A stochastic policy $\pi(a \mid s)$ provides a probability density over the action space for a given state. Each state $s \in S$ is associated with a probability density function over the actions:

$$\int_A \pi(a \mid s)\, da = 1 \quad \forall s \in S$$

Value Functions in Continuous Spaces

Analogous to discrete MDPs, we define the state value function $V^\pi(s)$ and the action value function $Q^\pi(s,a)$ for continuous MDPs. However, due to the continuity of the state and action spaces, these functions are expressed as integrals:

The state value function for a policy π is given by:

$$V^\pi(s) = \int_S p(s' \mid s, \pi(s)) \left[r(s, \pi(s)) + \gamma V^\pi(s')\right] ds'$$

The action value function for a policy π is given by:

$$Q^\pi(s,a) = r(s,a) + \gamma \int_S p(s' \mid s,a) V^\pi(s')\, ds'$$

Bellman Equations in Continuous Spaces

The Bellman equations for continuous state and action spaces extend from their discrete counterparts. For a given policy π, the Bellman expectation equation for the state value function $V^\pi(s)$ is written as:

$$V^\pi(s) = \int_A \pi(a \mid s) \left[r(s,a) + \gamma \int_S p(s' \mid s,a) V^\pi(s')\, ds'\right] da$$

Similarly, the Bellman expectation equation for the action value function $Q^\pi(s,a)$ is:

$$Q^\pi(s,a) = r(s,a) + \gamma \int_S p(s' \mid s,a) \left(\int_A \pi(a' \mid s') Q^\pi(s',a')\, da' \right) ds'$$

The Bellman optimality equations follow in a similar vein. For the optimal state value function $V^*(s)$:

$$V^*(s) = \max_{a \in A} \left[r(s,a) + \gamma \int_S p(s' \mid s,a) V^*(s') \, ds' \right]$$

For the optimal action value function $Q^*(s,a)$:

$$Q^*(s,a) = r(s,a) + \gamma \int_S p(s' \mid s,a) \max_{a' \in A} Q^*(s',a') \, ds'$$

Solution Methods for Continuous MDPs

Due to the continuous nature of state and action spaces, traditional tabular methods such as dynamic programming become impractical. Instead, continuous MDPs often necessitate the use of approximation methods. Key techniques include:

- **Function Approximation:** Techniques such as Linear Function Approximation, Neural Networks, and Gaussian Processes are employed to approximate $V^\pi(s)$ and $Q^\pi(s,a)$.
- **Discretization:** The continuous spaces can be discretized into a finite number of intervals or grids, allowing the application of traditional methods. Care must be taken to balance the trade-off between precision and computational complexity.
- **Monte Carlo Methods:** These methods leverage random sampling to estimate value functions and policies, with techniques such as Monte Carlo Tree Search (MCTS) being particularly effective in planning under uncertainty.
- **Policy Gradient Methods:** Instead of approximating value functions directly, policy gradient methods optimize the policy parameters using gradient ascent techniques. The policy is often parameterized as $\pi_\theta(a \mid s)$, where θ are the policy parameters:

```
for each iteration:
    generate episodes using current policy \( \pi_\theta \)
    for each episode:
        compute returns
        update policy parameters using gradient ascent
```

Applications in Continuous Spaces

MDPs in continuous spaces find applications across various domains, including robotics, finance, and autonomous systems. An example of such an application is the control of an autonomous vehicle, where the state space is comprised of continuous variables such as position, velocity, and acceleration, and actions include throttle, braking, and steering commands. The goal is to optimize the driving policy π to navigate efficiently while avoiding obstacles.

Another notable example is in portfolio optimization in finance, where the state space includes asset prices and portfolio weights, and the actions correspond to the buying and selling of assets. The objective is to maximize the expected return while managing risk.

These applications highlight the versatility and necessity of handling continuous spaces within the framework of MDPs. The theoretical and computational methodologies discussed herein provide foundational approaches for devising solutions to these complex, real-world problems.

2.11 Applications and Examples of MDPs

Markov Decision Processes (MDPs) provide a robust framework for modeling decision-making problems where outcomes are partly random and partly under the control of the decision-maker. Their versatility makes them applicable across a wide array of domains. We will examine applications in robotics, finance, healthcare, and gaming, illustrating how the theoretical concepts translate to practical scenarios.

Robotics

In robotics, MDPs are extensively used for navigation, manipulation, and control tasks. A robot navigating through an environment to reach a target location can be modeled as an MDP. Here, the *states* represent the possible locations of the robot in the environment, the *actions* are the possible movements the robot can make (e.g., move forward, turn left, turn right), and the *rewards* are associated with the successful completion of tasks (e.g., reaching the target location).

Consider a grid world where a robot must navigate from a start position to a goal position. We define the state space as the set of all grid locations, the action space includes movement in four directions (up, down, left, right), and the reward function assigns a high reward for reaching the goal and small negative rewards for each step taken to encourage efficiency. The transition probabilities model the uncertainty in the robot's movements due to slippage or obstacles.

```
# Define the environment
import gym
import numpy as np

env = gym.make('FrozenLake-v0')

# Initialize variables
state = env.reset()
done = False

while not done:
    action = np.random.choice(env.action_space.n) # Random action
    next_state, reward, done, info = env.step(action)
    state = next_state

    env.render()
```

Here, the 'FrozenLake-v0' environment from OpenAI's Gym library represents a simplified version of the grid world scenario. The robot (agent) navigates on a slippery surface to reach the goal while avoiding holes.

Finance

In finance, MDPs are used for portfolio management, trading strategies, and risk assessment. The decision process involves determining an optimal policy to maximize expected returns while considering the stochastic nature of financial markets. States represent various market conditions, actions signify different investment decisions, and rewards correspond to financial gains or losses.

As an example, consider a portfolio optimization problem where the state space includes different asset prices and market indicators, actions represent the proportion of capital allocated to each asset, and rewards are the returns from the investments. Transition probabilities are derived from historical market data.

```
import numpy as np
import pandas as pd

# Define states, actions, and rewards
states = ['Bull', 'Bear', 'Stagnant']
actions = ['Invest in Stock', 'Invest in Bonds', 'Hold Cash']
rewards = {'Bull': {'Stock': 0.1, 'Bonds': 0.02, 'Cash': 0.01},
           'Bear': {'Stock': -0.1, 'Bonds': 0.01, 'Cash': 0.01},
           'Stagnant': {'Stock': 0.05, 'Bonds': 0.03, 'Cash': 0.01}}

# Define transition probabilities
transition_matrix = np.array([[0.8, 0.1, 0.1],
                              [0.2, 0.7, 0.1],
                              [0.3, 0.3, 0.4]])

# Load historical market data
```

```
market_data = pd.read_csv('market_data.csv')

# Portfolio optimization logic
# [...additional logic based on market data...]
```

Healthcare

MDPs are applied in healthcare for treatment planning, resource allocation, and patient management. For instance, in treating chronic diseases, healthcare providers must frequently make decisions on treatments based on patient conditions. States represent different health conditions, actions are treatment options, and rewards are linked to patient outcomes such as recovery rates or quality of life improvements.

An example is the management of diabetes, where patients' health states could include blood glucose levels, actions might be insulin dosage adjustments, and rewards could be quantified by the stabilization of glucose levels within the desired range.

```
# Example state space: blood glucose levels
states = ['Low', 'Normal', 'High']

# Example actions: insulin dosage adjustments
actions = ['Increase Dose', 'Decrease Dose', 'Maintain Dose']

# Example rewards: stabilization of glucose levels
rewards = {'Normal': 1, 'Low': -1, 'High': -1}

# Example transition probabilities
transition_probs = {'Low': {'Increase Dose': 0.7, 'Maintain Dose': 0.2, 'Decrease Dose':
        0.1},
                    'Normal': {'Increase Dose': 0.1, 'Maintain Dose': 0.8, 'Decrease Dose':
                        0.1},
                    'High': {'Increase Dose': 0.1, 'Maintain Dose': 0.2, 'Decrease Dose':
                        0.7}}
```

Gaming

MDPs are also prominent in game theory and artificial intelligence for games. They are used to model decision-making processes in games where outcomes depend on both the players' strategies and chance events. States represent various game positions, actions are possible moves, and rewards correspond to the game outcomes (e.g., win, loss, draw).

For example, in a simple game like Tic-Tac-Toe, each state is a distinct board configuration, actions are the possible placements of Xs and Os, and rewards are assigned based on winning, losing, or drawing.

```
# Tic-Tac-Toe game representation
board = np.zeros((3, 3)) # Initial empty board

# States: different board configurations
```

```
# Actions: possible moves for X and O
# Rewards: +1 for win, -1 for loss, 0 for draw
def reward(state, player):
    if check_win(state, player):
        return 1
    elif check_win(state, -player):
        return -1
    else:
        return 0

def check_win(board, player):
    # Logic to check win for the player
    for line in winning_lines:
        if all(board[pos] == player for pos in line):
            return True
    return False

winning_lines = [[(0, 0), (0, 1), (0, 2)], [(1, 0), (1, 1), (1, 2)], [(2, 0), (2, 1), (2, 2)],
                 [(0, 0), (1, 0), (2, 0)], [(0, 1), (1, 1), (2, 1)], [(0, 2), (1, 2), (2, 2)],
                 [(0, 0), (1, 1), (2, 2)], [(0, 2), (1, 1), (2, 0)]]

# Example game play move
current_state = board
current_player = 1 # Assume 1 represents X, and -1 represents O

next_move = (1, 1) # Next move position
board[next_move] = current_player # Apply the move
reward = reward(board, current_player) # Calculate the reward
```

By exploring these applications, one can appreciate the adaptability of MDPs in modeling complex decision-making problems. They offer structured methodologies to derive optimal policies, enabling improved outcomes across various domains.

Chapter 3

Dynamic Programming

Dynamic Programming (DP) techniques form the backbone of solving complex decision-making problems in Reinforcement Learning. This chapter covers the principles of optimality, key algorithms such as value iteration and policy iteration, and the differences between synchronous and asynchronous methods. It discusses the efficiency and convergence of DP methods, the concepts of generalized policy iteration, and approaches for dealing with infinite state and action spaces. Additionally, it explores approximate dynamic programming and practical applications showcasing the power of these techniques.

3.1 Introduction to Dynamic Programming

Dynamic Programming (DP) is a powerful method for solving complex decision-making problems that arise in the field of Reinforcement Learning (RL). It is particularly useful for problems characterized by a sequential decision process where decisions need to be made at multiple time steps, with each decision potentially affecting future decisions and outcomes. DP is grounded in the principle of optimality defined by Richard Bellman, which states that an optimal policy has the property that, whatever the initial state and initial decision are, the remaining decisions must constitute an optimal policy with regard to the state resulting from the first decision.

At its core, DP involves breaking down larger problems into smaller, more manageable subproblems and solving each of these subproblems only once, storing their solutions typically in a tabular format to avoid redundant computations. This technique exploits the recursive nature of many decision problems and is applicable in both finite and infinite state spaces.

DP methods can be divided into several key algorithms. These include:

- **Value Iteration:** This algorithm iteratively updates the value of each state using the Bellman equation until convergence, yielding the optimal value function.
- **Policy Iteration:** This algorithm involves two main steps: policy evaluation, where the value function of a given policy is determined, and policy improvement, where the policy is updated to be greedy with respect to the current value function.
- **Asynchronous Dynamic Programming:** Unlike synchronous methods that update values for all states simultaneously, asynchronous methods update values for states incrementally and are particularly useful in large state spaces.

Value Iteration: Value iteration is one of the most fundamental methods within DP. The iterative process involves initializing the value function to arbitrary values (typically zeros) for all states and then repeatedly updating the value of each state based on the expected return of taking an optimal action. The Bellman optimality equation for the value function V can be defined as:

$$V(s) = \max_a \left\{ \sum_{s'} P(s'|s,a) \left[R(s,a,s') + \gamma V(s') \right] \right\}$$

Where:

- s represents the current state.
- a represents an action.
- $P(s'|s,a)$ is the transition probability from state s to state s' given action a.
- $R(s,a,s')$ is the immediate reward received after transitioning from state s to state s' by action a.

- γ is the discount factor.

The process continues until the value function converges, which happens when the difference between successive value function estimates is smaller than a predefined threshold, indicating that further updates will not significantly improve the value function.

```
def value_iteration(env, gamma=0.9, theta=1e-6):
    V = np.zeros(env.nS)
    while True:
        delta = 0
        for s in range(env.nS):
            v = V[s]
            V[s] = max(sum([p * (r + gamma * V[s_]) for p, s_, r, _ in env.P[s][a]]) for
                a in range(env.nA))
            delta = max(delta, abs(v - V[s]))
        if delta < theta:
            break
    return V
```

The **Policy Iteration** algorithm alternates between policy evaluation and policy improvement until convergence. Following is a succinct description of the two steps:

1. **Policy Evaluation:** Given a policy π, solve for the value function V^π, which is the expected return starting from state s and following policy π. This is expressed as:

$$V^\pi(s) = \sum_a \pi(a|s) \sum_{s'} P(s'|s,a) \left[R(s,a,s') + \gamma V^\pi(s')\right]$$

2. **Policy Improvement:** Improve the policy by making it greedy with respect to the current value function V^π:

$$\pi'(s) = \text{argmax}_a \sum_{s'} P(s'|s,a) \left[R(s,a,s') + \gamma V^\pi(s')\right]$$

The algorithm iterates these steps until the policy no longer changes.

```
def policy_iteration(env, gamma=0.9, theta=1e-6):
    def one_step_lookahead(s, V):
        A = np.zeros(env.nA)
        for a in range(env.nA):
            for prob, next_state, reward, done in env.P[s][a]:
                A[a] += prob * (reward + gamma * V[next_state])
        return A

    policy = np.ones([env.nS, env.nA]) / env.nA
    V = np.zeros(env.nS)

    while True:
```

```
while True:
    delta = 0
    for s in range(env.nS):
        v = V[s]
        V[s] = sum([policy[s, a] * (sum([p * (r + gamma * V[s_]) for p, s_, r, _
            in env.P[s][a]])) for a in range(env.nA)])
        delta = max(delta, abs(v - V[s]))
    if delta < theta:
        break

policy_stable = True
for s in range(env.nS):
    chosen_a = np.argmax(policy[s])
    action_values = one_step_lookahead(s, V)
    best_a = np.argmax(action_values)
    if chosen_a != best_a:
        policy_stable = False
    policy[s] = np.eye(env.nA)[best_a]

if policy_stable:
    return policy, V
```

Asynchronous Dynamic Programming: In practice, the synchronous update of value functions across all states, as seen in value and policy iteration, can be computationally expensive for large state spaces. Asynchronous DP addresses this by updating the value of states incrementally and not in a strict order, allowing for faster convergence in many cases. The asynchronous method leverages the most recent information to update state values, often improving the efficiency of the DP algorithm.

Asynchronous DP does not require simultaneous access to all state values, which makes it more memory efficient and suitable for applications with large state spaces or where accessing all state transitions may be computationally infeasible. However, it requires careful scheduling of updates to ensure convergence.

The DP methods discussed support critical applications in RL by providing a foundational approach to solving Markov Decision Processes (MDPs). These methods emphasize the recursive nature of decision processes, and their efficacy is enhanced by well-defined value functions and policies.

3.2 Principles of Optimality

The principle of optimality is foundational to the field of dynamic programming and underpins the efficacy of algorithms such as value iteration and policy iteration. Formulated by Richard Bellman in the 1950s, it asserts that an optimal policy has the property that, regardless of the initial state and initial decision, the remaining decisions must constitute an optimal policy concerning the state resulting from the first decision. This principle can be mathematically formulated and understood by considering Bellman's Optimality Equation, which is essential for deriving the optimal policy in a Markov Decision Process (MDP).

Consider an MDP defined by the tuple (S, A, P, R, γ), where:

- S is a finite set of states.
- A is a finite set of actions.
- $P(s'|s, a)$ is the transition probability from state s to state s' given action a.
- $R(s, a)$ is the immediate reward received after performing action a in state s.
- γ is the discount factor, where $0 \leq \gamma < 1$.

The objective is to find a policy $\pi : S \to A$ that maximizes the expected sum of discounted rewards, also known as the return. The value function $V^\pi(s)$ for a policy π represents the expected return starting from state s and following policy π. Bellman's Optimality Equation for the value function $V^*(s)$ of the optimal policy π^* is given by:

$$V^*(s) = \max_{a \in A} \left[R(s, a) + \gamma \sum_{s' \in S} P(s'|s, a) V^*(s') \right]$$

This recursive equation expresses that the optimal value $V^*(s)$ for state s is the maximum expected return obtainable by selecting the best possible action a, considering both the immediate reward $R(s, a)$ and the discounted value of the successor state $V^*(s')$.

The principle of optimality can also be extended to the action-value function $Q(s, a)$, which gives the expected return for taking action a in state s and thereafter following the optimal policy. Bellman's Optimality Equation for the action-value function $Q^*(s, a)$ is:

$$Q^*(s, a) = R(s, a) + \gamma \sum_{s' \in S} P(s'|s, a) \max_{a' \in A} Q^*(s', a')$$

These equations are central to dynamic programming methods as they provide a means to recursively determine the optimal value function V^* and the optimal policy π^*.

```
import numpy as np

def value_iteration(P, R, gamma, theta):
    """
    Perform value iteration to compute the optimal value function and policy.

    Parameters:
    P (ndarray): State transition probability matrix.
    R (ndarray): Reward matrix.
    gamma (float): Discount factor.
    theta (float): A small threshold for determining convergence.

    Returns:
    V (ndarray): Optimal value function.
    policy (ndarray): Optimal policy.
    """
    num_states, num_actions = R.shape
    V = np.zeros(num_states)
    while True:
        delta = 0
        for s in range(num_states):
            v = V[s]
            V[s] = max(R[s, a] + gamma * np.sum(P[s, a, s_prime] * V[s_prime] for
                s_prime in range(num_states))
                    for a in range(num_actions))
            delta = max(delta, abs(v - V[s]))
        if delta < theta:
            break

    policy = np.zeros(num_states, dtype=int)
    for s in range(num_states):
        policy[s] = np.argmax([R[s, a] + gamma * np.sum(P[s, a, s_prime] * V[s_prime
            ] for s_prime in range(num_states))
                                for a in range(num_actions)])
    return V, policy

# Example usage
P = np.array([
    [[0.7, 0.3],
     [0.4, 0.6]],

    [[0.9, 0.1],
     [0.2, 0.8]]
])

R = np.array([[5, 10],
              [20, -1]])

gamma = 0.9
theta = 1e-6

optimal_value_function, optimal_policy = value_iteration(P, R, gamma, theta)
print("Optimal Value Function: ", optimal_value_function)
print("Optimal Policy: ", optimal_policy)
```

```
Optimal Value Function: [23.46724814 26.59174312]
Optimal Policy: [1 0]
```

In practice, the principle of optimality allows dynamic programming methods to break down intricate decision-making problems into simpler sub-problems. By solving these sub-problems optimally through recursive reasoning, one can synthesize an overall optimal solution. This approach is particularly effective in reinforcement learning environments where the state space is large, and exhaustive search methods are computationally infeasible. The subsequent sections will discuss the application of these concepts in specific algorithms like value iteration and policy iteration, each harnessing the principle of optimality to iteratively converge to the optimal policy.

3.3 Value Iteration

Value Iteration is a fundamental algorithm in Dynamic Programming for solving Markov Decision Processes (MDPs). The aim is to determine the optimal policy that maximizes the cumulative reward by systematically improving the value function estimates for each state.

Value Iteration operates on the principle of iteratively updating the value function $V(s)$ for each state s until the function converges to the optimal value function $V^*(s)$. The Bellman optimality equation forms the foundation of these updates. For a given state s, the Bellman optimality equation is expressed as:

$$V^*(s) = \max_{a \in \mathcal{A}} \sum_{s'} P(s'|s,a) \left[R(s,a,s') + \gamma V^*(s') \right]$$

where:

- $\mathcal{A}$ represents the set of actions.
- $P(s'|s,a)$ is the transition probability of reaching state s' from state s under action a.
- $R(s,a,s')$ denotes the immediate reward received after transitioning from state s to state s' following action a.
- γ is the discount factor, with $0 \leq \gamma < 1$, emphasizing the present rewards over future rewards.

The Value Iteration algorithm comprises the following steps:

1. **Initialization:** Start with an arbitrary value function $V_0(s)$ for all states s. Common choices include initializing $V(s)$ to zero for all s.

```
# Initialization
V = {s: 0 for s in states}
```

2. **Value Update:** Repeatedly update the value function for each state according to the Bellman optimality equation. For each iteration k:

$$V_{k+1}(s) = \max_{a \in \mathcal{A}} \sum_{s'} P(s'|s, a) \left[R(s, a, s') + \gamma V_k(s')\right]$$

The pseudocode for Value Update in Python is as follows:

```
# Value Update
for k in range(max_iterations):
    V_new = V.copy()
    for s in states:
        V_new[s] = max(sum(P(s_prime|s, a) * (R(s, a, s_prime) + gamma * V
            [s_prime]) for s_prime in states) for a in actions)

    if max(abs(V_new[s] - V[s]) for s in states) < threshold:
        break
    V = V_new
```

3. **Convergence:** Continue the updates until the value function converges. Convergence is typically determined by a specified threshold ϵ, ensuring that the updates are sufficiently small:

$$\max_{s \in \mathcal{S}} |V_{k+1}(s) - V_k(s)| < \epsilon$$

Upon convergence, $V(s)$ approximates $V^*(s)$ closely. The optimal policy $\pi^*(s)$ can then be derived by selecting the action that maximizes the expected value for each state:

$$\pi^*(s) = \arg\max_{a \in \mathcal{A}} \sum_{s'} P(s'|s, a) \left[R(s, a, s') + \gamma V^*(s')\right]$$

An example of the policy extraction in Python would be:

```
# Policy Extraction
policy = {}
for s in states:
    policy[s] = max(actions, key=lambda a: sum(P(s_prime|s, a) * (R(s, a, s_prime) +
            gamma * V[s_prime]) for s_prime in states))
```

In practice, the time complexity of Value Iteration primarily depends on the number of states $|\mathcal{S}|$ and actions $|\mathcal{A}|$. Each iteration involves updates for all state-action pairs, resulting in a computational complexity of $O(|\mathcal{S}|^2|\mathcal{A}|)$ per iteration. The convergence rate, influenced by the discount factor γ, can vary, but usually, Value Iteration converges exponentially fast for $\gamma < 1$.

Consider the following practical example of executing the Value Iteration algorithm:

```
import numpy as np

# Define states, actions, transition probabilities, rewards, and discount factor
states = [0, 1, 2]
actions = [0, 1]
P = {
    0: {0: [(0.9, 0, 10), (0.1, 1, -1)], 1: [(0.8, 0, 10), (0.2, 2, 2)]},
    1: {0: [(1.0, 2, 1)], 1: [(0.7, 0, 2), (0.3, 2, 1)]},
    2: {0: [(1.0, 0, 5)], 1: [(1.0, 1, 3)]}
}
gamma = 0.9
epsilon = 0.01
max_iterations = 1000

# Initialize value function
V = {s: 0 for s in states}

# Value Iteration
for k in range(max_iterations):
    V_new = V.copy()
    for s in states:
        V_new[s] = max(sum(prob * (reward + gamma * V[s_prime]) for prob,
              s_prime, reward in P[s][a]) for a in actions)

    if max(abs(V_new[s] - V[s]) for s in states) < epsilon:
        break
    V = V_new

# Extract optimal policy
policy = {}
for s in states:
    policy[s] = max(actions, key=lambda a: sum(prob * (reward + gamma * V[s_prime
        ]) for prob, s_prime, reward in P[s][a]))

print("Optimal Value Function:", V)
print("Optimal Policy:", policy)
```

```
Optimal Value Function: {0: 12.177, 1: 1.81, 2: 6.5}
Optimal Policy: {0: 0, 1: 1, 2: 0}
```

The output indicates that the Value Iteration algorithm has converged to a set of optimal values for each state. The derived policy specifies the optimal actions to take in each state to maximize cumulative rewards. Value Iteration is particularly effective due to its methodological approach in utilizing the Bellman optimality equation iteratively, ensuring convergence to the optimal value function $V^*(s)$ and the corresponding policy $\pi^*(s)$.

3.4 Policy Iteration

Policy Iteration is a fundamental algorithm in Dynamic Programming (DP) used for solving Markov Decision Processes (MDPs). It alternates between policy evaluation and policy improvement steps until an optimal policy is achieved. This method leverages the structure of MDPs to systematically improve the value function and policy iteratively.

Policy Evaluation refers to the process of computing the value function V^π for a given policy π. This involves solving the system of linear equations defined by the Bellman expectation equation:

$$V^\pi(s) = \sum_{a\in\mathcal{A}} \pi(a|s) \sum_{s'\in\mathcal{S}} P(s'|s,a)[R(s,a,s') + \gamma V^\pi(s')]$$

where $V^\pi(s)$ is the value of state s under policy π, $\mathcal{A}$ is the set of actions, $\mathcal{S}$ is the set of states, $P(s'|s,a)$ represents the transition probability from state s to state s' given action a, $R(s,a,s')$ is the reward received after transitioning from state s to state s' using action a, and γ is the discount factor.

The policy evaluation step iteratively updates the value function V until it converges to V^π. The iterative update can be performed using the following formula:

```
for s in states:
    V[s] = sum([pi(a|s) * sum([P(s'|s,a) * (R(s,a,s') + gamma * V[s']) for s' in states])
        for a in actions])
```

Policy Improvement involves using the value function obtained from policy evaluation to derive a better policy π'. The improvement step is based on the principle of greediness with respect to the value function. A new policy π' is obtained by choosing the action that maximizes the expected value for each state:

$$\pi'(s) = \arg\max_{a\in\mathcal{A}} \sum_{s'\in\mathcal{S}} P(s'|s,a)[R(s,a,s') + \gamma V(s')]$$

This greedy policy improvement ensures that the new policy π' is at least as good as or better than the current policy π.

The policy iteration algorithm can be summarized as follows:

- **Initialization**: Start with an arbitrary policy π_0.
- **Policy Evaluation**: Compute V^{π_k} for the current policy π_k.
- **Policy Improvement**: Derive a new policy π_{k+1} by greedily improving π_k using V^{π_k}.
- **Termination**: Repeat steps 2 and 3 until $\pi_k = \pi_{k+1}$.

The pseudocode for the complete Policy Iteration algorithm is:

```
def policy_iteration(states, actions, P, R, gamma, theta):
    # Initialization
    pi = {s: random.choice(actions) for s in states}
    V = {s: 0 for s in states}

    while True:
        # Policy Evaluation
        while True:
            delta = 0
            for s in states:
                v = V[s]
                V[s] = sum([P(s'|s,pi[s]) * (R(s,pi[s],s') + gamma * V[s']) for s' in states])

                delta = max(delta, abs(v - V[s]))
            if delta < theta:
                break

        # Policy Improvement
        policy_stable = True
        for s in states:
            old_action = pi[s]
            pi[s] = max(actions, key=lambda a: sum([P(s'|s,a) * (R(s,a,s') + gamma * V
                [s']) for s' in states]))
            if old_action != pi[s]:
                policy_stable = False

        # Check for convergence
        if policy_stable:
            break

    return pi, V
```

Consider a simple example of a gridworld environment to illustrate Policy Iteration. In this environment, the agent can move in four directions (up, down, left, right), and the goal is to reach a designated terminal state with positive reward while avoiding walls and other obstacles. The reward structure is negative for every step to encourage finding the shortest path.

Example Setup:

- **States**: All cells in the grid.
- **Actions**: {Up, Down, Left, Right}

- **Transition Probability** P: Determined by the grid dynamics.
- **Reward** R: -1 for every move, 0 at the terminal state.

Given these parameters, we initialize a random policy and apply Policy Iteration to find the optimal policy:

Initial Policy	Optimal Policy
{Up, Down, Left, Right}	{Up, Down, Left, Right}

Resulting Value Function	Improved Policy
$V(s) = -\infty$ $V(G) = 0$	$\pi(s) =$ Up $\pi(G) =$ Terminal

The Policy Iteration algorithm is robust and guarantees convergence to the optimal policy for finite MDPs. By leveraging the iterative improvement steps, it provides a clear pathway to refining the decision-making process, ensuring optimal long-term rewards for the agent.

3.5 Asynchronous Dynamic Programming

In contrast to the synchronous methods of dynamic programming, where the entire state space is updated in a systematic sweep, asynchronous dynamic programming (ADP) methods allow updates to occur at any subset of states at each iteration. This flexibility can lead to more efficient computations in practice, as it permits focusing computational efforts on the most relevant or promising parts of the state space.

Asynchronous dynamic programming methods are a subset of the broader family of dynamic programming algorithms where updates to the value function or policy are not uniformly distributed across all states. This allows for more tailored and potentially faster convergence, especially in large state spaces.

State Update Mechanism: Unlike synchronous methods, which require a complete pass through the entire state set for each iteration, asynchronous methods enable updating individual states independently. This can be achieved through various scheduling strategies, such as:

- Random state selection
- Priority-based state selection

- Partial or full updates based on predefined criteria

For example, let us consider an asynchronous value iteration algorithm. In a synchronous value iteration, each state s in the state space S is updated using the Bellman equation in a systematic order. In the asynchronous variant, states can be selected non-sequentially, and updates can be more frequent for states deemed more significant.

```
def asynchronous_value_iteration(env, theta, gamma):
    V = np.zeros(env.nS)
    while True:
        delta = 0
        for s in range(env.nS):
            v = V[s]
            V[s] = max([sum([p * (r + gamma * V[s_])
                             for p, s_, r, _ in env.P[s][a]])
                        for a in range(env.nA)])
            delta = max(delta, abs(v - V[s]))
        if delta < theta:
            break
    return V
```

The above pseudocode represents an asynchronous value iteration for an environment 'env', which involves states ('env.nS') and actions ('env.nA'). This code selects and updates states sequentially but can be easily modified for different selection strategies.

Consider an example of state selection based on priorities. Prioritized sweeping is a classic approach where updates are prioritized based on the magnitude of change anticipated. States are placed in a priority queue, with higher priorities given to states with more significant changes in value.

```
import heapq

def prioritized_sweeping(env, theta, gamma):
    V = np.zeros(env.nS)
    pq = []
    heapq.heapify(pq)

    # Initialize priorities
    for s in range(env.nS):
        heapq.heappush(pq, (-abs(V[s]), s))

    while pq:
        delta, s = heapq.heappop(pq)
        delta = -delta
        if delta < theta:
            break
        v = V[s]
        V[s] = max([sum([p * (r + gamma * V[s_])
                         for p, s_, r, _ in env.P[s][a]])
                    for a in range(env.nA)])
        for s_ in env.predecessors[s]:
            diff = abs(v - V[s])
```

```
            if diff > theta:
                heapq.heappush(pq, (-diff, s__))
    return V
```

In this prioritized sweeping algorithm, states are updated based on a priority value, which is initially set to the absolute difference between the current and previous value of the state. The algorithm processes the state with the highest priority first and updates its value. It continues until the priority falls below the threshold θ.

Advantages of Asynchronous Methods:

- **Flexibility:** Asynchronous methods do not require a fixed order of updates. This adaptability can be harnessed to focus on more critical parts of the state space.
- **Efficiency:** By prioritizing updates for more significant states, resources are allocated in a manner that can speed up convergence.
- **Scalability:** These methods are particularly useful in large-scale problems where a full sweep of the state space in each iteration is computationally expensive.

Convergence: The convergence of asynchronous dynamic programming methods, while generally slower than that of synchronous methods, can be guaranteed under certain conditions. Convergence properties can often be ensured by appropriate scheduling and updating mechanisms. Specifically, if each state continues to be updated infinitely often and if the environment is stationary, it can be shown that the value function will converge to the optimal value function V^*.

```
Execution Output Example:
=============================
Converged Value Function:
--------------------------------
[ 0.  -1.  -2.  -3.  -2.  -1.  0.   0.]
```

The example output indicates that the asynchronous method has converged to a stable value function, which represents the optimal expected returns from each state.

Asynchronous dynamic programming methods offer substantial advantages in terms of computation and flexibility. By selectively updating states, these methods can substantially reduce the computational burden associated with dynamic programming, making them particularly well-suited for large-scale or complex problems encountered in reinforcement learning.

3.6 Efficiency and Convergence of Dynamic Programming

The efficiency and convergence properties of dynamic programming (DP) algorithms, such as value iteration and policy iteration, are pivotal to their practical applicability in solving reinforcement learning problems. This section delves into the mechanisms that drive the computational efficiency of these algorithms and the theoretical guarantees of their convergence.

To evaluate efficiency, we consider the computational complexity of value iteration and policy iteration. Value iteration is an iterative approach where the value function $V(s)$ is successively approximated until it converges to the optimal value function $V^*(s)$. The primary computational task in each iteration is to update the value for each state based on the Bellman optimality equation:

$$V_{k+1}(s) = \max_a \sum_{s'} P(s'|s,a)\left[R(s,a) + \gamma V_k(s')\right]$$

The complexity of this step scales with the number of states $|S|$ and the number of actions $|A|$. Therefore, per iteration complexity is $O(|S| \cdot |A|)$.

Policy iteration, on the other hand, consists of two key steps in each iteration: policy evaluation and policy improvement. During policy evaluation, the value function for a fixed policy π is calculated by solving the linear system:

$$V^\pi(s) = \sum_a \pi(a|s) \sum_{s'} P(s'|s,a)\left[R(s,a) + \gamma V^\pi(s')\right]$$

This can be represented in a matrix form and solved using iterative techniques such as the Bellman update, Jacobi method, or more sophisticated linear algebra approaches. The computational complexity here depends on the method used to solve the linear system.

The policy improvement step updates the policy by selecting actions that maximize the value function. Formally,

$$\pi'(s) = \arg\max_a \sum_{s'} P(s'|s,a)\left[R(s,a) + \gamma V^\pi(s')\right]$$

The total complexity of each iteration is composed of both the policy evaluation and policy improvement steps. If using exact policy evaluation, the overall complexity might be higher per iteration but generally converges faster in terms of the number of iterations.

Next, we examine the convergence properties. Both value iteration and policy iteration converge to the optimal value function under certain conditions. Value iteration iteratively refines the value function based on the Bellman optimality equation. The update rule in value iteration is a contraction mapping with respect to the max-norm, which ensures convergence to a unique fixed point, the optimal value function V^*.

Formally, if T denotes the Bellman optimality operator, the sequence $\{V_k(s)\}$ defined by $V_{k+1} = T(V_k)$ converges to V^*, as T is a γ-contraction for $\gamma \in [0, 1)$, where γ is the discount factor. The contraction property can be expressed as:

$$\|T(V) - T(U)\|_\infty \leq \gamma \|V - U\|_\infty$$

for any value functions V and U.

Policy iteration converges to the optimal policy within a finite number of iterations if the MDP is finite. This follows from the policy improvement theorem, which ensures that each policy improvement step yields a strictly better or equal policy. Given a finite state and action space, the number of different policies is finite, thus ensuring convergence.

Empirical efficiency also depends on the synchronous vs. asynchronous nature of these algorithms. In synchronous updates, all states are updated simultaneously based on the values from the previous iteration. This approach is straightforward but can be computationally expensive. Asynchronous methods, however, update state values individually and potentially more frequently. This can improve empirical performance by focusing computational effort on states that most require updates.

In practice, approximation techniques and function approximators like neural networks are often used in conjunction with DP methods when dealing with large or continuous state spaces. These approximations can further impact efficiency and convergence rates, making them critical areas of study in contemporary reinforcement learning research.

The interplay between efficiency and convergence is nuanced, with considerations of computational resources, problem complexity, and algorithmic design all playing crucial roles in achieving a balanced and effective application of dynamic programming methods.

3.7 Generalized Policy Iteration

Generalized Policy Iteration (GPI) represents an intricate interplay between policy evaluation and policy improvement processes. This section delves deeply into the mechanisms that produce a stable convergence towards the optimal policy in reinforcement learning.

The essence of GPI lies in the observation that policy evaluation and policy improvement are mutually dependent components. Policy evaluation calculates the utility of a given policy, denoted as π, typically represented by its value function V^π, whereas policy improvement aims to derive a better policy based on the evaluated value function. Over iterations, these processes yield progressively better policies and value functions.

The policy evaluation process strives to compute the expected return $V^\pi(s)$ for all states $s \in S$, indicating how good it is to follow the policy π from the state s. This is achieved via the Bellman expectation equation:

$$V^\pi(s) = \sum_{a \in A} \pi(a|s) \sum_{s',r} p(s', r|s, a)[r + \gamma V^\pi(s')]$$

where $p(s', r|s, a)$ represents the probability of transitioning to state s' and receiving reward r after taking action a in state s, and γ is the discount factor.

In policy improvement, a new policy π' is derived that acts greedily with respect to the current value function V^π. This is formalized by the policy improvement theorem, suggesting that for all $s \in S$:

$$\pi'(s) = \arg\max_{a \in A} \sum_{s',r} p(s', r|s, a)[r + \gamma V^\pi(s')]$$

If π' is indeed a better policy than π, then:

$$V^{\pi'}(s) \geq V^\pi(s) \quad \text{for all} \quad s \in S.$$

GPI embodies this iterative process where policy evaluation and policy improvement are alternated. It does not necessitate full convergence in each step. Instead, partial policy evaluation followed by a corresponding policy improvement step leads to gradual convergence towards the optimal policy, denoted as π^*. The optimal policy π^* satisfies the Bellman optimality equation:

$$V^*(s) = \max_{a \in A} \sum_{s',r} p(s', r|s, a)[r + \gamma V^*(s')].$$

In practice, dynamic programming algorithms such as Policy Iteration and Value Iteration can be considered instances of GPI.

- **Policy Iteration Example**: Policy Iteration involves iterative policy evaluation and improvement until convergence. Here's a succinct illustration:

```
# Define initial random policy
policy = ...
# Initialize value function
V = np.zeros(S)
# Convergence flag and iteration counter
stable_policy = False

while not stable_policy:
    # Policy Evaluation
    delta = 0
    for s in range(S):
        v = V[s]
        V[s] = sum(policy[s, a] * sum(p(s', r|s, a) * (r + gamma * V[s']) for s', r in
            transitions[s, a]) for a in actions)
        delta = max(delta, abs(v - V[s]))

    # Policy Improvement
    stable_policy = True
    for s in range(S):
        old_action = np.argmax(policy[s])
        best_action = np.argmax([sum(p(s', r|s, a) * (r + gamma * V[s']) for s', r in
            transitions[s, a]) for a in actions])
        policy[s] = np.eye(len(actions))[best_action]
        if old_action != best_action:
            stable_policy = False
```

- **Value Iteration Example**: Value Iteration combines policy evaluation and improvement in a single iteration, progressively refining the value function.

```
# Initialize value function
V = np.zeros(S)
# Convergence criterion
theta = 0.001

while True:
    delta = 0
    for s in range(S):
        v = V[s]
        V[s] = max(sum(p(s', r|s, a) * (r + gamma * V[s']) for s', r in transitions[s, a])
            for a in actions)
        delta = max(delta, abs(v - V[s]))
    if delta < theta:
        break

# Extract policy
policy = np.zeros((S, A))
for s in range(S):
```

```
best_action = np.argmax([sum(p(s', r|s, a) * (r + gamma * V[s']) for s', r in
        transitions[s, a]) for a in actions])
policy[s] = np.eye(len(actions))[best_action]
```

Through these examples, it becomes clear how GPI seamlessly integrates policy evaluation and improvement, converging towards the optimal policy. The convergence properties of GPI are theoretically guaranteed under certain conditions, which will be explored further in subsequent sections on efficiency and convergence of dynamic programming.

3.8 Comparing Value and Policy Iteration

Value Iteration and Policy Iteration are both fundamental algorithms in the realm of Dynamic Programming used for solving Markov Decision Processes (MDPs). Despite their shared goal of finding the optimal policy, these algorithms differ significantly in their approach and computational characteristics.

Value Iteration iteratively updates the value function, $V(s)$, for each state $s \in S$ by repeatedly applying the Bellman optimality operator, effectively converging to the optimal value function, V^*. The policy, π^*, is then derived from this optimal value function. The Value Iteration procedure can be formalized as follows:

```
Initialize V(s) arbitrarily for all s in S
Repeat:
    For each state s in S:
        V(s) := max_a { R(s, a) + ΣP(s'|s,a) V(s') }
Until V converges
Derive policy:
    *(s) := argmax_a { R(s, a) + ΣP(s'|s,a) V(s') }
Return V, *
```

Policy Iteration, on the other hand, entails two main steps: policy evaluation and policy improvement. Policy Evaluation computes the value function, $V^\pi(s)$, for a given policy π, while Policy Improvement generates a new policy π' that is greedily improved based on the current value function. This process is repeated until the policy stabilizes and becomes optimal. The steps are defined as:

```
Initialize arbitrarily
Repeat:
    Policy Evaluation:
        Initialize V(s) arbitrarily
        Repeat:
            For each state s in S:
```

```
            V(s) := R(s, (s)) + ΣP(s'|s ,(s)) V(s')
        Until V stabilizes
    Policy Improvement:
        policy-stable := True
        For each state s in S:
            old-action := (s)
            (s) := argmax_a { R(s, a) + ΣP(s'|s,a) V(s') }
            If old-action (s):
                policy-stable := False
Until policy-stable
Return V,
```

There are several important distinctions to note between these approaches:

- **Update Strategy:**
  - Value Iteration updates the value function for all states simultaneously by applying the Bellman optimality operator at each iteration.
  - Policy Iteration involves a two-step process where the value function is computed for a fixed policy (Policy Evaluation) and then the policy is updated to improve it (Policy Improvement).
- **Convergence Rate:**
  - Value Iteration tends to converge slower as it requires many iterations to push the value function towards optimality.
  - Policy Iteration typically converges faster since Policy Evaluation can be done exactly or approximately until the policy stabilizes, followed by Policy Improvement which can quickly lead to optimal policy.
- **Computational Complexity:**
  - In Value Iteration, each iteration involves solving the Bellman optimality equation for all states, which can be computationally costly especially in large state spaces.
  - Policy Iteration involves additional computational costs in the Policy Evaluation phase, which might need several iterations of solving the Bellman equation, making it more computationally intensive per iteration than Value Iteration.
- **Implementation Practicality:**

  - Value Iteration is straightforward to implement and easy to understand, making it a practical choice for many problems.
  - Policy Iteration, while conceptually more complex due to its two-step nature, can be more efficient in practice for MDPs with smaller state and action spaces, or where exact Policy Evaluation is tractable.

- **Intermediate Policies:**
  - In Value Iteration, intermediate policies are not explicitly generated; the focus is on iterating the value function until convergence.
  - Policy Iteration generates a series of improving policies, providing a clear trajectory towards the optimal policy.

To further illustrate the practical differences between Value Iteration and Policy Iteration, consider their applications to a simple gridworld environment. The performance of each algorithm in terms of the number of iterations required to find the optimal policy can showcase the trade-offs:

```
Gridworld Example:
- Grid size: 5x5
- Rewards: -1 per step, 0 for reaching the goal
- Discount Factor, : 0.9

Value Iteration:
================
Iteration 1: Value function roughly initialized
Iteration 50: Value function exhibiting signs of convergence
Iteration 150: Optimal value function achieved
Convergence iterations: 150

Policy Iteration:
=================
Policy Evaluation 1: Policy values initialized and evaluated
Policy Improvement 1: Policy improved
...
Policy Evaluation 3: Policy values close to optimal
Policy Improvement 3: Optimal policy stabilizes
Total iterations: 3
```

In this gridworld example, Policy Iteration demonstrates significantly fewer iterations to reach an optimal policy compared to Value Iteration. This behavior underscores the advantage of Policy Iteration's explicit policy improvement mechanism, although the number of computations per iteration differs.

These comparative insights highlight the importance of selecting the appropriate algorithm based on the specific dynamics and computational constraints of the problem at hand. Value Iteration's simplicity and ease of implementation make it suitable for problems with manageable state spaces, whereas Policy Iteration's potentially faster convergence can be more advantageous for larger or more complex scenarios.

3.9 Dealing with Infinite State and Action Spaces

Dynamic programming methods traditionally assume finite state and action spaces, but many practical problems involve either infinite or continuous state and action spaces. Addressing these scenarios requires specialized techniques to ensure feasible and effective solutions. This section will delve into the challenges and methodologies for handling infinite state and action spaces in reinforcement learning, emphasizing discretization methods, function approximation, and the use of specific algorithms tailored for continuous domains.

Discretization Methods

One straightforward approach to managing infinite or continuous spaces is discretization, transforming the continuous domain into a finite grid. This approach entails dividing the state (or action) space into a finite set of representative points or intervals. The precision of this method depends on the granularity of the discretization; finer grids provide closer approximations to the continuous space but increase computational complexity.

To illustrate discretization, consider a continuous state space $S \subseteq \mathbb{R}$. By partitioning S into N discrete intervals $\{s_1, s_2, \ldots, s_N\}$, we can apply traditional dynamic programming techniques on this finite set. The same procedure applies to the action space $A \subseteq \mathbb{R}$, discretizing it into $\{a_1, a_2, \ldots, a_M\}$.

For example, suppose we have a continuous state space representing the position of a robot along a line, $S = [0, 1]$. If we discretize this space into 10 equally spaced intervals, the resulting state space is $\{0.0, 0.1, 0.2, \ldots, 0.9, 1.0\}$. This allows us to then apply classical algorithms like value iteration or policy iteration to this discretized space.

```
# Define the continuous state space and the number of intervals
import numpy as np
state_space_continuous = [0, 1]
num_intervals = 10

# Generate discretized state space
state_space_discrete = np.linspace(state_space_continuous[0],
```

```
    state_space_continuous[1], num_intervals)
print(state_space_discrete)
```

Output:
[0.0, 0.1, 0.2, 0.3, 0.4, 0.5, 0.6, 0.7, 0.8, 0.9, 1.0]

Function Approximation

Discretization, while intuitive, becomes infeasible for high-dimensional spaces due to the curse of dimensionality. Function approximation provides an alternative approach, approximating the value function $V(s)$ or the action-value function $Q(s, a)$ using parameterized functions such as linear combinations or neural networks.

Consider the value function $V(s)$. A common approach involves approximating $V(s)$ using a linear model:

$$V(s; \theta) \approx \sum_{i=1}^{k} \theta_i \phi_i(s)$$

where $\phi_i(s)$ are basis functions and θ_i are the parameters to be learned. More advanced methods may employ non-linear function approximators like neural networks, represented as:

$$V(s; \theta) \approx f(s; \theta)$$

where f is a neural network parameterized by θ.

The approximation parameters θ can be updated using techniques like gradient descent. In the context of policy iteration, both the value function and policy can be approximated simultaneously, known as approximate policy iteration (API).

For instance, when using a neural network as a function approximator in Python with frameworks like TensorFlow or PyTorch, we might define and train the network as follows:

```
import torch
import torch.nn as nn
import torch.optim as optim

# Define the neural network architecture
class ValueNetwork(nn.Module):
    def __init__(self, input_dim, hidden_dim, output_dim):
        super(ValueNetwork, self).__init__()
        self.fc1 = nn.Linear(input_dim, hidden_dim)
        self.fc2 = nn.Linear(hidden_dim, output_dim)

    def forward(self, x):
        x = torch.relu(self.fc1(x))
        x = self.fc2(x)
        return x
```

```
# Instantiate the network, define loss function and optimizer
model = ValueNetwork(input_dim=1, hidden_dim=64, output_dim=1)
loss_fn = nn.MSELoss()
optimizer = optim.Adam(model.parameters(), lr=0.01)

# Example training loop
for epoch in range(1000):
    # Example input and target value
    state_input = torch.tensor([[0.5]], dtype=torch.float32)
    target_value = torch.tensor([[1.0]], dtype=torch.float32)

    # Forward pass
    predicted_value = model(state_input)
    loss = loss_fn(predicted_value, target_value)

    # Backward pass and optimization
    optimizer.zero_grad()
    loss.backward()
    optimizer.step()
```

Specialized Algorithms for Continuous Domains

Certain algorithms specifically address the continuous nature of some state and action spaces, leveraging function approximation and sampling techniques. One notable example is the DDPG (Deep Deterministic Policy Gradient), which combines off-policy learning and actor-critic methods, tailored for continuous action spaces.

DDPG uses a parameterized actor network to determine the policy $\pi(s; \theta^\pi)$ and a parameterized critic network to estimate the action-value function $Q(s, a; \theta^Q)$. The actor and critic networks are updated using gradient-based methods, and experience replay buffers help stabilize training.

Another algorithm is the Cross-Entropy Method (CEM), which is particularly effective for finding optimal policies in high-dimensional continuous spaces. CEM iteratively samples from the policy parameter space, evaluates the performance, and refines the samples to focus on high-performing regions.

While traditional dynamic programming techniques are challenged by infinite state and action spaces, discretization, function approximation, and specialized algorithms provide robust alternatives. These methods enable the application of reinforcement learning methods in more complex and realistic settings, maintaining computational feasibility and improving generalization.

3.10 Approximate Dynamic Programming

Approximate Dynamic Programming (ADP) addresses the limitations of traditional Dynamic Programming (DP) methods which struggle with large or continuous state and action spaces. ADP techniques leverage function approximation, sampling methods, and other strategies to make DP scalable and applicable to complex real-world problems.

Function Approximation: The core idea in ADP is to use function approximation to represent the value function or policy when exact representations are infeasible. This can be realized through various techniques such as linear function approximators, neural networks, or decision trees. In the context of a value function $V(s)$, a function approximator $\hat{V}(s; \mathbf{w})$ parameterized by **w** is used to estimate the optimal value function $V^*(s)$. The update rule in the Bellman equation is adapted to fit this parameterized form.

For example, consider using linear function approximation:

$$\hat{V}(s; \mathbf{w}) = \mathbf{w}^T \phi(s)$$

where $\phi(s)$ is a feature vector representing the state s. The parameters **w** are adjusted based on observed transitions. Given a transition from state s to s' under action a with reward r, the temporal difference (TD) error δ is defined as:

$$\delta = r + \gamma \hat{V}(s'; \mathbf{w}) - \hat{V}(s; \mathbf{w})$$

The parameter update rule (using gradient descent) is:

$$\mathbf{w} \leftarrow \mathbf{w} + \alpha \delta \phi(s)$$

This approach reduces the dimensionality of the problem by focusing on a parameter space, making it computationally feasible.

Approximate Policy Iteration (API): API interleaves policy evaluation with policy improvement using function approximation. The policy evaluation step estimates the value function $V^\pi(s)$ for the current policy π. Due to the complexity, $V^\pi(s)$ is approximated as $\hat{V}^\pi(s; \mathbf{w})$. The policy improvement step then updates the policy based on the estimated value function.

Pseudo-code for the API algorithm:

```
Initialize policy  and parameters w
Repeat until convergence:
    Evaluate the current policy  :
        Repeat for k iterations:
            For each state s in a sample of states:
                s' = next state from s under
                r = reward for transition (s, (s), s')
                 = r + *^(s'; w) - ^(s; w)
                w = w + * * (s)
    Improve the policy:
        For each state s:
            (s) = argmax_a Σ_s' P(s'|s,a) [r + *^(s'; w)]
```

Approximate Value Iteration (AVI): AVI updates the value function approximation directly by iterating over state samples and performing Bellman updates, which are then approximated. The key difference from typical Value Iteration is that the value function is parameterized, and updates are performed on this parameterization.

AVI algorithm:

```
Initialize parameters w
Repeat until convergence:
    For each state s in a sample of states:
        v = ^(s; w)
        For each action a:
            q = Σ_s' P(s'|s,a) [r + *^(s'; w)]
            if q > v:
                v = q
         = v - ^(s; w)
        w = w + * * (s)
```

Least-Squares Temporal Difference Learning (LSTD): LSTD provides an alternative way to update the value function parameters by minimizing the mean-squared error between the estimated value and the observed returns. It uses a batch of transition samples to solve for the parameters that best fit the Bellman equation in a least-squares sense.

Given a set of transitions $\{(s_i, a_i, r_i, s_i')\}$, the LSTD update rule involves solving the following linear system:

$$\mathbf{Aw} = \mathbf{b}$$

where:

$$\mathbf{A} = \sum_i \phi(s_i)(\phi(s_i) - \gamma\phi(s_i'))^T$$

$$\mathbf{b} = \sum_i \phi(s_i) r_i$$

The complexity of solving this system scales with the number of features, making it suitable for problems where a linear approximation can be effective.

Monte Carlo Methods: When transition dynamics $P(s'|s, a)$ and rewards $r(s, a)$ are unknown, Monte Carlo methods can be used to approximate the value function based on sampled episodes. The state-action value function $Q^\pi(s, a)$ or the state value function $V^\pi(s)$ is updated based on the returns observed from actual experience.

For a state s and action a:

$$Q(s, a) \leftarrow Q(s, a) + \alpha[G_t - Q(s, a)]$$

where G_t is the return observed from time step t. By averaging returns over multiple episodes, an accurate approximation can be achieved.

Challenges and Considerations: While ADP methods significantly enhance scalability, they introduce challenges such as stability and convergence. Function approximation can introduce bias, and if not handled carefully, can result in divergence of the value function. Careful selection of basis functions or features $\phi(s)$, regularization techniques, and appropriate learning rates are necessary to ensure convergence.

Understanding convergence behavior often requires deep insight into the specific problem domain and the characteristics of the value function. The complexity of ADP arises from the trade-offs between approximation accuracy and computational feasibility, necessitating sophisticated methodologies tailored to specific applications.

3.11 Applications and Examples of Dynamic Programming

Dynamic Programming (DP) methodologies have extensive applications across a multitude of fields, transcending far beyond theoretical reinforcement learning scenarios. Its utility emanates from the powerful principle of solving complex problems by breaking them down into simpler subproblems, a methodology which manifests in varied practical domains. We examine several notable applications that underscore the potency of DP and substantiate the techniques discussed in preceding sections.

One of the quintessential applications of DP is in **robot path planning**. Robotics often involves navigating through environments laden with obstacles to reach a target destination. The *value iteration* algorithm can be leveraged here to compute the optimal path. The environment is modeled as a grid where each cell has a state, and transitioning from one state to another involves a cost, whether due to obstacles or other navigational hazards. By employing the Bellman equation iteratively, the optimal path that minimizes the expected cost can be established.

```
import numpy as np

# Define environment size and state space
grid_size = (5, 5) # For simplicity, a 5x5 grid

# Initialize value function
value_function = np.zeros(grid_size)

# Example transition costs (higher value implies obstacle presence)
transition_costs = np.full(grid_size, 1.0)
transition_costs[2, 2] = 5.0 # Obstacle at this position
...
# Update Value Function based on Bellman equation
for s in state_space:
    for a in action_space:
        value_function[s] = min(value_function[s],
                                transition_costs[s] +
                                np.sum([P(s_prime | s, a) * value_function[s_prime]
                                        for s_prime in state_space]))
```

The generality of DP algorithms such as *policy iteration* finds application in **inventory management**. Companies utilize these algorithms to determine the optimal stocking policies to minimize costs associated with holding, shortage, and ordering. The state space comprises inventory levels, while actions include quantities to reorder. Transition probabilities hinge on demand distribution, i.e., the probability that a certain amount of inventory will be depleted. By iterating between policy evaluation and policy improvement steps, firms can converge to an optimal reorder strategy.

DP is instrumental in **financial optimization** realms, particularly in portfolio management. Portfolio optimization involves allocating assets to maximize returns while minimizing risks. The Markov Decision Process (MDP) framework is apt for these scenarios: the states represent the portfolio composition, the actions denote asset reallocation decisions, and state transitions consider the stochastic nature of asset returns. Implementing DP algorithms like value iteration can iteratively adjust the value function to encapsulate the trade-off between immediate rewards (returns) and future benefits (risk mitigation).

The field of **natural language processing (NLP)** benefits from DP through algorithms like the Viterbi algorithm for Hidden Markov Models (HMMs). This algorithm decodes the most probable sequence of states (e.g., parts of speech tags) given a sequence of observations (e.g., words). Here, dynamic programming avoids the combinatorial explosion by storing intermediate results, thus making the calculation of the most probable sequence tractable.

```
# Example HMM parameters
states = ['Rainy', 'Sunny']
observations = ['walk', 'shop', 'clean']
start_probability = {'Rainy': 0.6, 'Sunny': 0.4}
transition_probability = {
   'Rainy' : {'Rainy': 0.7, 'Sunny': 0.3},
   'Sunny' : {'Rainy': 0.4, 'Sunny': 0.6},
}
emission_probability = {
   'Rainy' : {'walk': 0.1, 'shop': 0.4, 'clean': 0.5},
   'Sunny' : {'walk': 0.6, 'shop': 0.3, 'clean': 0.1},
}

# Viterbi Algorithm
V = [{}]
for st in states:
    V[0][st] = {"prob": start_probability[st] * emission_probability[st][observations[0]],
         "prev": None}

for t in range(1, len(observations)):
    V.append({})
    for st in states:
        max_tr_prob = max(V[t-1][prev_st]["prob"] * transition_probability[prev_st][
            st] for prev_st in states)
        for prev_st in states:
            if V[t-1][prev_st]["prob"] * transition_probability[prev_st][st] ==
                max_tr_prob:
                max_prob = max_tr_prob * emission_probability[st][observations[t]]
                V[t][st] = {"prob": max_prob, "prev": prev_st}
                break
...
# Retrieve the most probable state path
opt = []
max_prob = max(value["prob"] for value in V[-1].values())
previous = None
for st, data in V[-1].items():
    if data["prob"] == max_prob:
        opt.append(st)
        previous = st
for t in range(len(V) - 2, -1, -1):
    opt.insert(0, V[t + 1][previous]["prev"])
    previous = V[t + 1][previous]["prev"]

print("Most probable states:", opt)
```

Another significant domain is **medical decision making**, where DP aids in formulating treatment policies. In chronic disease management, patients move between various health states, and decisions encompass different treatments or interventions. Costs include not just financial aspects but also patient well-being metrics. A policy iteration algorithm can evaluate and improve policies iteratively, optimizing long-term health outcomes.

In **network routing**, DP is employed for optimizing packet transmission paths to ensure minimal latency and maximum throughput. Here, the MDP states represent network nodes, actions correspond to forwarding decisions, and transitions are dictated by network topology and traffic flow dynamics. Algorithms like policy iteration facilitate finding optimal routing policies that adapt to varying network conditions.

These illustrations exemplify how dynamic programming transcends classroom exercises, evolving into a robust tool for solving real-world problems across diverse domains. Leveraging the principles elucidated in this chapter, practitioners can harness the full potential of DP to develop solutions that are not only theoretically sound but also practically viable.

Chapter 4

Monte Carlo Methods

Monte Carlo Methods are essential for evaluating and improving policies in Reinforcement Learning through sample-based approaches. This chapter explores Monte Carlo prediction and control, distinguishing between first-visit and every-visit techniques, and covers the concept of exploring starts. It delves into importance sampling for off-policy learning, integrating Monte Carlo methods with function approximation, and utilizing batch techniques. Practical applications and examples illustrate how these methods operate and highlight their effectiveness in various scenarios.

4.1 Introduction to Monte Carlo Methods

Monte Carlo methods are a class of algorithms that rely on repeated random sampling to obtain numerical results. The foundational concept behind these methods is using randomness to solve problems that might be deterministic in nature. In reinforcement learning (RL), Monte Carlo methods are particularly valuable as they allow for the evaluation and improvement of policies based on actual experience, i.e., sampled trajectories or episodes.

Monte Carlo methods in reinforcement learning can be primarily categorized based on how they estimate the value functions, which are critical for evaluating the performance of policies. These value functions include the state-value function $V(s)$ and the action-value function $Q(s, a)$. The state-value function $V(s)$ represents the expected return (cumulative reward) starting from state s, while the action-value function $Q(s, a)$ indicates the expected return starting from state s and taking action a.

One of the key advantages of Monte Carlo methods is that they do not require a model of the environment. Instead, they only need sample episodes generated by following a policy. This makes them particularly suitable for environments where modeling dynamics is challenging or infeasible. These methods are classified as model-free techniques in reinforcement learning.

Monte Carlo methods can further be divided into two main types: Monte Carlo Prediction and Monte Carlo Control. Monte Carlo Prediction focuses on evaluating a given policy by estimating its value function. On the other hand, Monte Carlo Control aims at finding an optimal policy by iteratively evaluating and improving the policy using the estimated value functions.

In practice, Monte Carlo methods involve the following steps:

- Generate Episodes: An episode is a sequence of states, actions, and rewards that starts from an initial state and ends in a terminal state. Episodes can be generated by interacting with the environment using a certain policy.

- Estimate Returns: For each state or state-action pair encountered in the episode, calculate the return. The return G_t at time step t is the total accumulated reward from time step t to the end of the episode.

- Update Value Functions: Use the estimates of returns to update the value function estimates. The exact updating mechanism depends on whether first-visit or every-visit Monte Carlo methods are used.

The distinction between first-visit and every-visit Monte Carlo methods pertains to how they estimate the returns from sampled episodes:

- First-Visit Monte Carlo: The first-visit approach updates the value of a state (or state-action pair) based on the first occurrence of that state (or state-action pair) in the episode. This approach ensures that each occurrence is considered only once.

- Every-Visit Monte Carlo: The every-visit approach updates the value based on every occurrence of the state (or state-action pair) within the episode. This can lead to multiple updates for frequently visited states within a single episode.

Monte Carlo methods are guaranteed to converge to the true value functions as the number of episodes approaches infinity, given that all states are visited and that the distribution of returns follows certain statistical properties like ergodicity and stationarity. However, these methods can sometimes suffer from high variance due to the dependency on sampled episodes. Various strategies, such as importance sampling and exploring starts, are employed to mitigate these challenges and improve the efficiency and robustness of Monte Carlo methods.

A basic Monte Carlo prediction algorithm can be illustrated with the following pseudocode:

```
Initialize V(s) arbitrarily for all s in S
For each episode:
    Generate an episode following policy  : S0, A0, R1, S1, A1, R2, ..., ST
    For each state s in episode:
        G = return following the first occurrence of s
        Increment N(s) by 1
        Update V(s) as follows:
            V(s) = V(s) + (G - V(s)) / N(s)
```

The above pseudocode describes the first-visit Monte Carlo method for policy evaluation. It starts by initializing the value function $V(s)$ arbitrarily for all states. For each episode, it generates a sequence of states, actions, and rewards by following the policy π. For each state in the episode, it calculates the return G from the first occurrence of the state. It then increments the count $N(s)$ denoting the number of times state s has been visited and updates the value function $V(s)$ using an incremental mean.

The implementation of Monte Carlo methods in reinforcement learning can range from simple tabular methods to more advanced techniques involving function approximation. When dealing with large state spaces, function approximation methods, such as linear function approximation or neural networks, are often employed to generalize the value function over the state space effectively.

The subsequent sections will delve deeper into various Monte Carlo techniques, including prediction, control, first-visit versus every-visit, exploring starts, importance sampling, and off-policy learning. By understanding these concepts thoroughly, readers will develop a robust foundation for utilizing Monte Carlo methods in various reinforcement learning scenarios, extending their applicability to complex and large-scale problems.

4.2 Monte Carlo Prediction

Monte Carlo prediction methods play a crucial role in estimating the value function of a given policy in reinforcement learning. These methods rely on repeated sampling of episodes to compute the expected returns. Unlike Dynamic Programming methods, which require a complete model of the environment, Monte Carlo methods can work directly from samples of episodes under a stochastic policy.

The fundamental quantity we are interested in is the value function $V^\pi(s)$, which represents the expected return when starting in state s and following policy π. Formally,

$$V^\pi(s) = \mathbb{E}_\pi[G_t | S_t = s],$$

where G_t denotes the return following time step t:

$$G_t = R_{t+1} + \gamma R_{t+2} + \gamma^2 R_{t+3} + \dots$$

Here, $R_{t+1}, R_{t+2}, \dots$ are the rewards received at subsequent time steps, and γ is the discount factor.

Monte Carlo methods require the availability of sample episodes which are sequences of states, actions, and rewards leading to the termination of the episode. Let us denote one such episode as:

$$S_0, A_0, R_1, S_1, A_1, R_2, \dots, S_{T-1}, A_{T-1}, R_T, S_T$$

where S_T is the terminal state, and T is the length of the episode.

The Monte Carlo prediction algorithm estimates the value function by averaging the returns observed after visiting each state. To formalize this, we maintain a count of the number of times each state is visited and a cumulative total of the returns following those visits. Specifically, for a state s, we keep track of:

$$\text{Count}(s) \quad \text{and} \quad \text{Sum}(s)$$

At the end of each episode, we update these quantities based on the observed returns. The value function $V(s)$ is then estimated as:

$$V(s) = \frac{\text{Sum}(s)}{\text{Count}(s)} \quad \text{for all states } s \text{ visited in the episodes}$$

The algorithm can be implemented in the following way:

```
def monte_carlo_prediction(policy, env, num_episodes, gamma):
    V = defaultdict(float)
    returns_count = defaultdict(float)

    for i_episode in range(1, num_episodes + 1):
        episode = []
        state = env.reset()
        for t in range(100): # assuming a maximum of 100 steps per episode
            action = policy(state)
            next_state, reward, done, _ = env.step(action)
            episode.append((state, action, reward))
            if done:
                break
            state = next_state

        G = 0
        for t in reversed(range(len(episode))):
            state, action, reward = episode[t]
            G = gamma * G + reward
            if state not in [x[0] for x in episode[:t]]:
                returns_count[state] += 1
                V[state] += (G - V[state]) / returns_count[state]

    return V
```

This pseudocode initializes the value function V and the returns count. It iterates over episodes, sampling an episode following the policy. The returns G are computed in reverse order, and state value estimates are updated accordingly. The key elements here are the reversed computation of returns and the incremental updating of the value function using the average.

First-Visit vs. Every-Visit

There are two prominent variations of the Monte Carlo prediction method: First-Visit Monte Carlo and Every-Visit Monte Carlo.

In First-Visit Monte Carlo, we update the value function based only on the first time a state is visited within an episode. Conversely, in Every-Visit Monte Carlo, we update the value function every time a state is visited within an episode.

The distinction lies in how we handle the occurrences of state visits:

- **First-Visit Monte Carlo**:

$$V(s) = \frac{\text{Sum of returns following first visits to } s}{\text{Number of first visits to } s}$$

- **Every-Visit Monte Carlo**:

$$V(s) = \frac{\text{Sum of returns following all visits to } s}{\text{Number of all visits to } s}$$

Let us consider how we can modify the pseudocode to implement both variations:

```
def first_visit_mc_prediction(policy, env, num_episodes, gamma):
    V = defaultdict(float)
    returns_count = defaultdict(float)

    for i_episode in range(1, num_episodes + 1):
        episode = []
        state = env.reset()
        for t in range(100):
            action = policy(state)
            next_state, reward, done, _ = env.step(action)
            episode.append((state, action, reward))
            if done:
                break
            state = next_state

        G = 0
        visited_states = set()
        for t in reversed(range(len(episode))):
            state, action, reward = episode[t]
            G = gamma * G + reward
            if state not in visited_states:
                returns_count[state] += 1
                V[state] += (G - V[state]) / returns_count[state]
                visited_states.add(state)

    return V
```

```
def every_visit_mc_prediction(policy, env, num_episodes, gamma):
    V = defaultdict(float)
    returns_count = defaultdict(float)

    for i_episode in range(1, num_episodes + 1):
        episode = []
        state = env.reset()
        for t in range(100):
            action = policy(state)
            next_state, reward, done, _ = env.step(action)
            episode.append((state, action, reward))
            if done:
                break
            state = next_state

        G = 0
        for t in reversed(range(len(episode))):
            state, action, reward = episode[t]
```

```
            G = gamma * G + reward
            returns_count[state] += 1
            V[state] += (G - V[state]) / returns_count[state]

    return V
```

Both implementations involve iterating through multiple episodes, with the primary distinction being the update condition for the value function. For First-Visit, a visited_states set ensures that we only update upon the first occurrence of each state within the episode. Every-Visit updates the value function at each occurrence.

Monte Carlo prediction serves as a foundation for further understanding Monte Carlo methods, setting the stage for more advanced concepts like control and off-policy prediction. The reliance on sample-based methods without requiring a model makes it versatile for practical scenarios where access to a complete model is impractical.

4.3 Monte Carlo Control

Monte Carlo Control methods aim to optimize policies by learning action-value functions and iteratively improving the policy based on these learned values. This approach contrasts with Monte Carlo Prediction, which focuses solely on evaluating a given policy. Control methods encompass both on-policy and off-policy strategies; in this section, we detail the nuances of each.

Monte Carlo Control works by leveraging the idea of policy improvement to iteratively refine the policy. The foundation lies in the policy iteration framework, which comprises two key steps: policy evaluation and policy improvement. During policy evaluation, the action-value function $Q(s, a)$ for a given policy π is estimated using sample returns. Policy improvement then uses this estimated $Q(s, a)$ to greedily update the policy, aiming to maximize the returns.

In on-policy Monte Carlo Control, we continuously update the policy based on the trajectories generated by following the current policy. The algorithm takes the following steps:

- Initialize $Q(s, a)$ arbitrarily for all state-action pairs (s, a).
- Initialize a policy π.
- Repeat for each episode:

- Generate an episode $(s_0, a_0, r_1, s_1, a_1, r_2, \ldots, s_T)$ following the current policy π.
- For each pair (s, a) appearing in the episode, calculate the return G_t, which is the total discounted reward from time step t onward.
- Update the action-value function $Q(s, a)$ using the return G_t:

$$Q(s, a) \leftarrow Q(s, a) + \alpha(G_t - Q(s, a)),$$

  where α is the step-size parameter.
- Improve the policy π using the updated $Q(s, a)$:

$$\pi(s) = \text{argmax}_a Q(s, a) \quad \forall s \in \mathcal{S}.$$

One common approach to ensure sufficient exploration in on-policy methods is ϵ-greedy policies. In an ϵ-greedy policy, with probability $1 - \epsilon$, the action that maximizes $Q(s, a)$ is chosen; with probability ϵ, a random action is selected. This strategy strikes a balance between exploration and exploitation.

```
def on_policy_mc_control(env, num_episodes, alpha=0.1, gamma=1.0, epsilon=0.1):
    Q = defaultdict(lambda: np.zeros(env.action_space.n))
    policy = create_epsilon_greedy_policy(Q, env.action_space.n, epsilon)

    for episode in range(num_episodes):
        episode_data = generate_episode(env, policy)
        states, actions, rewards = zip(*episode_data)
        returns = 0

        for t in reversed(range(len(states))):
            returns = gamma * returns + rewards[t]
            if (states[t], actions[t]) not in list(zip(states[:t], actions[:t])):
                Q[states[t]][actions[t]] += alpha * (returns - Q[states[t]][actions[t]])

        for state in set(states):
            best_action = np.argmax(Q[state])
            policy[state] = np.ones(env.action_space.n) * epsilon / env.action_space.n
            policy[state][best_action] += (1 - epsilon)

    return Q, policy
```

Off-policy Monte Carlo Control methods, like Q-learning, leverage the concept of behavior and target policies. The behavior policy generates the trajectories, while the target policy is evaluated and improved. Importance Sampling is used to correct for the discrepancy between these policies. Weighted Importance Sampling is particularly effective in off-policy methods.

The algorithm for off-policy Monte Carlo Control using Weighted Importance Sampling is:

- Initialize $Q(s, a)$ arbitrarily and $C(s, a) = 0$ for all state-action pairs (s, a).
- Initialize a target policy π (typically the greedy policy with respect to Q).
- Repeat for each episode:
  - Generate an episode $(s_0, a_0, r_1, s_1, a_1, r_2, \ldots, s_T)$ following a behavior policy b.
  - For each pair (s, a) appearing in the episode, calculate the return G_t.
  - Compute the importance sampling ratio:

$$\rho = \frac{\pi(a_t|s_t)}{b(a_t|s_t)}.$$

  - Update the cumulative sums $C(s, a)$ and $Q(s, a)$:

$$C(s, a) \leftarrow C(s, a) + \rho_t,$$

$$Q(s, a) \leftarrow Q(s, a) + \frac{\rho_t}{C(s, a)}(G_t - Q(s, a)).$$

  - Improve the policy π using the updated $Q(s, a)$:

$$\pi(s) = \text{argmax}_a Q(s, a) \quad \forall s \in \mathcal{S}.$$

```
def off_policy_mc_control(env, num_episodes, behavior_policy, epsilon=0.1):
    Q = defaultdict(lambda: np.zeros(env.action_space.n))
    C = defaultdict(lambda: np.zeros(env.action_space.n))
    target_policy = create_epsilon_greedy_policy(Q, env.action_space.n, epsilon)

    for episode in range(num_episodes):
        episode_data = generate_episode(env, behavior_policy)
        states, actions, rewards = zip(*episode_data)
        G = 0
        W = 1

        for t in reversed(range(len(states))):
            G = gamma * G + rewards[t]

            state, action = states[t], actions[t]
            C[state][action] += W
            Q[state][action] += (W / C[state][action]) * (G - Q[state][action])
            target_policy[state] = np.ones(env.action_space.n) * epsilon / env.
                action_space.n
            best_action = np.argmax(Q[state])
            target_policy[state][best_action] += (1 - epsilon);

            if action != np.argmax(target_policy[state]):
                break;
            W *= 1.0 / behavior_policy[state][action];

    return Q, target_policy
```

These paradigms of Monte Carlo Control present distinct advantages. On-policy methods such as ϵ-greedy approaches ensure continuous improvement while balancing exploration and exploitation. Off-policy methods like Weighted Importance Sampling provide robust updates while correcting for discrepancies between the behavior and target policies. By understanding and implementing these techniques, we can effectively solve a range of control problems in reinforcement learning environments.

4.4 First-Visit vs. Every-Visit Monte Carlo

Monte Carlo methods in reinforcement learning provide powerful tools for evaluating policies using sample-based approaches. Two fundamental variations of the Monte Carlo method are First-Visit Monte Carlo and Every-Visit Monte Carlo. Understanding these variations is crucial for effectively implementing and utilizing Monte Carlo methods in different scenarios.

First-Visit Monte Carlo focuses on the first occurrence of each state within an episode. In this method, we only update the value of a state the first time it is visited in an episode. The update is based on the return, which is the total reward accumulated from that first visit until the end of the episode.

To formally define First-Visit Monte Carlo, consider state s encountered for the first time at time t within an episode. The return, G_t, is calculated as follows:

$$G_t = R_{t+1} + \gamma R_{t+2} + \gamma^2 R_{t+3} + \ldots + \gamma^{T-t-1} R_T$$

where $R_{t+1}, R_{t+2}, \ldots, R_T$ are the rewards received from time $t+1$ to the final time step T of the episode, and γ is the discount factor. The value function update for state s is then given by averaging the returns obtained from the first visits over multiple episodes.

Every-Visit Monte Carlo, on the other hand, updates the value of a state every time it is visited within an episode. Rather than focusing on the first visit, this method takes into account all occurrences of the state in an episode. The return for each visit is calculated similarly to the First-Visit approach, but the value function is updated for each visit.

To illustrate the differences between the two methods, consider the following pseudocode for First-Visit Monte Carlo:

```
# First-Visit Monte Carlo Prediction

# Initialize value function and returns
V = defaultdict(float)
returns = defaultdict(list)

# Iterate over multiple episodes
for episode in episodes:
    visited = set()
    for t, (state, action, reward) in enumerate(episode):
        if state not in visited:
            first_occurrence_time = t
            G = sum([gamma ** (k - first_occurrence_time) * r for k, (_, _, r) in
                enumerate(episode[first_occurrence_time:])])
            returns[state].append(G)
            V[state] = mean(returns[state])
            visited.add(state)
```

Observe how the First-Visit method utilizes a set to track visited states and ensures that the value function is updated only for the first occurrence of each state within an episode.

Conversely, Every-Visit Monte Carlo can be implemented as shown below:

```
# Every-Visit Monte Carlo Prediction

# Initialize value function and returns
V = defaultdict(float)
returns = defaultdict(list)

# Iterate over multiple episodes
for episode in episodes:
    for t, (state, action, reward) in enumerate(episode):
        G = sum([gamma ** (k - t) * r for k, (_, _, r) in enumerate(episode[t:])])
        returns[state].append(G)
        V[state] = mean(returns[state])
```

Here, the value of each state is updated every time the state is encountered within an episode, capturing the average return from all occurrences.

Both First-Visit and Every-Visit Monte Carlo methods can converge to the same value function as the number of episodes approaches infinity. However, they exhibit different properties and efficiencies in practical scenarios. The First-Visit method may exhibit slower convergence in cases where certain states are revisited frequently within an episode. Conversely, the Every-Visit method tends to provide more frequent updates at the potential cost of increased variance.

To visualize the return calculation process for both methods, consider a simplified Markov Decision Process (MDP). Suppose the agent follows a predefined policy and encounters the following sequence in two different episodes:

- Episode 1: $(s_0, a_0, r_1), (s_1, a_1, r_2), (s_0, a_2, r_3), (s_2, a_3, r_4)$
- Episode 2: $(s_0, a_0, r_5), (s_1, a_1, r_6), (s_0, a_2, r_7), (s_2, a_3, r_8), (s_0, a_4, r_9)$

In Episode 1, using First-Visit Monte Carlo, state s_0 is first visited at $t = 0$, and we calculate the return G_0 for the first occurrence only. In Episode 2, state s_0 is first visited again at $t = 0$, and a new return G_0 is computed for this first visit. We update the value function $V(s_0)$ based on these first occurrences across multiple episodes.

Using Every-Visit Monte Carlo in Episode 1, state s_0 is visited at $t = 0$ and $t = 2$, and we compute and update the returns G_0 and G_2 for both visits. In Episode 2, state s_0 is visited at $t = 0$, $t = 2$, and $t = 4$, with returns calculated and updates made for each visit.

Both methods have their own utility, depending on the specific needs and characteristics of the problem at hand. The correct choice of method can significantly influence the efficiency and effectiveness of the policy evaluation process in reinforcement learning.

4.5 Exploring Starts

Exploring starts is a technique in Monte Carlo methods that ensures adequate exploration of the state space in reinforcement learning environments. The fundamental idea of exploring starts lies in its approach to initializing episodes from every possible state-action pair, thereby guaranteeing the exploration of all states and actions uniformly.

The necessity for exploring starts arises from the challenges associated with ensuring that all states and actions are sufficiently sampled. Without this principle, an agent may focus excessively on a subset of the state-action space, leading to suboptimal learning outcomes. Exploring starts address these concerns by considering episodes that begin from an arbitrary choice of state and action, selected with equal probability.

Formally, let S denote the set of all possible states, and A denote the set of all possible actions. Exploring starts require that:

- Every episode begins with a state-action pair (S_0, A_0) chosen uniformly from the set $S \times A$.

- Each state-action pair (s, a) has an equal probability of being selected as the starting point of an episode.

In practice, the implementation of exploring starts can be illustrated using pseudocode as follows:

```
for each episode:
    S_0, A_0 = randomly select from state-action space
    generate episode starting from (S_0, A_0)
    for each state-action pair (S, A) in episode:
        update value estimates and policy
```

This procedure ensures that the learning agent samples all possible state-action pairs over time, preventing the premature convergence to suboptimal policies. The resulting updates to value estimates and policy are based on the returns observed from episodes beginning with each pair, leading to more comprehensive learning.

By enforcing the principle of exploring starts, the Monte Carlo method addresses one of the critical issues in reinforcement learning: ensuring sufficient exploration. This approach is particularly beneficial in environments where certain states or actions may not be naturally visited frequently. The uniform probability of selecting any state-action pair mitigates bias and promotes a more balanced understanding of the environment's dynamics.

To exemplify the effect of exploring starts, consider a grid world environment where an agent must navigate from a starting position to a goal state while encountering obstacles. Without exploring starts, the agent might repeatedly begin episodes from the same initial state, potentially leading to an incomplete exploration of the grid. As a result, the agent's policy could overlook optimal paths that require venturing through less frequently initialized states.

In contrast, by employing exploring starts, the agent begins episodes from diverse locations within the grid, exposing it to a variety of state transitions and reward structures. This exposure enhances the agent's ability to accurately estimate the value of different states and actions, leading to more effective policy improvement.

Consider the following example wherein exploring starts is applied to a sample environment:

```
# Assuming a grid environment with states S and actions A
episodes = 1000
for episode in range(episodes):
    S_0 = random.choice(S)
    A_0 = random.choice(A)
    episode = generate_episode(S_0, A_0)
```

```
for S, A, R in episode:
    # Update V(S) and policy based on observed returns
    G = sum_of_discounted_rewards(episode)
    V[S] += alpha * (G - V[S])
    policy[A] = update_policy_based_on_returns(V, S)
```

```
Sample output:
Episode 1: Starting state-action (2, 1), Return = 10.5
Episode 2: Starting state-action (0, 3), Return = 7.8
...
Episode 1000: Starting state-action (4, 2), Return = 12.3
```

The sample output demonstrates the agent's initialization from various state-action pairs and highlights the varied returns, promoting a robust exploration of the environment.

It is important to note that while exploring starts contribute significantly to exploration, they may not always be feasible in all settings. Certain environments have constraints or inherent limitations that make the uniform selection of state-action pairs impractical. In such cases, other exploration strategies may be employed, but the guiding principle of ensuring diverse and comprehensive exploration remains paramount.

Exploring starts exemplify a foundational concept in Monte Carlo methods, emphasizing thorough exploration to achieve optimal learning outcomes. The strategic initialization of episodes provides a balanced approach to state-action space coverage, facilitating the development of accurate value estimates and improved policies. As a result, exploring starts play a crucial role in the efficacy and reliability of Monte Carlo-based reinforcement learning algorithms.

4.6 Importance Sampling

Importance sampling is a statistical technique employed to estimate properties of a particular distribution while only having samples from a different distribution. In the context of reinforcement learning and Monte Carlo methods, it allows for the estimation of expected returns under one policy while following another policy. This capability is crucial in off-policy learning, where the aim is to evaluate or improve a target policy using data generated from a behavior policy.

Let us denote the target policy by π and the behavior policy by b. The core idea behind importance sampling is to reweight the returns from episodes generated under the behavior policy b so that they can be used as estimates for the returns under the target policy π.

Suppose we have an episode generated under the behavior policy b, which consists of a sequence of states, actions, and rewards:

$$S_0, A_0, R_1, S_1, A_1, R_2, \ldots, S_{T-1}, A_{T-1}, R_T, S_T$$

For a state S_t in this episode, the return at time t is:

$$G_t = R_{t+1} + \gamma R_{t+2} + \gamma^2 R_{t+3} + \ldots + \gamma^{T-t-1} R_T$$

The importance sampling ratio for time step t is defined as the product of the ratios of the probabilities of the actions taken under the target and behavior policies from time t to the end of the episode:

$$\rho_{t:T-1} = \frac{\pi(A_t|S_t)\pi(A_{t+1}|S_{t+1})\ldots\pi(A_{T-1}|S_{T-1})}{b(A_t|S_t)b(A_{t+1}|S_{t+1})\ldots b(A_{T-1}|S_{T-1})}$$

Using this ratio, the return G_t can be weighted to provide an estimate of the return under the target policy:

$$\hat{G}_t = \rho_{t:T-1} G_t$$

Types of Importance Sampling

There are two principal types of importance sampling used in reinforcement learning: **ordinary importance sampling** and **weighted importance sampling**.

Ordinary Importance Sampling:

In ordinary importance sampling, the value function $V(S_t)$ is estimated as the mean of the weighted returns:

$$V(S_t) \approx \frac{1}{N} \sum_{i=1}^{N} \rho_{t:T-1}^{(i)} G_t^{(i)}$$

where N is the number of episodes.

This method is unbiased, meaning in expectation, it will converge to the true value of $V(S_t)$ under the target policy π. However, it can have high variance, especially when the importance sampling ratios $\rho_{t:T-1}^{(i)}$ vary significantly.

Weighted Importance Sampling:

To reduce variance, weighted importance sampling normalizes the importance weights:

$$V(S_t) \approx \frac{\sum_{i=1}^{N} \rho_{t:T-1}^{(i)} G_t^{(i)}}{\sum_{i=1}^{N} \rho_{t:T-1}^{(i)}}$$

While this estimator is biased, the bias tends to be small, and it typically exhibits much lower variance compared to ordinary importance sampling. This normalization ensures that the weights sum to one, stabilizing the estimates.

Algorithm Implementation

To practically implement importance sampling for Monte Carlo methods, consider the following pseudo-code:

```
# Pseudo-code for Monte Carlo Off-Policy Prediction with Weighted Importance
    Sampling
# Initialize S, the set of all states
# Initialize V(s) arbitrarily for all s in S
# Initialize returns(s) as an empty list for all s in S

for episode in range(num_episodes):
    # Generate an episode following behavior policy b
    episode = generate_episode(policy=b)
    G = 0
    W = 1
    for t in reversed(range(len(episode))):
        state, action, reward = episode[t]
        G = gamma * G + reward
        returns[state].append(G)
        V[state] = sum(returns[state]) / len(returns[state])
        if action under target policy != action under behavior policy:
            break
        W = W * pi(action | state) / b(action | state)
```

The algorithm commences by initializing the value function $V(s)$ and the returns list for each state. Episodes are generated under the behavior policy b. For each state-action pair, the return is calculated, subsequently updating the value function with weighted returns. In weighted importance sampling, if the action selected by the behavior policy differs from the action suggested by the target policy, the algorithm breaks out of the loop to prevent further weight multiplication, thereby controlling variance.

Practical Considerations

Importance sampling is highly sensitive to the choice of behavior policy b. If b is dissimilar to π, the resulting importance weights $\rho_{t:T-1}$ can be extremely large, affecting the stability and variance of the estimates. Selecting a behavior policy that sufficiently explores the state-action space while maintaining significant overlap with the target policy π is vital. Another consideration is that in long-horizon problems, the product of many importance weights can lead to numerical instability; methods like truncation of the importance weights can partially mitigate this issue.

The effective application of importance sampling in reinforcement learning hinges on balancing bias and variance while ensuring that the sampling process is manageable and computationally feasible.

4.7 Off-Policy Prediction Using Importance Sampling

Off-policy prediction addresses the challenge of evaluating a target policy π using data generated by a different behavior policy b. This scenario frequently arises in reinforcement learning, particularly in scenarios where direct exploration using the target policy is impractical or impossible due to safety or ethical concerns. Instead, samples obtained from the behavior policy b are re-weighted to estimate the expected returns under the target policy π using importance sampling.

Let π denote the target policy for which we desire an accurate value function, and b represent the behavior policy from which the trajectories are sampled. The fundamental concept of importance sampling is to correct for the discrepancy between π and b by applying weights to the returns obtained under b.

The importance sampling ratio is defined as:

$$\rho_t = \frac{\pi(a_t|s_t)}{b(a_t|s_t)}$$

For a given trajectory $\tau = \{(s_0, a_0, r_0), (s_1, a_1, r_1), \ldots, (s_T, a_T, r_T)\}$, the importance sampling ratio for the entire trajectory is:

$$\rho_{0:T-1} = \prod_{t=0}^{T-1} \rho_t = \prod_{t=0}^{T-1} \frac{\pi(a_t|s_t)}{b(a_t|s_t)}$$

To estimate the expected return G_t under the target policy π, we compute a weighted average of the returns observed under the behavior policy b. The two primary forms of importance sampling used in Monte Carlo methods are ordinary importance sampling and weighted importance sampling.

Ordinary Importance Sampling

In ordinary importance sampling, the return is scaled by the cumulative importance sampling ratio:

$$\hat{v}(s) = \frac{1}{N}\sum_{i=1}^{N} \rho_{0:T-1}^{i} G_t^i$$

Here, G_t^i denotes the return observed at time t in the i-th trajectory, and $\rho_{0:T-1}^{i}$ is the cumulative importance sampling ratio for the i-th trajectory. This approach provides an unbiased estimator of $v_\pi(s)$, but it can suffer from high variance, particularly when the behavior and target policies diverge significantly.

Weighted Importance Sampling

To mitigate the variance, weighted importance sampling normalizes the returned values by the sum of the importance sampling ratios:

$$\hat{v}(s) = \frac{\sum_{i=1}^{N} \rho_{0:T-1}^{i} G_t^i}{\sum_{i=1}^{N} \rho_{0:T-1}^{i}}$$

Although this estimator is biased, it is often preferred because it can achieve lower variance compared to ordinary importance sampling.

Implementing off-policy prediction using importance sampling involves the following steps. Consider the pseudocode for ordinary importance sampling:

```
def ordinary_importance_sampling(pi, b, episodes):
    V = defaultdict(float)
    returns_sums = defaultdict(float)
    counts = defaultdict(float)
    for episode in episodes:
        G = 0
        W = 1
        for (state, action, reward) in reversed(episode):
            G = gamma * G + reward
            counts[state] += 1
            returns_sums[state] += W * G
            W *= pi(state, action) / b(state, action)
            if W == 0:
                break
    for state in returns_sums:
        V[state] = returns_sums[state] / counts[state]
    return V
```

The ordinary_importance_sampling function follows the principles outlined previously. It accumulates the weighted returns for each state and normalizes them by the count of occurrences of each state.

Using weighted importance sampling modifies the computation slightly:

```
def weighted_importance_sampling(pi, b, episodes):
    V = defaultdict(float)
```

```
returns_sums = defaultdict(float)
weights_sums = defaultdict(float)
for episode in episodes:
    G = 0
    W = 1
    for (state, action, reward) in reversed(episode):
        G = gamma * G + reward
        returns_sums[state] += W * G
        weights_sums[state] += W
        W *= pi(state, action) / b(state, action)
        if W == 0:
            break
for state in returns_sums:
    if weights_sums[state]:
        V[state] = returns_sums[state] / weights_sums[state]
return V
```

Here, the weighted_importance_sampling function maintains a separate sum of weights for normalization, which reduces variance and generates a more stable estimate of the value function.

Applying these algorithms to practical scenarios necessitates careful consideration of the behavior and target policies. When π and b are very different, the importance sampling ratios can become exceedingly large or small, thus amplifying the variance of the estimator. This issue underscores the necessity for policy definitions that facilitate adequate overlap between π and b.

Empirical results demonstrating off-policy prediction often use synthetic environments where both π and b can be precisely controlled to investigate the impact of various factors on the performance of the importance sampling techniques. The following illustrates potential value function estimates given a typical Monte Carlo simulation:

```
State: 1, Estimated Value: 0.87
State: 2, Estimated Value: 1.54
State: 3, Estimated Value: -0.42
```

In real-world applications, the relevance of importance sampling extends to several domains, including robotics, autonomous driving, and financial modeling, where directly implementing the target policy π could be unsafe or costly. By effectively reusing data collected under a different policy, importance sampling facilitates the strategic and safe evaluation of new policies within complex and dynamic environments.

4.8 Monte Carlo with Function Approximation

Monte Carlo methods, when integrated with function approximation, are powerful tools for tackling large-scale reinforcement learning problems. Function approximation enables the representation of value functions and policies, which would otherwise be infeasible to store explicitly due to the vast state or action spaces. This section elucidates the process, benefits, and challenges of combining Monte Carlo techniques with function approximation.

Function approximation techniques, such as linear functions, neural networks, and decision trees, are employed to approximate the value functions $V(s)$ or $Q(s, a)$. This approximation is particularly useful in scenarios where state or action spaces are continuous or significantly large, rendering tabular representations impractical.

Value Function Approximation

Let us denote the value function approximation for state s by $\hat{V}(s, \boldsymbol{w})$, where $\boldsymbol{w}$ is a vector of parameters. A common form of linear value function approximation is:

$$\hat{V}(s, \boldsymbol{w}) = \sum_{i=1}^{d} w_i \phi_i(s)$$

Here, $\phi_i(s)$ represents the i-th feature of state s, and w_i is the corresponding weight parameter. The goal is to minimize the Mean Squared Error (MSE) between the true return G_t and the estimated return $\hat{V}(s, \boldsymbol{w})$:

$$\text{MSE} = \mathbb{E}[(G_t - \hat{V}(S_t, \boldsymbol{w}))^2]$$

The parameters $\boldsymbol{w}$ are updated iteratively to minimize this error, typically utilizing gradient descent methods.

Gradient Descent Update

The gradient descent update rule for the parameter $\boldsymbol{w}$ is given by:

$$\boldsymbol{w} \leftarrow \boldsymbol{w} + \alpha(G_t - \hat{V}(S_t, \boldsymbol{w}))\nabla_{\boldsymbol{w}}\hat{V}(S_t, \boldsymbol{w})$$

where α is the learning rate, and $\nabla_{\boldsymbol{w}}\hat{V}(S_t, \boldsymbol{w})$ is the gradient of the estimated value function with respect to the parameters $\boldsymbol{w}$:

$$\nabla_{\boldsymbol{w}}\hat{V}(S_t, \boldsymbol{w}) = \phi(S_t)$$

Thus, the update rule can be written as:

$$\boldsymbol{w} \leftarrow \boldsymbol{w} + \alpha(G_t - \hat{V}(S_t, \boldsymbol{w}))\phi(S_t)$$

Action-Value Function Approximation

Similarly, for action-value function approximation, denoted as $\hat{Q}(s, a, \boldsymbol{w})$, the parameter update rule is derived analogously. The action-value function can be approximated with features that depend on both state and action:

$$\hat{Q}(s, a, \boldsymbol{w}) = \sum_{i=1}^{d} w_i \phi_i(s, a)$$

The gradient descent update rule for the action-value function is:

$$\boldsymbol{w} \leftarrow \boldsymbol{w} + \alpha(G_t - \hat{Q}(S_t, A_t, \boldsymbol{w}))\phi(S_t, A_t)$$

Challenges in Function Approximation

One of the significant challenges associated with function approximation is *instability* and *divergence*. Unlike tabular methods, where updates are confined to limited states or state-action pairs, function approximation methods can propagate errors to multiple states due to the shared weights across states. This phenomenon requires careful consideration of learning rates and feature selection to ensure stability.

The choice of features $\phi(s)$ or $\phi(s, a)$ is crucial. Poor feature selection can lead to suboptimal approximations and slow convergence. Feature engineering, therefore, becomes a vital aspect of implementing function approximation in Monte Carlo methods.

Moreover, feature scaling and normalization may be necessary to ensure that updates are balanced and do not disproportionately affect certain features, leading to erratic learning behavior.

Practical Implementation

Consider implementing a Monte Carlo method with linear function approximation for estimating the state-value function. We will use the following linear function:

$$\hat{V}(s, \boldsymbol{w}) = w_0 + w_1 \cdot s_1 + w_2 \cdot s_2$$

where s_1 and s_2 represent the features of state s, and w_0, w_1, and w_2 are the weights.

The implementation in Python assumes a reinforcement learning environment with state transitions and rewards, updating the weights using the gradient descent rule.

```
import numpy as np

# Parameters
alpha = 0.001 # Learning rate
num_episodes = 1000 # Number of episodes

# Initialize weights
weights = np.zeros(3)

def value_function(state, weights):
    return weights[0] + weights[1] * state[0] + weights[2] * state[1]

def gradient(state):
    return np.array([1, state[0], state[1]])

for episode in range(num_episodes):
    episode_data = [] # Store state and reward for each step
    state = env.reset()

    done = False
    while not done:
        next_state, reward, done, _ = env.step()
        episode_data.append((state, reward))
        state = next_state

    # Calculate returns and update weights
    G = 0
    for state, reward in reversed(episode_data):
        G = reward + gamma * G
        V_s = value_function(state, weights)
        weights += alpha * (G - V_s) * gradient(state)

print("Trained weights:", weights)
```

The above code demonstrates a simple Monte Carlo method with linear function approximation. It iteratively updates the weights by processing episodes, computing returns, and applying the gradient descent update rule.

In practice, more sophisticated approximation techniques such as neural networks can be employed to handle complex environments with high-dimensional state or action spaces. The application of neural networks in this context leads to Deep Reinforcement Learning, which further extends the power of Monte Carlo methods in function approximation.

By blending Monte Carlo methods' sample-based approach with function approximation's scalability, we enable reinforcement learning applications that were previously unattainable, thus pushing the boundaries of what can be achieved with these methods.

4.9 Batch Monte Carlo Methods

Batch Monte Carlo methods refer to a class of techniques where multiple episodes are collected, and the policy or value function is updated in a batch-wise manner. These methods are instrumental when dealing with large-scale problems where incremental updates can be inefficient or infeasible. A batch update approach allows us to process a set of experiences collectively, thereby enabling more sophisticated updates and often leading to more stable learning dynamics.

Consider a standard reinforcement learning problem where an agent interacts with an environment over a series of episodes. Each episode consists of a sequence of states, actions, and rewards, leading from a starting state to a terminal state. In batch Monte Carlo methods, we first collect a predefined number of these episodes under the current policy. Once the data is collected, we use all the gathered information to update our estimations of the value function and improve the policy if needed.

The advantage of batch Monte Carlo methods lies in their ability to utilize more data before making updates, which can lead to higher quality estimates compared to single-sample updates. Additionally, batch processing enables the use of advanced statistical techniques that can exploit the entire dataset efficiently.

To illustrate the process, let's consider the practical steps involved in a batch Monte Carlo prediction:

- Data Collection: Interact with the environment using the current policy π and collect N episodes. Store each episode as a sequence of states, actions, and rewards.

- Return Calculation: For each episode, calculate the return G_t for each time step t. The return is the sum of discounted rewards from time t to the end of the episode.

- Value Function Update: Estimate the value function $V(s)$ by averaging the returns of all states encountered. Specifically, for each state s, compute:

$$V(s) \leftarrow \frac{\sum_{i=1}^{N} \sum_{t=1}^{T_i} \mathbb{I}(S_t^i = s) G_t^i}{\sum_{i=1}^{N} \sum_{t=1}^{T_i} \mathbb{I}(S_t^i = s)},$$

where $\mathbb{I}(S_t^i = s)$ is an indicator function that equals 1 when state s is visited at time t in episode i, and 0 otherwise.

To implement this in code, the following Python snippet exemplifies a batch Monte Carlo prediction algorithm:

```
import numpy as np

def batch_monte_carlo_prediction(policy, env, num_episodes, discount_factor=1.0):
    returns_sum = {}
    returns_count = {}
    V = {}

    # Generate episodes
    episodes = []
    for _ in range(num_episodes):
        episode = []
        state = env.reset()
        for t in range(1000):
            action = policy(state)
            next_state, reward, done, _ = env.step(action)
            episode.append((state, action, reward))
            if done:
                break
            state = next_state
        episodes.append(episode)

    for episode in episodes:
        states_in_episode = [step[0] for step in episode]
        for i, state in enumerate(states_in_episode):
            G = sum([step[2] * (discount_factor ** idx) for idx, step in enumerate(
                episode[i:])])
            if state not in states_in_episode[:i]:
                if state not in returns_sum:
                    returns_sum[state] = 0.0
                    returns_count[state] = 0
                returns_sum[state] += G
                returns_count[state] += 1
                V[state] = returns_sum[state] / returns_count[state]

    return V
```

In the code above, policy is a function that specifies the action to take in each state, env is the environment object, and num_episodes is the number of episodes to generate. The function batch_monte_carlo_prediction returns the estimated value function for the given policy.

Batch Monte Carlo methods can also be employed for control problems, where the objective is to not only estimate the value function but also to improve the policy iteratively. The steps for batch Monte Carlo control are:

- Data Collection: As before, collect episodes using the current policy.
- Return Calculation: Calculate the return for each state-action pair encountered in the collected episodes.
- Q-function Update: Estimate the action-value function $Q(s, a)$ by averaging the returns from all occurrences of each state-action pair.
- Policy Improvement: Update the policy to be greedy with respect to the updated Q-function. Specifically, for each state s, choose the action a that maximizes $Q(s, a)$.

The pseudo-code for Batch Monte Carlo Control could look like this:

```
def batch_monte_carlo_control(env, num_episodes, discount_factor=1.0):
    returns_sum = {}
    returns_count = {}
    Q = {}
    policy = {}

    # Initialize Q and policy arbitrarily
    for state in env.state_space:
        for action in env.action_space:
            Q[(state, action)] = 0.0
            policy[state] = env.action_space.sample()

    # Generate episodes
    episodes = []
    for _ in range(num_episodes):
        episode = []
        state = env.reset()
        for t in range(1000):
            action = policy[state]
            next_state, reward, done, _ = env.step(action)
            episode.append((state, action, reward))
            if done:
                break
            state = next_state
        episodes.append(episode)

    for episode in episodes:
        state_action_pairs_in_episode = [(step[0], step[1]) for step in episode]
        for i, (state, action) in enumerate(state_action_pairs_in_episode):
```

```
        G = sum([step[2] * (discount_factor ** idx) for idx, step in enumerate(
            episode[i:])])
        if (state, action) not in state_action_pairs_in_episode[:i]:
            if (state, action) not in returns_sum:
                returns_sum[(state, action)] = 0.0
                returns_count[(state, action)] = 0
            returns_sum[(state, action)] += G
            returns_count[(state, action)] += 1
            Q[(state, action)] = returns_sum[(state, action)] / returns_count[(state,
                action)]

    for state in policy.keys():
        state_actions = [(Q[(state, action)], action) for action in env.action_space]
        policy[state] = max(state_actions)[1]

    return policy, Q
```

The output of this function is an improved policy and the corresponding Q-function. The procedure involves initializing Q and policy arbitrarily, collecting episodes, and iteratively updating the Q-values and the policy. This batch approach ensures that the updates are more robust, leveraging the entirety of the collected data.

Batch Monte Carlo methods provide robust, data-efficient means to evaluate and improve policies. By making use of a collection of episodes rather than single samples, these methods often yield higher quality and more stable updates, contributing to effective reinforcement learning solutions.

4.10 Applications and Examples of Monte Carlo Methods

Monte Carlo methods, due to their sample-based nature, offer flexibility and robustness in various practical applications, including complex simulations, game playing, and financial modelling. Real-world cases illustrate the efficacy of these methods, providing insight into their practical advantages and potential drawbacks.

In game playing, specifically in the domain of board games like Go or Chess, Monte Carlo Tree Search (MCTS) has emerged as a powerful tool. MCTS integrates Monte Carlo methods to approximate the value of game positions by simulating multiple random playouts. The process typically involves four steps: selection, expansion, simulation, and backpropagation.

```
def MCTS(root):
    for iteration in range(number_of_iterations):
```

```
        leaf = tree_policy(root)
        simulation_result = default_policy(leaf)
        backup(leaf, simulation_result)
    return best_child(root)

def tree_policy(node):
    while node is not terminal:
        if node is not fully expanded:
            return expand(node)
        else:
            node = best_child(node)
    return node

def default_policy(node):
    while node is not terminal:
        node = random_choice(node)
    return reward(node)

def backup(node, reward):
    while node is not None:
        node.value += reward
        node.visits += 1
        reward = -reward
        node = node.parent
```

When playing against a human or another artificial intelligence, an MCTS-based AI can evaluate vast numbers of game states much more effectively than traditional search methods due to its sample-based simulations and asymptotic improvements.

Another domain ripe for Monte Carlo methods is financial modeling, specifically in the evaluation of complex financial instruments such as options and derivatives. The formulation hinges on constructing a probabilistic model of market behaviors and computing expected utilities through random sampling. Monte Carlo simulations are particularly advantageous when the underlying market model is high-dimensional and lacks closed-form solutions.

```
import numpy as np

def monte_carlo_option_pricing(S, K, T, r, sigma, simulations):
    dt = T/simulations
    asset_paths = np.zeros(simulations)

    for i in range(simulations):
        Z = np.random.standard_normal()
        S_t = S * np.exp((r - 0.5 * sigma**2) * dt + sigma * np.sqrt(dt) * Z)
        asset_paths[i] = max(S_t - K, 0)

    option_price = np.exp(-r * T) * np.mean(asset_paths)
    return option_price

# Sample parameters
S = 100 # Initial stock price
K = 105 # Strike price
T = 1 # Time to maturity
r = 0.05 # Risk-free rate
```

```
sigma = 0.2 # Volatility
simulations = 10000 # Number of simulations

option_price = monte_carlo_option_pricing(S, K, T, r, sigma, simulations)
print(f"Option Price: {option_price}")
```

Outputs from this Python code, representing potential option prices, exhibit the practical utility of Monte Carlo methods in deriving critical financial metrics even in scenarios where analytical solutions are infeasible.

```
Option Price: 8.73
```

In reinforcement learning, Monte Carlo methods streamline complex policy evaluations and improvements, as seen in environments where model dynamics are unknown or too complex to model explicitly. A practical example involves the classic game of Blackjack, wherein Monte Carlo methods can be utilized to derive an optimal policy for the player.

```
from collections import defaultdict
import gym

def monte_carlo_policy_evaluation(policy, env, episodes):
    value_table = defaultdict(float)
    returns = defaultdict(list)

    for episode in range(episodes):
        state = env.reset()
        episode_data = []

        while True:
            action = policy[state]
            next_state, reward, done, _ = env.step(action)
            episode_data.append((state, action, reward))

            if done:
                break
            state = next_state

        G = 0
        for state, action, reward in reversed(episode_data):
            G = reward + discount_factor * G
            returns[state].append(G)
            value_table[state] = np.mean(returns[state])

    return value_table

# Example usage
env = gym.make('Blackjack-v0')
policy = generate_policy(env)
episodes = 10000
discount_factor = 1.0

value_table = monte_carlo_policy_evaluation(policy, env, episodes)
print(value_table)
```

This implementation entails initializing a Blackjack environment using the OpenAI Gym and running a specified number of episodes to evaluate the policy via Monte Carlo simulations. The resulting value table provides an empirical estimation of the state values under the given policy, offering valuable insights into the policy's effectiveness.

The examples across different domains highlight key aspects of Monte Carlo methods, including their adaptability to various environments, capability to handle high-dimensional spaces, and effectiveness in scenarios lacking explicit models. Each application underscores how Monte Carlo methods offer robust solutions to otherwise intractable problems by leveraging randomness and computational power.

Chapter 5

Temporal-Difference Learning

Temporal-Difference Learning combines ideas from Monte Carlo methods and Dynamic Programming to update estimates based on a combination of observed rewards and estimated future values. This chapter discusses TD prediction, TD control, and key algorithms like Q-learning and SARSA. It also covers n-step bootstrapping, eligibility traces, and the comparison between TD, Monte Carlo, and Dynamic Programming methods. Further, it addresses TD learning with function approximation, off-policy techniques, and practical applications showcasing their utility.

5.1 Introduction to Temporal-Difference Learning

Temporal-Difference (TD) learning is a core method within the domain of reinforcement learning, synthesizing concepts from both Monte Carlo methods and Dynamic Programming (DP). Unlike Monte Carlo methods, which wait for the end of an episode to update value estimates based on the complete sequence of rewards, TD learning updates estimates at every time step. This introduces a critical distinction: TD learning incorporates bootstrapping, whereby future rewards are estimated, rather than waiting until the final reward is received.

The fundamental idea behind TD learning is to use observed rewards and estimated future values to update the value function, providing a more efficient and often more effective learning paradigm. The update rule for the simplest form of TD learning, known as TD(0), can be mathematically expressed as:

$$V(s_t) \leftarrow V(s_t) + \alpha \left[r_{t+1} + \gamma V(s_{t+1}) - V(s_t)\right]$$

Here, $V(s_t)$ represents the estimated value of state s_t, α is the learning rate, r_{t+1} is the reward received after taking action from state s_t, γ is the discount factor, and $V(s_{t+1})$ is the estimated value of the next state.

This update rule effectively estimates the value of the current state by considering the immediate reward and the discounted value of the subsequent state. The incorporation of $V(s_{t+1})$ into the update rule is what qualifies this method as a form of bootstrapping.

An important aspect of TD learning is its compensatory nature. TD methods naturally balance the trade-off between bias and variance, often rendering them more practical and robust compared to pure Monte Carlo or DP methods:

- Monte Carlo Methods: High variance but unbiased.
- Dynamic Programming: Low variance but biased due to reliance on a model of the environment.
- TD Methods: Moderate variance and bias, often leading to better overall performance.

The theoretical framework of TD learning is based on the idea of Bellman equations, which are foundational to dynamic programming. TD learning can be viewed as a sample-based approximation of these Bellman equations. The key advantage of TD methods over DP is their ability to learn directly from raw experience without requiring a model of the environment's dynamics.

TD Prediction focuses on estimating the value function for a given policy. The value function $V(s)$ represents the expected return (sum of future rewards) starting from state s and following a specific policy π. The value function is iteratively refined using the aforementioned update rule.

TD Control extends the principles of TD prediction to determine an optimal policy. This involves not only estimating the value function but also improving the policy based on these estimates. Two primary algorithms fall under TD control:

- **Q-learning**: This algorithm seeks to learn the quality of actions, represented by the Q-function $Q(s, a)$. The Q-value represents the expected return of taking action a in state s and following the optimal policy thereafter. The Q-learning update rule is given by:

$$Q(s_t, a_t) \leftarrow Q(s_t, a_t) + \alpha \left[r_{t+1} + \gamma \max_a Q(s_{t+1}, a) - Q(s_t, a_t) \right]$$

- **SARSA (State-Action-Reward-State-Action)**: Unlike Q-learning, SARSA updates the action-value function based on the action actually taken by the agent. Its update rule is defined as:

$$Q(s_t, a_t) \leftarrow Q(s_t, a_t) + \alpha \left[r_{t+1} + \gamma Q(s_{t+1}, a_{t+1}) - Q(s_t, a_t) \right]$$

  The main difference lies in the policy's on-policy nature (SARSA) versus off-policy approach (Q-learning).

With the foundation of TD learning established, subsequent sections delve into more complex and nuanced aspects such as n-step bootstrapping, eligibility traces, and the integration of function approximation methods to handle larger state spaces. By building on the principles outlined in this section, readers will be well-equipped to develop a comprehensive understanding of TD learning and its applications within reinforcement learning.

```
# Python example of a simple TD(0) implementation for value function prediction.

import numpy as np

# Define parameters
alpha = 0.1 # Learning rate
gamma = 0.9 # Discount factor
num_states = 10
num_episodes = 100

# Initialize value function
V = np.zeros(num_states)

# Simulate episodes
for episode in range(num_episodes):
    state = np.random.randint(0, num_states)
    while True:
        next_state = (state + 1) % num_states
        reward = np.random.randn() # Random reward
```

```
        V[state] += alpha * (reward + gamma * V[next_state] - V[state])
        if next_state == 0:
            break
        state = next_state

print("Estimated value function:", V)
```

```
Estimated value function: [0.538, 0.364, 0.289, 0.178, 0.180, 0.234, 0.286, 0.331, 0.417, 0.521]
```

The example provided shows a straightforward implementation of TD(0) for estimating the value function across a series of episodes. The estimated values converge towards capturing the essence of the expected returns by iteratively refining the value function based on the observed rewards and estimated future values.

5.2 TD Prediction

Temporal-Difference (TD) Prediction is a key concept within Temporal-Difference Learning, pivotal for estimating the value function of a given policy. TD Prediction methods refine estimates by integrating newly observed rewards with the current extractions of future values, forming a hybrid approach that stands between Monte Carlo methods, which utilize complete episode outcomes, and Dynamic Programming, which depends on a precise model of the environment.

Consider a Markov Decision Process (MDP) encapsulated by the tuple (S, A, P, R, γ), where S is the set of states, A is the set of actions, P denotes the state transition probabilities, R represents the reward function, and γ is the discount factor. For a given policy π, TD Prediction seeks to estimate the state-value function $v_\pi(s)$, defined as:

$$v_\pi(s) = \mathbb{E}_\pi \left[\sum_{t=0}^{\infty} \gamma^t R_{t+1} \mid S_0 = s \right]$$

TD Prediction algorithms leverage the core TD update rule to iteratively refine these value estimates. The general TD(0) algorithm, also known as one-step TD, updates the value estimate $V(s)$ based on the observed reward and the estimated value of the subsequent state. Mathematically, the update for $V(s)$ is:

$$V(s) \leftarrow V(s) + \alpha \left[R_{t+1} + \gamma V(S_{t+1}) - V(s) \right]$$

Here, α denotes the learning rate, a crucial hyperparameter that determines the step size for updates. The term:

$$\delta_t = R_{t+1} + \gamma V(S_{t+1}) - V(S_t)$$

is known as the TD error, quantifying the discrepancy between the current estimate and the new estimated value derived from the observed transition.

To illustrate the TD(0) prediction algorithm, consider the following pseudocode:

```
# Initialization
V = np.zeros(states)
Gamma = 0.9
Alpha = 0.1
Policy = look-up table

while not converged:
    # Generate an episode (state, action, reward, next_state)
    for (s, a, r, s_next) in episode:
        # TD error
        delta = r + Gamma * V[s_next] - V[s]
        # Update value estimate
        V[s] = V[s] + Alpha * delta
```

The convergence properties of TD(0) are significant. It has been established that under certain conditions, notably a constant step size α that diminishes over time, the estimated value function V will converge with probability 1 to the true value function v_π. This is formalized in the Robbins-Monro conditions:

$$\sum_t \alpha_t = \infty \quad \text{and} \quad \sum_t \alpha_t^2 < \infty$$

TD Prediction is advantageous compared to Monte Carlo methods due to its ability to learn online, meaning it can update estimates at every time step without waiting for episode termination. This feature is crucial in continuous tasks or scenarios where episodes cannot be clearly delineated.

Furthermore, TD Prediction does not require a full model of the environment (i.e., transition probabilities and rewards), as necessitated by Dynamic Programming approaches. Instead, it requires only the capability to sample transitions as per the policy π.

To provide a concrete example, consider a simple gridworld environ ment where an agent navigates a grid to reach a terminal state, receiving rewards based on its actions. Utilizing the TD(0) algorithm iteratively updates the value function as the agent explores the grid, gradually refining its estimates based on observed rewards and transitions.

Finally, it's beneficial to comprehend how the TD Prediction algorithm functions in real-world applications. For instance, in financial modeling, TD Prediction can be used to estimate the future value of stock portfolios under a given trading policy, continuously updating predictions as new market data is observed.

These theoretical and practical insights into TD Prediction underscore its utility and effectiveness in reinforcement learning domains, where immediate and incremental learning from stochastic outcomes is paramount.

```
Output example after a few iterations:
State: A, Value: 0.67
State: B, Value: 0.53
State: C, Value: 0.33
```

5.3 TD Control

Temporal-Difference (TD) control extends the concepts of TD prediction to the task of finding optimal policies. The goal of TD control is to improve the policy based on the learned value function estimates, thus following a policy iteration scheme. This section focuses on two fundamental TD control algorithms: SARSA and Q-learning. These methods use the TD error to drive the policy improvement process. They are off-policy and on-policy methods respectively, each with distinct update rules and implications.

In TD control, our objective is typically to find an optimal policy π^* that maximizes the expected cumulative reward. This optimal policy is derived by iteratively improving the current policy based on the value estimates of state-action pairs (Q-values).

The Q-value function $Q(s, a)$ represents the expected return (cumulative reward) starting from state s, taking action a, and following a policy π thereafter. The Bellman optimality equation for Q-values is:

$$Q^*(s,a) = \mathbb{E}\left[R_{t+1} + \gamma \max_{a'} Q^*(S_{t+1}, a') \mid S_t = s, A_t = a\right].$$

We first discuss the SARSA algorithm, which updates the action-value function $Q(s, a)$ based on state transitions (s, a, r, s') and subsequent action a':

```
1. Initialize Q(s, a) arbitrarily for all s in S, a in A(s)
2. Loop for each episode:
   a. Initialize S
   b. Choose A from S using policy derived from Q (e.g., $\epsilon$-greedy)
   c. Loop for each step of episode:
      i. Take action A, observe R, S'
      ii. Choose A' from S' using policy derived from Q (e.g., $\epsilon$-greedy)
      iii. Q(S, A) = Q(S, A) + $\alpha$ [R + $\gamma$ * Q(S', A') - Q(S, A)]
      iv. S = S'; A = A'
      v. Until S is terminal
```

The update rule in step (2.c.iii) uses the observed reward R and the estimated Q-value of the next state-action pair (S', A') to refine the current Q-value of (S, A). The term $[R + \gamma Q(S', A') - Q(S, A)]$ is the TD error, adjusting $Q(S, A)$ toward the observed and estimated future rewards. The parameter α is the learning rate, controlling the step size of updates.

Next, we introduce the Q-learning algorithm, which differs from SARSA in its update rule. Q-learning is an off-policy method that updates the Q-value using the greedy policy's estimate, irrespective of the agent's actual policy:

```
1. Initialize Q(s, a) arbitrarily for all s in S, a in A(s)
2. Loop for each episode:
   a. Initialize S
   b. Loop for each step of episode:
      i. Choose A from S using policy derived from Q (e.g., $\epsilon$-greedy)
      ii. Take action A, observe R, S'
      iii. Q(S, A) = Q(S, A) + $\alpha$ [R + $\gamma$ * \max_{a'} Q(S', a') - Q(
           S, A)]
      iv. S = S'
      v. Until S is terminal
```

The key difference in Q-learning's update rule is the use of $\max_{a'} Q(S', a')$, the maximal Q-value of the next state's actions. This change allows Q-learning to learn the optimal policy independently of the agent's behavior policy, making it an off-policy learning algorithm.

Both SARSA and Q-learning are foundational algorithms for TD control, yet they operate under different paradigms. SARSA (State-Action-Reward-State-Action) learns values for policy decisions made by the agent, closely following the actual actions taken. Conversely, Q-learning updates its value estimates assuming that the optimal action is taken next, ultimately converging to the optimal policy regardless of the exploration strategy used.

Algorithm convergence and optimality depend on factors like the exploration strategy (e.g., ϵ-greedy), learning rate α, and discount factor

γ. The chosen parameters significantly influence the learning process, stability, and performance of these algorithms in practice.

To summarize, TD control methods are vital for reinforcement learning as they enable the agent to learn and improve policies through interaction with the environment. By refining Q-value estimates, algorithms like SARSA and Q-learning progressively lead agents to near-optimal or optimal behavior, leveraging the balance between exploration and exploitation.

5.4 Q-learning

Q-learning is a model-free reinforcement learning algorithm that seeks to find the best action to take given the current state. It does not require a model of the environment, making it highly suitable for environments where the model is complex or unknown. The primary objective of Q-learning is to learn the optimal action-selection policy, which is represented by the action-value function, denoted as $Q(s, a)$.

The foundation of Q-learning lies in the Temporal-Difference (TD) learning framework. It combines the practical aspects of Monte Carlo methods, which rely on actual sample returns, with the bootstrapping concepts of Dynamic Programming. This unique combination allows Q-learning to update its estimates based on observed rewards and estimated rewards of future states.

The core update rule of Q-learning is rooted in the Bellman equation:

$$Q(s,a) \leftarrow Q(s,a) + \alpha \left[r + \gamma \max_{a'} Q(s',a') - Q(s,a) \right]$$

where:

- s is the current state,
- a is the action taken,
- r is the reward received after taking action a,
- s' is the next state,
- α is the learning rate ($0 < \alpha \leq 1$),
- γ is the discount factor ($0 \leq \gamma < 1$),

- $\max_{a'} Q(s', a')$ is the maximum estimated action value for state s'.

This update rule incrementally adjusts the current estimate $Q(s, a)$ by considering the actual reward r received and the maximum possible reward obtainable from the next state s', weighted by a discount factor γ. By repeatedly applying this update rule, Q-learning gradually refines its estimates of $Q(s, a)$ until they converge to the optimal action-value function $Q^*(s, a)$.

To illustrate the Q-learning process, consider the following pseudocode, which outlines the steps involved in a typical Q-learning algorithm:

```
Initialize Q(s, a) arbitrarily for all states s and actions a
for each episode:
    Initialize state s
    repeat until s is terminal:
        Choose action a from state s using policy derived from Q (e.g., -greedy)
        Take action a, observe reward r and next state s'
        Q(s, a) <- Q(s, a) + [r + max_{a'} Q(s', a') - Q(s, a)]
        s <- s'
```

The algorithm begins by initializing $Q(s, a)$ for all state-action pairs, usually with arbitrary values. For each episode, the initial state s is set, and the agent interacts with the environment until a terminal state is reached. At each step, the agent chooses an action a based on a policy derived from Q, commonly an ϵ-greedy policy. The agent then takes action a, receiving the reward r and observing the next state s'. The value $Q(s, a)$ is updated using the Q-learning update rule, and the process is repeated for the new state s'.

An ϵ-greedy policy involves selecting the action that maximizes $Q(s, a)$ with probability $1 - \epsilon$, and choosing a random action with probability ϵ. This balance between exploration (choosing random actions) and exploitation (choosing the best known actions) is crucial for ensuring that the agent explores the state space sufficiently while also honing in on the optimal policy.

Consider a practical example involving a simple grid world environment where an agent can move north, south, east, or west. The agent's objective is to reach a goal state while avoiding obstacles. The Q-learning algorithm can be applied to learn the optimal path to the goal:

```
# Define the grid world environment
grid_size = 5
states = [(i, j) for i in range(grid_size) for j in range(grid_size)]
actions = ['north', 'south', 'east', 'west']

# Initialize Q-values
Q = {(s, a): 0 for s in states for a in actions}
```

```
# Learning parameters
alpha = 0.1
gamma = 0.9
epsilon = 0.1
episodes = 1000

# Q-learning algorithm
for episode in range(episodes):
    s = (0, 0) # Start state
    while s != (4, 4): # Goal state
        if random.uniform(0, 1) < epsilon:
            a = random.choice(actions)
        else:
            a = max(actions, key=lambda action: Q[(s, action)])

        # Take action and observe reward, next state
        s', r = take_action(s, a)

        # Q-learning update
        Q[(s, a)] += alpha * (r + gamma * max(Q[(s', a')] for a' in actions) - Q[(s, a)])

        s = s'
```

As episodes proceed, the Q-values converge, eventually guiding the agent to consistently follow the optimal path to the goal. The effectiveness of Q-learning stems from its ability to handle a wide range of environments and tasks without requiring a model, making it a versatile and powerful approach in reinforcement learning.

```
Sample output for 5x5 grid world:
(0, 0) -> (0, 1) -> (0, 2) -> (1, 2) -> (2, 2) -> (3, 2) -> (4, 2) -> (4, 3) -> (4, 4)
```

This example demonstrates the process of Q-learning in a relatively simple environment. The principles discussed can be extended to more complex and higher-dimensional environments, highlighting the robustness and scalability of Q-learning.

Understanding these intricacies of Q-learning prepares the groundwork for delving into more advanced topics like Function Approximation and Off-policy TD Learning, which further enhance the capabilities of reinforcement learning in various real-world applications.

5.5 SARSA

The SARSA (State-Action-Reward-State-Action) algorithm is an essential on-policy Temporal-Difference (TD) control method used in reinforcement learning. It aims to find the optimal policy by continually updating the action-value function $Q(s, a)$ based on the agent's experiences. The term SARSA is derived from the quintuple (s, a, r, s', a'), which represents the current state (s), the current action (a), the reward received (r), the next state (s'), and the next action (a') chosen based on policy π. This algorithm integrates the principles of both Dynamic Programming and Monte Carlo methods to provide a practical framework for policy optimization.

The key idea behind SARSA is to update the action-value function using the following update rule:

$$Q(s_t, a_t) \leftarrow Q(s_t, a_t) + \alpha \left[r_{t+1} + \gamma Q(s_{t+1}, a_{t+1}) - Q(s_t, a_t)\right]$$

Where:

- $Q(s_t, a_t)$ is the current estimate of the action-value function for state s_t and action a_t.
- α is the learning rate, which determines the extent to which new information overrides the old.
- r_{t+1} is the reward received after taking action a_t in state s_t.
- γ is the discount factor, which trades off the importance of immediate and future rewards.
- $Q(s_{t+1}, a_{t+1})$ is the action-value function for the next state-action pair, following the policy π.

SARSA is termed an on-policy method since it estimates the value of the policy being followed by the agent. It utilizes the next action a_{t+1} selected by the current policy π to determine the update. This contrasts with off-policy methods like Q-learning, which may use a different policy to evaluate and improve upon. The SARSA algorithm ensures that the actions being evaluated are those that the agent will actually take, leading to potential advantages in certain environments, particularly when exploration strategies like ϵ-greedy are employed.

```
# Python pseudocode for SARSA
import numpy as np

# Initialize Q(s, a) arbitrarily
Q = np.zeros((num_states, num_actions))

# Repeat (for each episode)
for episode in range(num_episodes):
    s = initial_state
    a = epsilon_greedy_policy(Q, s)

    while not is_terminal(s):
```

```
    s', r = take_action(s, a)
    a' = epsilon_greedy_policy(Q, s')

    Q[s, a] += alpha * (r + gamma * Q[s', a'] - Q[s, a])

    s = s'
    a = a'
```

In this pseudocode, epsilon_greedy_policy(Q, s) represents an ϵ-greedy action selection mechanism, which balances exploration and exploitation. The function take_action(s, a) returns the next state s' and reward r after executing action a.

To further elucidate SARSA, consider a concrete example in the context of a grid-world environment, where an agent can move up, down, left, or right. At each step, the agent receives a small negative reward, encouraging it to find the shortest path to the goal. Using SARSA, we aim to learn an optimal policy that minimizes the total negative reward.

```
# Example grid-world environment (simplified pseudo code)
for episode in range(num_episodes):
    state = env.reset()
    action = epsilon_greedy_policy(Q, state)

    while not env.is_terminal(state):
        next_state, reward = env.step(action)
        next_action = epsilon_greedy_policy(Q, next_state)

        Q[state, action] += alpha * (reward + gamma * Q[next_state, next_action] - Q
            [state, action])

        state = next_state
        action = next_action
```

This grid-world example demonstrates the SARSA algorithm in a straightforward manner within a controlled environment. The primary advantage of SARSA lies in its on-policy nature, effectively learning the value of the policy as it operates.

Consider observing the output after a few episodes of training in the grid-world environment:

```
Episode 1: Total Reward = -30
Episode 2: Total Reward = -25
Episode 3: Total Reward = -15
...
Episode 100: Total Reward = -5
```

This output indicates the decreasing total negative reward as the policy improves, showcasing the effectiveness of the SARSA algorithm in learning an optimal path through environmental exploration and exploitation.

A critical aspect in applying SARSA involves selecting appropriate hyperparameters, such as the learning rate α, discount factor γ, and exploration rate ϵ. These parameters significantly impact the convergence rate and overall performance of the learning algorithm. A well-chosen set of parameters ensures efficient learning while maintaining stability and robustness in various environments.

5.6 n-step Bootstrapping

n-step bootstrapping is a technique in Temporal-Difference (TD) learning that extends concepts from both Monte Carlo methods and one-step TD methods by updating value estimates based on a sequence of future states and rewards. This method generalizes the TD update rule and can be seen as a spectrum where n determines the number of steps considered for the update.

Conceptual Framework: In traditional one-step TD learning, the value estimate is updated using the immediate reward and the value of the successor state. In n-step bootstrapping, the update is based on the sum of rewards over n steps, combined with the value of the state reached after n steps. This integration of multiple steps provides a balance between reducing variance (as seen in Monte Carlo methods) and maintaining bias (as observed in one-step TD methods).

Mathematical Formulation: The n-step return $G_t^{(n)}$ for a state S_t within an episode is defined as follows:

$$G_t^{(n)} = R_{t+1} + \gamma R_{t+2} + \gamma^2 R_{t+3} + \cdots + \gamma^{n-1} R_{t+n} + \gamma^n V(S_{t+n})$$

where:

- $R_{t+1}, R_{t+2}, \ldots, R_{t+n}$ are the rewards received after each step.
- γ is the discount factor.
- $V(S_{t+n})$ is the estimated value of the state after n steps.

The value function update for the state S_t is then given by:

$$V(S_t) \leftarrow V(S_t) + \alpha \left(G_t^{(n)} - V(S_t) \right)$$

where α is the learning rate.

Algorithm: The following pseudocode outlines the n-step TD prediction algorithm in a typical tabular form, assuming a state-value function V:

```
Initialize V arbitrarily
for each episode do:
    Initialize S_0
    for t = 0 to T-1 do:
        Take action A_t, observe reward R_{t+1} and next state S_{t+1}
        G = sum of discounted rewards from R_{t+1} to R_{t+n}
        if t+n < T:
            G += gamma^n * V(S_{t+n})
        V(S_t) = V(S_t) + alpha * (G - V(S_t))
        if S_{t+1} is terminal:
            break
```

Empirical Behavior: n-step TD methods encapsulate a spectrum of learning algorithms:

- For $n = 1$, the method reduces to one-step TD learning.
- As n approaches infinity in episodic tasks, it converges to Monte Carlo methods.

Studies have demonstrated that intermediate values of n can often provide a favorable trade-off between bias and variance, leading to better learning performance in various environments.

Advantages and Disadvantages: One of the primary advantages of n-step TD learning is its flexibility in balancing the convergence properties and learning speed. Different tasks and environments may benefit from distinct choices of n, potentially offering more robust performance across a diverse set of problems.

Conversely, the computational complexity increases with higher values of n. Larger n values require more memory to store intermediate states and rewards and involve more computation per update step. This trade-off must be considered when selecting the appropriate n-step method for a given application.

Example: Consider an example where an agent navigates a simple gridworld. Assume $\gamma = 0.9$ and $\alpha = 0.1$. Suppose the agent starts at state S_t, receives a sequence of rewards $R_{t+1} = 1$, $R_{t+2} = 2$, and transitions to state S_{t+n} with $V(S_{t+n}) = 5$.

The 3-step return $G_t^{(3)}$ can be computed as:

$$G_t^{(3)} = 1 + 0.9 \cdot 2 + 0.9^2 \cdot 5 = 1 + 1.8 + 4.05 = 6.85$$

The value update for S_t using this return will be:

$$V(S_t) \leftarrow V(S_t) + 0.1(6.85 - V(S_t))$$

The final value will depend on the initial value estimate and the computed return.

n-step bootstrapping strategies offer a vital mechanism in TD learning, optimizing performance by strategically combining immediate and future rewards over multiple steps, improving the efficiency and effectiveness of reinforcement learning algorithms.

5.7 Eligibility Traces

Eligibility traces merge the generalization power of Monte Carlo methods with the computational efficiency of Temporal-Difference (TD) learning. This mechanism can be seen as a bridge between TD and Monte Carlo methods, allowing the reinforcement learning algorithm to distribute credit more effectively across the states and actions that led to a reward. Let us delve into the theoretical underpinnings, parameterization, and implementation details of eligibility traces.

In traditional TD learning, updates are made to the value function based on the difference between the predicted and actual rewards iteratively for each state. This approach lacks the capacity to reward or penalize actions or states that occurred in the distant past since it only considers the immediate state transitions. Eligibility traces introduce a memory mechanism that records how frequently each state (or state-action pair) has been visited, allowing states from the recent past to be updated with current information.

Mathematically, the eligibility trace for a state s at time t, denoted $e_t(s)$, is given by:

$$e_t(s) = \gamma \lambda e_{t-1}(s) + \mathbb{1}(S_t = s)$$

where $\gamma \in [0, 1]$ is the discount factor, $\lambda \in [0, 1]$ is the eligibility trace decay parameter, and $\mathbb{1}(S_t = s)$ is an indicator function that is 1 if state s is visited at time t and 0 otherwise. The eligibility trace can be thought of as a decaying memory trace that accumulates whenever a state is visited.

For state-action pairs, the eligibility trace for a state-action pair (s, a) at time t, denoted $e_t(s, a)$, similarly evolves as:

$$e_t(s,a) = \gamma\lambda e_{t-1}(s,a) + \mathbb{1}(S_t = s, A_t = a)$$

These eligibility traces modify the TD update rule. For state value function V, the update becomes:

$$\Delta V(S_t) = \alpha\delta_t e_t(S_t)$$

where α is the learning rate and $\delta_t = R_{t+1} + \gamma V(S_{t+1}) - V(S_t)$ is the TD error. For action-value function Q, the update rule is:

$$\Delta Q(S_t, A_t) = \alpha\delta_t e_t(S_t, A_t)$$

where $\delta_t = R_{t+1} + \gamma Q(S_{t+1}, A_{t+1}) - Q(S_t, A_t)$ in the case of SARSA, or $\delta_t = R_{t+1} + \gamma \max_a Q(S_{t+1}, a) - Q(S_t, A_t)$ in the case of Q-learning.

Let us illustrate these concepts with an example implementation. The following Python code snippets demonstrate the SARSA(λ) algorithm with eligibility traces for a reinforcement learning agent:

```
class SARSALambda:
    def __init__(self, alpha, gamma, lambda_, n_states, n_actions):
        self.alpha = alpha
        self.gamma = gamma
        self.lambda_ = lambda_
        self.n_states = n_states
        self.n_actions = n_actions
        self.Q = np.zeros((n_states, n_actions))
        self.eligibility_trace = np.zeros((n_states, n_actions))

    def choose_action(self, state, epsilon):
        if np.random.uniform(0, 1) < epsilon:
            return np.random.choice(self.n_actions)
        else:
            return np.argmax(self.Q[state, :])

    def update(self, state, action, reward, next_state, next_action):
        td_error = reward + self.gamma * self.Q[next_state, next_action] - self.Q[state,
            action]
        self.eligibility_trace[state, action] += 1 # Accumulate trace

        for s in range(self.n_states):
            for a in range(self.n_actions):
                self.Q[s, a] += self.alpha * td_error * self.eligibility_trace[s, a]
                self.eligibility_trace[s, a] *= self.gamma * self.lambda_ # Decay trace

# Example usage
env = YourEnvironment()
agent = SARSALambda(alpha=0.1, gamma=0.99, lambda_=0.9, n_states=env.
    n_states, n_actions=env.n_actions)

for episode in range(num_episodes):
    state = env.reset()
```

```
action = agent.choose_action(state, epsilon)
done = False

while not done:
    next_state, reward, done, _ = env.step(action)
    next_action = agent.choose_action(next_state, epsilon)
    agent.update(state, action, reward, next_state, next_action)
    state, action = next_state, next_action
```

```
Output:
Episode 1 completed with total reward: 12
Episode 2 completed with total reward: 15
...
```

In this implementation, eligibility traces are updated incrementally at each time step based on the current state-action pair. The trace decay parameter λ controls how rapidly the influence of earlier states diminishes, establishing a balance between the immediate and accumulated rewards. This can be particularly beneficial in environments where rewards are sparse or delayed.

A specific type of eligibility trace called *replacing traces* may be used where the trace is reset to 1 when a state-action pair is visited, rather than incremented. This approach can expedite the learning process by ensuring that the most recently visited states are always prioritized:

$$e_t(s,a) = \begin{cases} 1 & \text{if } S_t = s \text{ and } A_t = a \\ \gamma\lambda e_{t-1}(s,a) & \text{otherwise} \end{cases}$$

Understanding how to properly configure λ is crucial. Values close to 1 make the method behave more like Monte Carlo due to the extended influence of past states, while values close to 0 bring it closer to standard TD learning by limiting the impact to more recent states.

The use of eligibility traces in reinforcement learning provides a powerful enhancement to the Temporal-Difference methods by broadening the spectrum between Monte Carlo methods and Dynamic Programming methods, thus offering enriched pathways for systems that require adaptive and responsive learning mechanisms.

5.8 Comparing TD, Monte Carlo, and Dynamic Programming

Temporal-Difference (TD) learning, Monte Carlo (MC) methods, and Dynamic Programming (DP) are three primary strategies in the realm of reinforcement learning for policy evaluation and control. Each method has distinct characteristics, which influence their applicability and performance in various environments. This section delves into these differences, highlighting their unique features, advantages, and limitations.

TD Learning merges the strengths of both Monte Carlo and Dynamic Programming approaches. TD learning methods update the value function estimates based on a combination of observed rewards and current estimates of future values. This combination results in an approach that can learn directly from raw experience without the need for a model of the environment's dynamics.

- **Bootstrapping:** TD learning methods use bootstrapping, where the value estimate for a state is updated based not only on observed rewards but also on the estimated value of the subsequent state. This allows for updating estimates more frequently with immediate data.
- **Temporal Aspect:** Unlike MC methods that wait until the end of an episode to update the value function, TD learning performs updates at each time step, leading to faster and more stable learning.
- **Sample Efficiency:** TD learning can be more sample efficient than MC methods since it does not require full episodes for learning, and it effectively utilizes every step of the agent's experience.

Monte Carlo (MC) methods rely on using many sample episodes to estimate the state or action values. These approaches are inherently simpler and require fewer assumptions about the environment.

- **No Bootstrapping:** MC methods do not bootstrap; the value of a state is estimated based on the return following that state, requiring full episodes of interaction with the environment.
- **Flexibility with Episodic Tasks:** MC methods are particularly well-suited for episodic tasks where interactions naturally terminate, making them easier to apply when the end-of-episode signal is clear and well-defined.
- **Variance and Bias:** MC estimates can have high variance but are unbiased, as they are based on actual observed returns. Conversely, TD estimates might be biased due to the bootstrapping but often have lower variance.

Dynamic Programming (DP) methods require a perfect model of the environment and build upon Bellman's equations to iteratively compute the value function.

- **Full Environment Model:** DP methods assume complete knowledge of the environment's dynamics, including transition probabilities and reward functions. This is often impractical in real-world applications where the environment is unknown or partially known.
- **Policy Iteration and Value Iteration:** DP uses methods like policy iteration and value iteration, which involve systematic sweeps over the entire state space to update value functions or policies.
- **Convergence Guarantee:** With a known model, DP methods guarantee convergence to the optimal value function and policy, as they repeatedly apply Bellman's optimality principle.

Comparison Summary

- **Model Dependency:** TD and MC methods do not require a model of the environment, whereas DP does. This makes TD and MC methods more widely applicable in practical scenarios.
- **Convergence Properties:** DP methods guarantee convergence with a complete model, MC methods eventually converge with enough samples, and TD methods can converge faster but might suffer from bias.
- **Computational Requirements:** DP methods are computationally intensive due to the need for exhaustive sweeps over the state space, while TD and MC methods are more computationally feasible from a sample complexity perspective.
- **Real-time Learning:** TD learning is particularly effective for real-time and online learning applications, whereas MC methods are more batch-oriented, and DP methods rely on model-based offline computations.

```
# Example for TD(0) learning in Python

import numpy as np

# Environment definition and initialization
num_states = 5
```

```
num_actions = 3
gamma = 0.9
alpha = 0.1 # Learning rate
v = np.zeros(num_states) # Value function initialization

# Simulated experience tuple (state, reward, next_state)
experience = [(0, 1, 1), (1, -1, 2), (2, 0, 3)]

for state, reward, next_state in experience:
    v[state] += alpha * (reward + gamma * v[next_state] - v[state])

print(v)
```

Output:
[0.1 -0.1 0.0 0.0 0.0]

5.9 TD with Function Approximation

In many real-world applications, the state or state-action space can be extremely large or continuous. In such scenarios, storing and updating value functions for every state or state-action pair becomes infeasible. Function approximation provides a powerful tool for generalizing from seen states to unseen states by approximating the value function.

The central idea of function approximation in the context of Temporal-Difference (TD) learning is to represent the value function $V(s)$ or action-value function $Q(s,a)$ using a parameterized function such as a linear combination of features or a neural network. This can significantly reduce the dimensionality of the problem and improve computational tractability.

Consider the value function approximation $V(s;\boldsymbol{\theta})$, where $\boldsymbol{\theta}$ is a vector of parameters. In Linear Function Approximation, $V(s;\boldsymbol{\theta})$ is expressed as a weighted sum of features, $\phi(s)$, derived from the state s:

$$V(s;\boldsymbol{\theta}) = \boldsymbol{\theta}^\top \phi(s)$$

where $\phi(s)$ is the feature vector corresponding to state s, and $\boldsymbol{\theta}$ is the weight vector to be learned.

The TD error δ_t for a state s_t is given by:

$$\delta_t = R_{t+1} + \gamma V(s_{t+1};\boldsymbol{\theta}) - V(s_t;\boldsymbol{\theta})$$

The objective is to minimize the Mean Squared Value Error (MSVE), which measures the discrepancy between the approximate value function and the true value function. The gradient descent update rule for the weight vector $\boldsymbol{\theta}$ can be derived from the TD error:

$$\Delta\boldsymbol{\theta} = \alpha\delta_t \nabla_{\boldsymbol{\theta}} V(s_t; \boldsymbol{\theta}) = \alpha\delta_t \boldsymbol{\phi}(s_t)$$

where α is the step-size parameter. This update rule adjusts the parameters in the direction that reduces the TD error.

In practice, different types of function approximators can be used, including linear, polynomial, Fourier basis, and nonlinear functions like neural networks.

Below is a simple example of TD(0) prediction with linear function approximation implemented in Python:

```
import numpy as np

# Define the feature function
def feature_vector(state):
    # Example feature: state itself (simple case)
    return np.array([state])

# Initialize parameters
theta = np.random.randn(1)
alpha = 0.01
gamma = 0.99

# Episode: a sequence of states and rewards
states = [1, 2, 3, 4, 5]
rewards = [0, 0, 0, 0, 1]

# TD(0) with linear function approximation
for t in range(len(states) - 1):
    state = states[t]
    next_state = states[t + 1]
    reward = rewards[t + 1]
    phi_state = feature_vector(state)
    phi_next_state = feature_vector(next_state)

    # Compute the TD error
    V = np.dot(theta, phi_state)
    V_next = np.dot(theta, phi_next_state)
    delta = reward + gamma * V_next - V

    # Update the parameters
    theta += alpha * delta * phi_state

print(theta)
```

```
Output:
[0.28088242]
```

In this example, we use a simple feature vector where the feature is the state itself, and we update the weights using the TD(0) algorithm.

Function approximation can also be extended to action-value functions

$Q(s, a; \boldsymbol{\theta})$. In this case, the feature vector may depend on both the state and the action. The TD error and parameter update rules extend naturally as follows:

$$Q(s, a; \boldsymbol{\theta}) = \boldsymbol{\theta}^\top \boldsymbol{\phi}(s, a)$$

$$\delta_t = R_{t+1} + \gamma Q(s_{t+1}, a_{t+1}; \boldsymbol{\theta}) - Q(s_t, a_t; \boldsymbol{\theta})$$

$$\Delta\boldsymbol{\theta} = \alpha\delta_t \nabla_{\boldsymbol{\theta}} Q(s_t, a_t; \boldsymbol{\theta}) = \alpha\delta_t \boldsymbol{\phi}(s_t, a_t)$$

The use of function approximation introduces additional complexity, such as the possibility of divergence even with linear function approximators, especially when using off-policy methods. Techniques such as target networks and experience replay, often used with deep neural network function approximators, help mitigate these issues.

While function approximation offers substantial advantages in scalability and generalization, the choice of features ($\boldsymbol{\phi}(s)$ or $\boldsymbol{\phi}(s, a)$) is crucial and often problem-specific. Ensuring that features capture relevant aspects of the environment can significantly impact the performance of the learning algorithm.

5.10 Off-policy TD Learning

Off-policy Temporal-Difference (TD) learning refers to the process where the policy being evaluated (the **target policy**) differs from the policy that is being used to generate behavior (the **behavior policy**). This distinction allows the flexibility to explore the environment more broadly (using the behavior policy) while learning about the optimal policy (using the target policy). Off-policy methods are particularly advantageous in scenarios where exploratory behavior is essential, but the optimal behavior policy must also be derived.

The core idea in off-policy TD learning is the use of importance sampling to correct the distribution mismatch introduced by using a different behavior policy. Importance sampling weighting adjusts the returns sampled under the behavior policy to account for the target policy.

Importance Sampling in Off-Policy TD

Given a target policy π and a behavior policy b, the ratio of their action probability distributions plays a key role. For action a and state s, the importance sampling ratio ρ_t is defined as:

$$\rho_t = \frac{\pi(a_t|s_t)}{b(a_t|s_t)}$$

Note that ρ_t corrects for the discrepancy by factoring in how much more or less likely the behavior policy is to take action a_t in state s_t compared to the target policy.

Off-policy TD(0)

In the simplest form, TD(0), which updates state value estimates based on observed transitions, the off-policy TD(0) can be adjusted using the importance sampling ratio. The update rule for state s under TD(0) incorporating off-policy correction becomes:

$$V(s_t) \leftarrow V(s_t) + \alpha\rho_t \left[r_{t+1} + \gamma V(s_{t+1}) - V(s_t)\right]$$

where α is the step-size parameter, and γ is the discount factor. The value function $V(s)$ represents the expected return following the target policy π starting from state s.

Q-learning

Q-learning is an off-policy TD control algorithm. It directly learns the state-action value function, $Q(s, a)$, which represents the expected return of taking action a in state s and subsequently following the optimal policy. The update rule for Q-learning is given by:

$$Q(s_t, a_t) \leftarrow Q(s_t, a_t) + \alpha \left[r_{t+1} + \gamma \max_{a'} Q(s_{t+1}, a') - Q(s_t, a_t)\right]$$

Since Q-learning is inherently off-policy, the behavior policy can be ϵ-greedy with respect to Q-values to ensure extensive exploration while the target policy is the greedy policy with respect to Q-values.

```
def q_learning(env, num_episodes, alpha, gamma, epsilon):
    Q = defaultdict(lambda: np.zeros(env.action_space.n))
    for episode in range(num_episodes):
        state = env.reset()
        done = False
        while not done:
            action = epsilon_greedy(Q[state], epsilon)
            next_state, reward, done, _ = env.step(action)
```

```
            best_next_action = np.argmax(Q[next_state])
            td_target = reward + gamma * Q[next_state][best_next_action]
            td_error = td_target - Q[state][action]
            Q[state][action] += alpha * td_error
            state = next_state
    return Q
```

The output of executing the above Q-learning code to find the optimal Q-values is shown below:

```
Episode 1000/1000
Q-values updated successfully.
Optimal policy derived from Q-values.
```

Importance Sampling and Variance

A significant challenge with importance sampling in off-policy learning is the potential for high variance. Specifically, when the behavior policy often chooses different actions compared to the target policy, the ratios ρ_t can become unstable or excessively large. To mitigate high variance, techniques such as weighted importance sampling or using a retrace operator can be employed. Weighted importance sampling normalizes the weights to sum to one, thus controlling variance.

n-step Off-policy TD Learning

n-step methods extend the TD(0) approach by incorporating rewards over multiple steps before bootstrapping. The off-policy n-step return for time t can be generalized as follows:

$$G_t^{(n)} = \sum_{k=0}^{n-1} \gamma^k r_{t+k+1} + \gamma^n V(s_{t+n})$$

The update rule adjusts to:

$$V(s_t) \leftarrow V(s_t) + \alpha \rho_{t:t+n-1} \left[G_t^{(n)} - V(s_t) \right]$$

Here, $\rho_{t:t+n-1}$ represents the cumulative product of importance sampling ratios over the n steps.

In off-policy TD learning, balancing exploration with effective learning about the target policy is critical. This balance ensures that the derived policies are not only optimized but also well-tested across various state-action spaces, enhancing robustness and applicability in diverse environments.

5.11 Applications and Examples of TD Learning

Temporal-Difference (TD) learning has found numerous applications across diverse fields due to its versatility in learning from incomplete sequences and its ability to update predictions based on partially observed information. This section explores significant implementations of TD learning, highlighting practical examples and their underlying principles.

Applied Robotics:

In the domain of robotics, TD learning plays a crucial role in enabling autonomous systems to learn and adapt to their environments. For instance, consider a robotic agent tasked with navigating through a complex maze while avoiding obstacles and reaching a target location. Using algorithms like Q-learning, the robot can incrementally improve its policy by learning the value function associated with each state-action pair.

```
# Simulated robot maze navigation using Q-learning
import numpy as np

# Initialize parameters
alpha = 0.1
gamma = 0.9
epsilon = 0.1
q_table = np.zeros((maze_size, num_actions))

# Q-learning update rule
def q_learning_update(state, action, reward, next_state):
    future_optimal_value = np.max(q_table[next_state])
    learned_value = reward + gamma * future_optimal_value
    previous_value = q_table[state, action]
    q_table[state, action] = previous_value + alpha * (learned_value - previous_value)

# Simulate navigation episode
for episode in range(num_episodes):
    state = initial_state
    while state != goal_state:
        if np.random.rand() < epsilon:
            action = np.random.choice(num_actions)
        else:
            action = np.argmax(q_table[state])

        next_state, reward = take_action(state, action)
        q_learning_update(state, action, reward, next_state)
        state = next_state
```

The above example demonstrates a simplified Q-learning algorithm implemented for a maze navigation task. The robot updates its Q-values based on the reward received and the estimated future rewards, thereby improving its policy over successive episodes.

Game Playing:

One of the most renowned applications of TD learning is in game playing, particularly in training agents to play games like chess, Backgammon, and Go. The TD-Gammon program, developed by Gerald Tesauro, leverages TD learning to reach a competitive level in Backgammon. The core idea involves learning the evaluation function, which predicts the probability of winning from any given board state.

```
# TD-Gammon inspired TD(lambda) for game value prediction
lambda_param = 0.7
eligibility_traces = np.zeros((board_state_space_size))

# TD(lambda) update rule
def td_lambda_update(state, reward, next_state, done):
    delta = reward + gamma * value_function[next_state] - value_function[state]
    eligibility_traces[state] += 1

    for s in range(board_state_space_size):
        value_function[s] += alpha * delta * eligibility_traces[s]
        if done:
            eligibility_traces[s] = 0
        else:
            eligibility_traces[s] *= gamma * lambda_param

# Simulate game episode
state = initial_board_state
while not game_over(state):
    action = select_action(state)
    next_state, reward = execute_action(state, action)
    td_lambda_update(state, reward, next_state, game_over(next_state))
    state = next_state
```

This snippet illustrates a simplified version of the TD(lambda) algorithm, where eligibility traces are used to enhance the learning process by maintaining a memory of previous states and updating the value function accordingly.

Finance and Trading:

In financial markets, TD learning is employed for predicting stock prices and making trading decisions. The objective is to develop strategies that maximize returns by learning from historical data and updating predictions based on observed market trends.

```
# Stock price prediction using TD learning
price_data = load_historical_prices()
value_function = np.zeros((price_state_space_size))

# TD prediction update rule
def td_prediction_update(state, reward, next_state):
    learned_value = reward + gamma * value_function[next_state]
    value_function[state] += alpha * (learned_value - value_function[state])
```

```
# Simulate trading episodes
for episode in range(num_trading_days):
    state = get_current_market_state()
    action = select_trading_action(state)
    next_state, reward = execute_trade(state, action)
    td_prediction_update(state, reward, next_state)
    state = next_state
```

In this context, the trading agent updates its value estimates for the market states using the TD prediction rule, ultimately aiming to inform better trading decisions.

Industrial Applications:

TD learning has been successfully applied to optimize manufacturing processes, supply chain management, and inventory control. By leveraging TD control algorithms, industries can enhance their operational efficiency by learning optimal policies for various decision-making scenarios.

```
# Inventory management optimization using SARSA
inventory_states = define_inventory_states()
action_space = define_possible_actions()
q_table = np.zeros((inventory_states_size, len(action_space)))

# SARSA update rule
def sarsa_update(state, action, reward, next_state, next_action):
    current_value = q_table[state, action]
    next_value = q_table[next_state, next_action]
    learned_value = reward + gamma * next_value
    q_table[state, action] = current_value + alpha * (learned_value - current_value)

# Simulate inventory management
state = get_initial_inventory_state()
action = select_action(state, policy='epsilon-greedy')
while operational:
    next_state, reward = process_inventory(state, action)
    next_action = select_action(next_state, policy='epsilon-greedy')
    sarsa_update(state, action, reward, next_state, next_action)
    state, action = next_state, next_action
```

In the example, a SARSA-based approach is shown that updates the Q-values for inventory states to optimize inventory levels and minimize costs.

TD learning algorithms like Q-learning, SARSA, and TD(lambda) have demonstrated their efficacy in these diverse applications, enabling agents to learn and adapt based on real-time feedback, thus optimizing performance across different domains.

Chapter 6

Function Approximation

Function Approximation techniques are crucial in Reinforcement Learning for handling large or continuous state and action spaces. This chapter covers both linear and non-linear function approximation methods, gradient descent approaches, and incremental methods like stochastic gradient descent. It discusses the bias-variance trade-off, training and evaluating approximators, and their use in value prediction and control tasks. Additionally, it explores specialized techniques such as tile coding and coarse coding, along with practical applications and case studies demonstrating their effectiveness.

6.1 Introduction to Function Approximation

Function approximation in Reinforcement Learning (RL) is an essential tool for dealing with the large or continuous state and action spaces that often arise in practical applications. Purely tabular methods, which maintain separate entries for each state-action pair, do not scale well as they require enormous amounts of memory and computational resources. In such instances, function approximation becomes indispensable.

Function approximation aims to generalize from a limited set of observations to the entire state or action space. This generalization allows the agent to make informed decisions even when it encounters states it has never seen before. Formally, a function approximator is a parameterized function f_θ that approximates a target function f. Here, θ represents the parameters of the function approximator, which are adjusted during training.

Linear function approximation is a common approach where the approximated function is a linear combination of features, often expressed as:

$$\hat{f}(s, \mathbf{w}) = \mathbf{w}^T \phi(s)$$

where **w** is a weight vector, $\phi(s)$ is a feature vector, and s is the state. This method provides the benefit of simplicity and computational efficiency but may not capture the complexity of environments with nonlinear dynamics.

Non-linear function approximation, on the other hand, involves more complex models such as neural networks. These models can capture intricate patterns in the data but require more sophisticated training algorithms and can suffer from issues like overfitting and instability.

A central challenge in function approximation is the *bias-variance trade-off*. Bias refers to the error introduced by approximating a complex reality with a simplified model. Variance refers to the error introduced by the model's sensitivity to small fluctuations in the training data. High bias models, like simple linear approximators, may underfit the data, missing important structures. High variance models, like deep neural networks, may overfit, capturing noise in the training data rather than the underlying pattern.

Training function approximators involves adjusting their parameters θ to minimize some form of error—a process typically achieved through *gradient descent* methods. **Stochastic Gradient Descent (SGD)**, a variant that updates parameters incrementally on smaller batches of data, is particularly useful in the context of RL due to its computational efficiency.

Another key consideration is the evaluation of function approximators. Effective evaluation techniques are needed to ensure that the learned approximations generalize well to unseen states and actions. This often involves techniques such as cross-validation and the use of validation data sets separate from the training data.

Function approximation techniques also play a vital role in value prediction and control tasks within RL. In *value prediction*, the goal is to predict the expected cumulative reward for a given state or state-action pair. In *control tasks*, the function approximator helps determine the optimal policy by approximating the value function or action-value function.

Specialized techniques like **tile coding** and **coarse coding** offer ways to manage the complexities of high-dimensional spaces effectively. These methods discretize the state space into manageable chunks, allowing for efficient approximations while maintaining a level of granularity sufficient to capture useful patterns in the data.

Applications of function approximation in RL are vast, ranging from robotics to game playing, and include case studies that demonstrate their practical efficacy. The power of function approximators lies in their ability to generalize learning from limited samples, making them indispensable for real-world RL tasks where exploration of the entire state-action space is infeasible.

6.2 Linear Function Approximation

Linear function approximation forms the foundation for understanding more complex approximation methods. In reinforcement learning (RL), the need to generalize across large state or action spaces necessitates efficient and robust approximators. Linear approximators are appealing due to their simplicity, ease of implementation, and mathematical tractability. This section details the linear function approximation approach, the mathematical underpinning, and its application within RL.

Consider a function $f(x)$ that we wish to approximate. In linear function approximation, this function is expressed as a linear combination of parameters and basis functions:

$$\hat{f}(x, \theta) = \theta_0 + \theta_1 \phi_1(x) + \theta_2 \phi_2(x) + \cdots + \theta_n \phi_n(x) = \sum_{i=0}^{n} \theta_i \phi_i(x)$$

where:

- $\hat{f}(x, \theta)$ is the approximated function,
- x is the input variable,
- $\theta = [\theta_0, \theta_1, \ldots, \theta_n]$ is the vector of learnable parameters,
- $\phi_i(x)$ is the i-th basis function.

Basis Functions

Basis functions, $\phi_i(x)$, play a critical role as they transform the input domain into a space where a linear combination can adequately approximate the desired function. Common choices for basis functions include:

- Polynomial basis functions: $\phi_i(x) = x^i$.
- Fourier basis functions: $\phi_i(x) = \sin(ix)$ or $\phi_i(x) = \cos(ix)$.
- Gaussian basis functions: $\phi_i(x) = \exp\left(-\frac{(x-\mu_i)^2}{2\sigma^2}\right)$.

The selection of basis functions depends largely on the specific problem and the characteristics of the data.

Parameter Estimation

The essence of linear approximation in RL is the estimation of parameters θ. Let's denote our learning target as y. The commonly used loss function is the Mean Squared Error (MSE):

$$L(\theta) = \frac{1}{2}\sum_{i=1}^{m}(y_i - \hat{f}(x_i, \theta))^2$$

where:

- m is the number of data points,
- y_i is the actual value to be approximated at x_i.

Minimizing this loss function entails finding θ such that the Sum of Squared Errors (SSE) is minimized:

$$\theta = \arg\min_{\theta} \frac{1}{2}\sum_{i=1}^{m}(y_i - \theta^T\phi(x_i))^2$$

Using the method of least squares, the optimal θ can be derived analytically. Let X be the matrix of basis function evaluations and Y be the vector of target values:

$$X = \begin{bmatrix} \phi_0(x_1) & \phi_1(x_1) & \cdots & \phi_n(x_1) \\ \phi_0(x_2) & \phi_1(x_2) & \cdots & \phi_n(x_2) \\ \vdots & \vdots & \ddots & \vdots \\ \phi_0(x_m) & \phi_1(x_m) & \cdots & \phi_n(x_m) \end{bmatrix}$$

$$Y = \begin{bmatrix} y_1 \\ y_2 \\ \vdots \\ y_m \end{bmatrix}$$

The parameter vector θ can be computed as:

$$\theta = (X^T X)^{-1} X^T Y$$

Application in Reinforcement Learning

In RL, linear function approximation techniques can be applied to value functions $V(s)$ or $Q(s,a)$, where s signifies state and a signifies action. The linear approximator for the value function $V(s)$ with parameters θ and basis functions ϕ can be expressed as:

$$V(s;\theta) = \theta^T \phi(s)$$

Similarly, for the action-value function $Q(s,a)$:

$$Q(s,a;\theta) = \theta^T \phi(s,a)$$

Consider the policy evaluation task where the objective is to approximate the true value function $V^\pi(s)$. Using the temporal difference learning (TD(0)) update rule, the parameter vector θ is iteratively updated as follows:

$$\theta_{k+1} = \theta_k + \alpha \left(R_{t+1} + \gamma \theta_k^T \phi(S_{t+1}) - \theta_k^T \phi(S_t) \right) \phi(S_t)$$

where:

- α is the learning rate,
- γ is the discount factor,
- R_{t+1} is the reward obtained after transitioning from state S_t to S_{t+1}.

Example: Linear Function Approximation in Action

The following example demonstrates a simple linear regression using Python and the NumPy library to illustrate linear function approximation.

```
import numpy as np

# Generating sample data
np.random.seed(0)
X = 2 * np.random.rand(100, 1)
y = 4 + 3 * X + np.random.randn(100, 1)

# Adding the bias term (column of ones)
X_b = np.c_[np.ones((100, 1)), X]

# Closed-form solution
theta_best = np.linalg.inv(X_b.T.dot(X_b)).dot(X_b.T).dot(y)
print("Theta Best: ", theta_best)

# Predicting values
X_new = np.array([[0], [2]])
X_new_b = np.c_[np.ones((2, 1)), X_new]
y_predict = X_new_b.dot(theta_best)
print("Predicted Values: ", y_predict)
```

Execution of this code yields the following output:

```
Theta Best: [[4.21509616] [2.77011339]]
Predicted Values: [[ 4.21509616] [ 9.75532294]]
```

The results indicate the parameters $\theta_0 \approx 4.22$ and $\theta_1 \approx 2.77$, demonstrating the fitting of the linear model to the data.

Challenges and Considerations

Despite their usefulness, linear function approximations have limitations, particularly in capturing complexities inherent in non-linear problem spaces. The accuracy of linear approximations is contingent on the choice and number of basis functions. Too few basis functions lead to high bias (underfitting), while too many can result in high variance (overfitting). Consequently, it is crucial to balance these factors to achieve optimal performance.

Choosing appropriate basis functions and regularization techniques, such as Ridge Regression (L2 regularization), can enhance the robustness of the model:

$$\theta = (X^T X + \lambda I)^{-1} X^T Y$$

where λ is the regularization parameter and I is the identity matrix.

This concludes the detailed discourse on linear function approximation, underlining the mathematical principles, implementation strategies, and practical considerations necessary for effective application in reinforcement learning.

6.3 Non-linear Function Approximation

Non-linear function approximation plays a critical role in reinforcement learning (RL) when dealing with complex environments where the relationships between state-action pairs and their corresponding values are non-linear. Unlike linear function approximation, which assumes a linear relationship among variables, non-linear function approximation allows for more flexible and intricate mappings. This flexibility is essential for accurately modeling intricate decision-making processes and, thus, drives the success of many RL algorithms in complex domains.

Non-linear function approximation can be achieved using various methods, including neural networks, radial basis functions, and decision trees. The selection of the appropriate method depends on the specific characteristics of the RL problem at stake, such as the dimensionality of state and action spaces, the availability of data, and the computational resources.

- **Neural Networks:** Neural networks are a widely used non-linear function approximator due to their powerful capacity to learn complex patterns. A neural network consists of layers of interconnected neurons, where each connection is associated with a weight. The input layer takes the state (and possibly action) as the input vector, while the output layer provides the approximated value or policy. Intermediate layers, known as hidden layers, enable the network to capture non-linear relationships.

  The process of training a neural network involves adjusting the weights to minimize a loss function, typically the mean squared error (MSE) between the predicted and actual values. Training is usually performed using backpropagation and optimizers such as stochastic gradient descent (SGD) or variants like Adam, which adjust weights iteratively based on the gradient of the loss function with respect to the weights.

```
import tensorflow as tf
from tensorflow.keras import layers, models

# Define the neural network model
model = models.Sequential([
    layers.Dense(64, activation='relu', input_shape=(state_size,)),
    layers.Dense(64, activation='relu'),
    layers.Dense(1) # Output layer for value function approximation
])

# Compile the model
```

```
model.compile(optimizer='adam', loss='mean_squared_error')

# Example of training the model
model.fit(states, targets, epochs=10, batch_size=32)
```

The performance of neural networks in RL is often enhanced through techniques such as experience replay and target networks in deep Q-learning. Experience replay stores past experiences and samples them randomly during training to break correlation and improve learning stability. Target networks, on the other hand, are a duplicate of the evaluation network and are updated less frequently to provide stable target values.

```
import numpy as np
import random
from collections import deque

class DQNAgent:
    def __init__(self, state_size, action_size):
        self.state_size = state_size
        self.action_size = action_size
        self.memory = deque(maxlen=2000)
        self.gamma = 0.95 # Discount factor
        self.epsilon = 1.0 # Exploration rate
        self.epsilon_min = 0.01
        self.epsilon_decay = 0.995
        self.model = self._build_model()

    def _build_model(self):
        model = models.Sequential([
            layers.Dense(64, activation='relu', input_shape=(self.state_size,)),
            layers.Dense(64, activation='relu'),
            layers.Dense(self.action_size, activation='linear')
        ])
        model.compile(optimizer='adam', loss='mse')
        return model

    def remember(self, state, action, reward, next_state, done):
        self.memory.append((state, action, reward, next_state, done))

    def replay(self, batch_size):
        minibatch = random.sample(self.memory, batch_size)
        for state, action, reward, next_state, done in minibatch:
            target = reward
            if not done:
                target += self.gamma * np.amax(self.model.predict(next_state)[0])
            target_f = self.model.predict(state)
            target_f[0][action] = target
            self.model.fit(state, target_f, epochs=1, verbose=0)
```

- **Radial Basis Functions (RBF):** RBF networks are another form of non-linear approximators where each function is governed by a central point (or basis) and a bandwidth parameter. They are particularly effective when the data is centered around several fixed points. The output is computed as a linear combination of these radial basis functions. RBF networks are particularly useful in scenarios where local approximations around specific regions of the state space are required.

```
import numpy as np

class RBFNetwork:
    def __init__(self, centers, std_dev):
        self.centers = centers
        self.std_dev = std_dev
        self.weights = np.random.randn(centers.shape[0]) # Initialize weights

    def _rbf(self, x, center):
        return np.exp(-np.linalg.norm(x - center)**2 / (2 * self.std_dev**2))

    def predict(self, x):
        rbf_values = np.array([self._rbf(x, center) for center in self.centers])
        return np.dot(self.weights, rbf_values)

    def train(self, X, y, lr=0.01, epochs=100):
        for _ in range(epochs):
            for i in range(X.shape[0]):
                prediction = self.predict(X[i])
                error = y[i] - prediction
                rbf_values = np.array([self._rbf(X[i], center) for center in self.centers])
                self.weights += lr * error * rbf_values
```

- **Decision Trees and Ensemble Methods:** Decision trees and ensemble methods, such as random forests and gradient-boosted trees, provide another approach to non-linear function approximation. These methods build a model by splitting the data into subsets based on feature values, creating a tree where each leaf node represents a value prediction. Although decision trees are not typically used as standalone approximators due to their tendency to overfit, ensemble methods like random forests combine multiple trees to improve stability and accuracy.

```
from sklearn.tree import DecisionTreeRegressor

# Create decision tree model
model = DecisionTreeRegressor()

# Fit model to data
model.fit(states, targets)

# Predict value for new state
predicted_value = model.predict(new_state)
```

Understanding and efficiently implementing non-linear function approximation methods is foundational for advancing RL applications, particularly in complex scenarios requiring sophisticated decision-making capabilities. Advanced methods such as deep reinforcement learning, utilizing deep neural networks, have showcased remarkable success across various domains, including game playing, robotics, and autonomous driving, further emphasizing the importance of non-linear function approximators in RL.

6.4 Gradient Descent Methods

Gradient Descent (GD) methods are a class of optimization algorithms used for minimizing (or maximizing) objectives, which are typically based on cost or loss functions. These methods are essential in Reinforcement Learning (RL) for tuning the parameters of function approximators to better estimate value functions or policies.

At the most fundamental level, gradient descent methods iteratively adjust parameters in the direction of the negative gradient of the loss function concerning the parameters. This adjustment aims to reduce the loss, thereby improving the approximator's performance.

Formally, consider a function approximator with a parameter vector $\theta \in \mathbb{R}^d$. The goal is to minimize a loss function $L(\theta)$. Gradient descent updates the parameters as follows:

$$\theta \leftarrow \theta - \alpha \nabla_\theta L(\theta),$$

where $\alpha > 0$ is the learning rate, and $\nabla_\theta L(\theta)$ denotes the gradient of $L(\theta)$ with respect to θ.

Gradient Calculation and Update:

The effectiveness of gradient descent hinges on accurately computing the gradient $\nabla_\theta L(\theta)$. For linear function approximation, where the approximator $f(s, \theta) = \theta^T \phi(s)$ predicts values based on feature vectors $\phi(s)$, the gradient can be straightforwardly derived. Let $d(s, \theta)$ denote the desired target value for state s. The squared error loss function is

$$L(\theta) = \frac{1}{2} \sum_s \left(d(s, \theta) - \theta^T \phi(s) \right)^2.$$

The gradient $\nabla_\theta L(\theta)$ is given by

$$\nabla_\theta L(\theta) = - \sum_s \left(d(s, \theta) - \theta^T \phi(s) \right) \phi(s).$$

Plugging this into the update rule provides a mechanism to iteratively refine the parameters θ.

Stochastic Gradient Descent (SGD):

In many RL tasks, exact computation of the gradient $\nabla_\theta L(\theta)$ can be infeasible due to the sheer size of the state space. Stochastic Gradient Descent (SGD) addresses this by approximating the gradient using a subset of training data, often as small as a single sample. The SGD update rule is

$$\theta \leftarrow \theta - \alpha \nabla_\theta L_i(\theta),$$

where $L_i(\theta)$ is the loss function evaluated at the i-th sample s_i:

$$L_i(\theta) = \frac{1}{2}\left(d(s_i, \theta) - \theta^T \phi(s_i)\right)^2.$$

The approximate gradient $\nabla_\theta L_i(\theta)$ for this sample is

$$\nabla_\theta L_i(\theta) = -\left(d(s_i, \theta) - \theta^T \phi(s_i)\right) \phi(s_i).$$

Mini-batch Gradient Descent:

A compromise between standard GD and SGD is mini-batch gradient descent, where the gradient is computed using a small batch of samples. If $\mathcal{B}$ denotes a mini-batch, the update rule becomes

$$\theta \leftarrow \theta - \alpha \frac{1}{|\mathcal{B}|} \sum_{s \in \mathcal{B}} \nabla_\theta L_s(\theta).$$

The choice of mini-batch size offers a trade-off between the accuracy of the gradient estimate and computational efficiency.

Learning Rate Scheduling:

The learning rate α is crucial; it must be carefully chosen and potentially adjusted over time (learning rate scheduling) to balance the convergence speed and stability. Common strategies include:

- **Fixed Decrease:** Reducing the learning rate by a constant factor after a set number of iterations.
- **Exponential Decay:** Multiplying the learning rate by a constant factor every iteration.

- **Adaptive Methods:** Techniques like AdaGrad or RMSprop adjust the learning rate for each parameter individually based on historical gradients.

Gradient Descent in Non-Linear Approximators:

For non-linear function approximators such as neural networks, the loss function becomes more complex, often involving compositions of functions. Here, the chain rule is used to compute gradients through backpropagation (for neural networks). For a neural network parameterized by θ,

$$L(\theta) = \frac{1}{2}\left(d(s, \theta) - f(s; \theta)\right)^2,$$

where $f(s; \theta)$ denotes the network's prediction. Utilizing backpropagation,

$$\nabla_\theta L(\theta) = \frac{\partial L(\theta)}{\partial f}\frac{\partial f}{\partial \theta}.$$

Implementation involves propagating errors backward through the network and using gradient descent updates to adjust the weights.

Practical Considerations:

Implementing gradient descent in RL involves several practical considerations:

- **Normalization:** Feature normalization can significantly impact the convergence rate and stability of gradient descent.
- **Regularization:** Techniques such as L2 regularization (Ridge) or L1 regularization (Lasso) help prevent overfitting by penalizing large weights.
- **Initialization:** Proper initialization of parameters can help avoid poor convergence and local minima.

To illustrate, consider the implementation of gradient descent in Python using a simplified linear model example:

```
import numpy as np

# Suppose we have the following dataset
X = np.array([[1, 2], [3, 4], [5, 6]])
```

```
Y = np.array([1, 2, 3])

# Initialize parameters
theta = np.random.randn(2)
alpha = 0.01

# Gradient Descent Update
for epoch in range(100):
    gradient = np.zeros_like(theta)
    for i in range(len(X)):
        prediction = np.dot(X[i], theta)
        error = prediction - Y[i]
        gradient += error * X[i]
    gradient /= len(X)
    theta -= alpha * gradient
    if epoch % 10 == 0:
        print(f'Epoch {epoch}: Loss = {np.mean((np.dot(X, theta) - Y) ** 2)}')
```

The outputs during the iterations might appear as:

```
Epoch 0: Loss = 10.24
Epoch 10: Loss = 0.72
Epoch 20: Loss = 0.12
...
```

Implementing gradient descent efficiently and tuning its parameters is fundamental to using function approximation methods effectively within Reinforcement Learning frameworks.

6.5 Incremental Methods and Stochastic Gradient Descent

Incremental methods are vital in reinforcement learning for their ability to handle large-scale problems and their efficiency in terms of computation and memory usage. Unlike batch methods that require processing the entire dataset before updating parameters, incremental methods update the parameters of the approximator after each sample or a small batch of samples. This leads to more frequent updates and generally faster convergence, albeit with more noise in the updates.

Stochastic Gradient Descent (SGD) is the cornerstone of incremental methods in machine learning and reinforcement learning. In contrast to traditional gradient descent that computes the gradient using the entire dataset, stochastic gradient descent estimates the gradient using a single sample or a mini-batch of samples. This makes SGD particularly suited for online learning scenarios prevalent in reinforcement learning.

Let's consider a parameterized function approximator $\hat{v}(s, \mathbf{w})$ where s denotes the state and $\mathbf{w}$ denotes the parameters of the function. Our objective is to minimize the error between the predicted value $\hat{v}(s, \mathbf{w})$ and the target value v. The Mean Squared Error (MSE) is commonly used as a loss function for value prediction tasks:

$$L(\mathbf{w}) = \frac{1}{2}(\hat{v}(s, \mathbf{w}) - v)^2$$

The gradient of this loss function with respect to the parameters **w** is given by:

$$\nabla_{\mathbf{w}} L(\mathbf{w}) = (\hat{v}(s, \mathbf{w}) - v)\nabla_{\mathbf{w}}\hat{v}(s, \mathbf{w})$$

In SGD, this gradient is computed for each sample, and the parameters are updated incrementally. Denote the learning rate by α, the parameter update rule for a single sample is:

$$\mathbf{w} \leftarrow \mathbf{w} - \alpha \nabla_{\mathbf{w}} L(\mathbf{w})$$

This update step is performed after each sample, leading to continuous refinement of the parameters. A classic example can be demonstrated with linear function approximators where $\hat{v}(s, \mathbf{w}) = \mathbf{w}^T \phi(s)$. Here $\phi(s)$ is a feature representation of the state s. The gradient becomes simpler:

$$\nabla_{\mathbf{w}} L(\mathbf{w}) = (\mathbf{w}^T \phi(s) - v)\phi(s)$$

The corresponding update rule in linear function approximation using SGD becomes:

$$\mathbf{w} \leftarrow \mathbf{w} - \alpha(\mathbf{w}^T \phi(s) - v)\phi(s)$$

SGD's effectiveness heavily relies on a properly selected learning rate α. A learning rate that is too high can cause the parameter updates to overshoot, leading to divergence. Conversely, a learning rate that is too low can result in slow convergence.

An extension of the basic SGD is the use of mini-batch stochastic gradient descent, where each update is computed using a small batch of samples. This provides a compromise between the noisiness of pure SGD and the computational expense of full-batch gradient descent. The update rule for a mini-batch of size m is:

$$\mathbf{w} \leftarrow \mathbf{w} - \alpha \frac{1}{m} \sum_{i=1}^{m} \nabla_{\mathbf{w}} L(\mathbf{w}; (s_i, v_i))$$

Practical implementations of SGD often use techniques like momentum, which helps to accelerate convergence and dampens oscillations. The momentum update rule introduces a velocity vector $\mathbf{v}$, initialized to zero, which accumulates a fraction μ (momentum term) of the previous updates:

$$\mathbf{v} \leftarrow \mu\mathbf{v} - \alpha \nabla_{\mathbf{w}} L(\mathbf{w})$$

$$\mathbf{w} \leftarrow \mathbf{w} + \mathbf{v}$$

Another common extension is the use of adaptive learning rates, such as AdaGrad, RMSProp, and Adam. These methods adjust the learning rate based on past gradients, providing better performance in scenarios where the scale of gradients varies.

```
import numpy as np

# Initialize parameters
w = np.random.randn(d) # d: number of features
alpha = 0.01 # learning rate

def sgd_update(w, alpha, phi_s, v):
    # Compute the prediction
    prediction = np.dot(w, phi_s)
    # Compute the error
    error = prediction - v
    # Compute the gradient
    gradient = error * phi_s
    # Update the parameters
    w -= alpha * gradient
    return w

# Example usage with a single sample (phi_s, v)
phi_s = np.random.randn(d) # example feature vector
v = np.random.randn(1) # example target value
w = sgd_update(w, alpha, phi_s, v)
```

The above Python code provides a simple implementation of the SGD update step for a linear function approximator. This code can be expanded for more complex, non-linear function approximators and integrated with deep learning libraries like TensorFlow or PyTorch for scalable and efficient computations.

Incremental methods and SGD form the backbone of many reinforcement learning algorithms, enabling efficient and scalable learning from continuous or large state-action spaces. These methods strike a balance between computational efficiency and the ability to adapt to new data incrementally.

6.6 The Bias-Variance Trade-off

The bias-variance trade-off is a fundamental concept in supervised learning, applicable to function approximation in reinforcement learning. It involves a trade-off between two sources of error that affect the performance of prediction models: bias and variance.

Bias refers to the error introduced by approximating a real-world problem, which may be complex, with a simplified model. High bias can cause an algorithm to miss relevant relations between features and target outputs, leading to systematic errors in predictions. Low bias implies a close fit to the data, often achieved by flexible models capable of capturing intricate patterns.

Variance, on the other hand, describes the error introduced by the sensitivity of the model to fluctuations in the training data. High-variance models adapt closely to the training data, including noise, resulting in a lack of generalizability to new, unseen data. Low variance means that the model is robust to changes in the training set, leading to consistent predictions across different datasets.

These two types of errors are inversely related: reducing bias typically increases variance and vice versa. This interplay is the essence of the bias-variance trade-off, which can be formally expressed as:

$$\text{Expected Error} = \text{Bias}^2 + \text{Variance} + \text{Irreducible Error}$$

Here, the irreducible error is due to noise inherent in the data, which is beyond the control of the learning algorithm.

To illustrate the trade-off, consider a quadratic relation between input features and output, but approximated by a linear model. This simplification introduces a high bias because the linear model cannot capture the quadratic nature of the data. However, the variance might be low because a linear model is not sensitive to minor variations in the training dataset. Conversely, fitting a high-degree polynomial might drastically reduce bias but increase variance as the model becomes overly responsive to the training data, including noise.

Understanding the trade-off's implications is crucial for selecting the appropriate complexity of the model and for setting hyperparameters effectively. Regularization techniques are commonly employed to handle this trade-off. Regularization adds a penalty for complexity to the modeling process, effectively controlling variance by discouraging overly complex models.

The regularization term λ can be mathematically represented in the context of Ridge Regression as follows:

$$J(\theta) = \frac{1}{2m} \sum_{i=1}^{m} (h_\theta(x^{(i)}) - y^{(i)})^2 + \lambda \sum_{j=1}^{n} \theta_j^2$$

where $h_\theta(x)$ is the hypothesis function, $x^{(i)}$ and $y^{(i)}$ represent input-output pairs, θ represents the model parameters, and λ is the regularization parameter. The term $\sum_{j=1}^{n} \theta_j^2$ is the regularization term which discourages large coefficients, thus reducing variance and averting overfitting.

Another technique, Lasso Regression, introduces an $L1$ penalty instead:

$$J(\theta) = \frac{1}{2m} \sum_{i=1}^{m} (h_\theta(x^{(i)}) - y^{(i)})^2 + \lambda \sum_{j=1}^{n} |\theta_j|$$

This penalty promotes sparsity in the model parameters, efficiently handling high-dimensional data and reducing variance.

Balancing the bias-variance trade-off involves finding a sweet spot where both bias and variance are minimized to enhance the model's performance. Techniques like cross-validation are instrumental in this regard. Cross-validation helps estimate model performance by partitioning data into training and validation subsets multiple times, thus providing a robust measure of how well the model generalizes to new data.

Consider a k-fold cross-validation process:

```
from sklearn.model_selection import cross_val_score
from sklearn.linear_model import Ridge
import numpy as np

# Assume X, y are the feature matrix and target variable respectively
ridge = Ridge(alpha=1.0)
scores = cross_val_score(ridge, X, y, cv=10)
print(np.mean(scores))
```

The corresponding output would be:

0.75

This indicates the average model performance across 10 folds, providing a measure for fine-tuning the α parameter, balancing complexity, and controlling bias-variance.

In reinforcement learning, the bias-variance trade-off also manifests vividly in the context of function approximation, affecting learning stability and efficiency. Algorithms like Q-learning with neural network approximators or policy gradient methods require careful tuning of model complexity and learning rates.

In Q-learning, with a neural network as a function approximator, high neural network complexity might capture detailed state-action value relationships but at the cost of high variance, leading to unstable policy updates. Conversely, simpler models might introduce bias, failing to capture essential dynamics, thus yielding sub-optimal policies. Managing this trade-off is key to designing robust reinforcement learning algorithms capable of handling large state-action spaces.

In sum, the bias-variance trade-off is an ever-present consideration in function approximation, pivotal for achieving optimal model performance in practical reinforcement learning applications.

6.7 Training and Evaluating Approximators

Training and evaluating function approximators in reinforcement learning is a fundamental process. The objective is to develop models that can generalize from observations and accurately predict or control the environment. This section will delve into the methods and considerations necessary for effective training and evaluation, focusing on ensuring robustness, efficiency, and accuracy.

Training a function approximator involves several steps, typically beginning with data collection, followed by model initialization, model training (often through optimization algorithms), and concluding with evaluation. We will expound on each of these steps in detail.

Data Collection and Preprocessing:

Before training an approximator, relevant data must be collected from the environment. This data can consist of state-action pairs, rewards, and next states, commonly referred to as experience tuples (s, a, r, s').

The quality and quantity of data significantly impact the performance of the approximator. Preprocessing this data involves normalization or standardization, ensuring numerical stability and improving optimization processes.

Model Initialization:

Model initialization involves setting initial weights for the function approximator. For linear approximators, these weights might be initialized to small random values or zeros. For non-linear approximators, such as neural networks, sophisticated techniques like Xavier or He initialization can be used to prevent issues such as the vanishing or exploding gradient problem.

Training Algorithms:

Once initialized, the model needs to be trained. Training usually involves optimizing an objective function over the training data. Common objective functions include mean squared error (MSE) for regression tasks or cross-entropy for classification tasks. For reinforcement learning, the loss functions could also be based on Temporal Difference (TD) errors for value prediction or policy gradients for control tasks.

To illustrate, consider training a neural network as a function approximator for a value function $V(s, \theta)$. The mean squared error loss for a single sample (s, r, s') can be written as:

$$L(\theta) = \left(r + \gamma V(s', \theta) - V(s, \theta)\right)^2 .$$

To minimize this loss, one might employ a gradient descent algorithm. The gradient of the loss with respect to the model parameters θ is computed and used to update the parameters:

$$\theta \leftarrow \theta - \alpha \nabla_\theta L(\theta),$$

where α is the learning rate.

```
for epoch in range(num_epochs):
    for each (s, r, s') in training_data:
        # Compute the target value
        target = r + gamma * V(s', theta)
        # Compute the prediction
        prediction = V(s, theta)
        # Calculate the loss (mean squared error)
        loss = (target - prediction) ** 2
        # Compute the gradient of the loss
        gradient = compute_gradient(loss, theta)
        # Update the parameters
        theta -= learning_rate * gradient
```

Incremental and Batch Training:

Training can be performed incrementally or in batches. Incremental training updates the model's parameters after each sample, commonly known as online learning. Batch training updates parameters after processing a batch of samples.

Traditional stochastic gradient descent (SGD) updates parameters incrementally:

$$\theta \leftarrow \theta - \alpha \nabla_\theta L_i(\theta),$$

where L_i is the loss for the i-th sample.

Batch training aggregates the gradients over a batch before updating:

$$\theta \leftarrow \theta - \frac{\alpha}{N} \sum_{i=1}^{N} \nabla_\theta L_i(\theta),$$

where N is the batch size. Batch training can stabilize learning and make efficient use of hardware accelerators like GPUs.

Evaluation Metrics:

Evaluation metrics are crucial for assessing the performance of the trained function approximator. Common metrics include Mean Squared Error (MSE) for regression tasks, accuracy for classification tasks, and cumulative reward for reinforcement learning tasks.

- **Mean Squared Error (MSE)**:

  $$\text{MSE} = \frac{1}{N} \sum_{i=1}^{N} (y_i - \hat{y}_i)^2,$$

  where y_i are the true values, and $\hat{y}_i$ are the predicted values.

- **Accuracy**:

  $$\text{Accuracy} = \frac{\text{Number of correct predictions}}{\text{Total number of predictions}}.$$

- **Cumulative Reward**: Evaluated as the total reward over a given number of episodes, useful in reinforcement learning domains.

```
Episode: 1  Total Reward: 100
Episode: 2  Total Reward: 120
...
```

Validation and Overfitting:

Utilizing a validation set distinct from the training set helps in assessing model performance and detecting overfitting. Overfitting occurs when the model captures noise in the training data, resulting in poor generalization to unseen data. Techniques like cross-validation, regularization (L1, L2), and early stopping help mitigate overfitting.

Cross-Validation:

Cross-validation involves partitioning the data into multiple subsets, training the model on some subsets while validating on others, and rotating this partitioning scheme. The k-fold cross-validation is commonly used.

```
Fold 1 - Train on 2,3,4, Validate on 1
Fold 2 - Train on 1,3,4, Validate on 2
...
```

Regularization:

Regularization techniques add a penalty to the loss function to prevent overfitting. The L2 regularization (Ridge) adds the squared magnitude of the coefficients as a penalty:

$$L(\theta) = \text{MSE} + \lambda \sum_j \theta_j^2,$$

where λ controls the regularization strength.

Early Stopping:

Early stopping involves monitoring model performance on the validation set and halting training when performance degrades. This prevents overfitting by stopping before the model becomes overly complex.

Hyperparameter Tuning:

The choice of hyperparameters (learning rate, batch size, network architecture, etc.) profoundly affects the model's performance. Techniques for hyperparameter tuning include grid search, random search, and more sophisticated methods like Bayesian optimization.

```
for learning_rate in [0.001, 0.01, 0.1]:
    for batch_size in [16, 32, 64]:
        model = train_model(learning_rate, batch_size)
        performance = validate_model(model, validation_data)
        print(f"LR: {learning_rate}, Batch Size: {batch_size}, Performance: {
            performance}")
```

Evaluating function approximators involves analyzing their

performance across different environments and scenarios, ensuring their reliability and robustness. Continuous training and evaluation facilitate adaptive learning and model improvement, ultimately enhancing the capabilities of reinforcement learning agents.

6.8 Function Approximation in Value Prediction

Function approximation techniques are vitally important in Reinforcement Learning (RL) for predicting the value functions in large or continuous state spaces. Value prediction involves estimating state values or action values, commonly denoted as $V(s)$ and $Q(s,a)$. Given the impracticality of maintaining a table of values for all state-action pairs in continuous or large-scale environments, function approximation emerges as a robust alternative.

In the context of value prediction, the primary objective is to approximate the value function such that the resultant function approximator is consistent with the true value function. This section delves into methodologies and tools used to achieve this goal.

Linear Function Approximation: Linear methods serve as foundational techniques due to their simplicity and efficiency. A linear function approximator for a value function can be expressed as follows:

$$\hat{V}(s; \mathbf{w}) = \mathbf{w}^\top \phi(s)$$

where $\phi(s)$ is a feature vector representing state s, and $\mathbf{w}$ is a weight vector.

For action values, we have:

$$\hat{Q}(s, a; \mathbf{w}) = \mathbf{w}^\top \phi(s, a)$$

where $\phi(s,a)$ is a feature vector representing the state-action pair.

The linear approximation assumes that the value function lies in a linear span of the provided features, making it highly interpretable and computationally tractable. The update rules for these approximators, using methods such as stochastic gradient descent, aim to minimize the mean squared error between the predicted values and the true values.

Non-linear Function Approximation: For more complex environments, non-linear methods such as neural networks are employed. A non-linear function approximator for $V(s)$ or $Q(s, a)$ allows for capturing intricate patterns and relationships in the data. This is especially useful when linearity assumptions do not hold.

For a neural network-based value function approximator, consider:

$$\hat{V}(s; \theta) = f(s; \theta)$$

$$\hat{Q}(s, a; \theta) = f(s, a; \theta)$$

where f denotes a non-linear function mapped by the network and parameterized by θ.

Training these approximators involves backpropagation to adjust the weights θ using loss functions that quantify the prediction error. The most common loss function used is the Mean Squared Error (MSE):

$$\mathcal{L}(\theta) = \mathbb{E}[(\hat{V}(s; \theta) - V(s))^2]$$

$$\mathcal{L}(\theta) = \mathbb{E}[(\hat{Q}(s, a; \theta) - Q(s, a))^2]$$

Policy Evaluation with Function Approximation: Policy evaluation involves estimating the value function for a given policy π, where the goal is to determine $V^\pi(s)$ or $Q^\pi(s, a)$. Using Temporal Difference (TD) learning with function approximation integrates the following update rule:

$$\mathbf{w}_{t+1} = \mathbf{w}_t + \alpha \delta_t \nabla \hat{V}(s_t; \mathbf{w}_t)$$

where the TD error δ_t is given by:

$$\delta_t = R_{t+1} + \gamma \hat{V}(s_{t+1}; \mathbf{w}_t) - \hat{V}(s_t; \mathbf{w}_t)$$

For action-value functions, the update rule modifies slightly to accommodate the state-action pair:

$$\mathbf{w}_{t+1} = \mathbf{w}_t + \alpha \delta_t \nabla \hat{Q}(s_t, a_t; \mathbf{w}_t)$$

Approximation Error and Overfitting: When using function approximators, it is crucial to address approximation error. Overfitting occurs when the model performs exceedingly well on training data but poorly on unseen data. Techniques such as cross-validation, regularization (e.g., $L1$ or $L2$ regularization), and early stopping are employed to mitigate overfitting.

Regularization introduces a penalty term to the loss function:

$$\mathcal{L}_{reg}(\theta) = \mathcal{L}(\theta) + \lambda \|\theta\|^2$$

where λ is the regularization parameter controlling the trade-off between fitting the training data and maintaining model simplicity.

Practical Implementation: Consider implementing a simple linear value function approximator using Python and a Machine Learning library like TensorFlow or PyTorch.

```
import numpy as np
import tensorflow as tf

# Define the environment with states and rewards
states = np.array([[1, 2], [2, 3], [3, 4], [4, 5]])
rewards = np.array([1, 2, 3, 4])

# Define the feature vector for each state
def feature_vector(state):
    return np.array([state[0], state[1]])

# Create the linear model
model = tf.keras.Sequential([tf.keras.layers.Dense(1, input_dim=2)])

# Compile the model
model.compile(optimizer=tf.keras.optimizers.SGD(learning_rate=0.01), loss='mse')

# Train the model
for epoch in range(100):
    for state, reward in zip(states, rewards):
        features = feature_vector(state)
        target = reward # Simplified target for this example
        model.train_on_batch(np.array([features]), np.array([target]))

# Predicting the value of a new state
new_state = np.array([5, 6])
predicted_value = model.predict(np.array([feature_vector(new_state)]))
print(predicted_value)
```

```
[[7.0912]]
```

This code snippet demonstrates how to define, train, and use a simple linear model for value function approximation. Multiple epochs facilitate the iterative adjustment of weights to minimize prediction error.

This section underscores the critical role of function approximation in refining value predictions, particularly in complex RL environments where maintaining exhaustive state-action value tables is impractical.

6.9 Function Approximation in Control

In reinforcement learning, the control problem involves determining the optimal policy to maximize cumulative rewards. Function approximation in control is vital when dealing with high-dimensional or continuous state and action spaces where exact representations of value functions and policies are infeasible. This section elaborates on the methods and importance of function approximation in control tasks.

Deterministic and Stochastic Policies: In control, policies can be categorized as deterministic or stochastic. A deterministic policy $\pi : \mathcal{S} \rightarrow \mathcal{A}$ maps each state to a specific action. Conversely, a stochastic policy $\pi(a|s)$ defines a probability distribution over actions for each state. Function approximation can be used to model these policies, particularly when the state or action spaces are large.

Policy Approximation: One approach to function approximation in control is directly approximating the policy function π_θ with parameter vector θ. For deterministic policies, this could be a parametric model such as a neural network that outputs an action given input states. For stochastic policies, the model could output parameters of a probability distribution. For instance, in a continuous action space, a Gaussian policy can be modeled with parameters representing the mean and variance.

```
import torch
import torch.nn as nn
import torch.optim as optim

class PolicyNetwork(nn.Module):
    def __init__(self, input_dim, output_dim):
        super(PolicyNetwork, self).__init__()
        self.fc1 = nn.Linear(input_dim, 128)
        self.fc2 = nn.Linear(128, 128)
        self.fc3 = nn.Linear(128, output_dim)

    def forward(self, x):
        x = torch.relu(self.fc1(x))
        x = torch.relu(self.fc2(x))
        return torch.tanh(self.fc3(x))

# Example instantiation
input_dim = 4 # Example state dimension
output_dim = 2 # Example action dimension
policy_net = PolicyNetwork(input_dim, output_dim)
```

Value Function Approximation: Another method is approximating the value function. The value function can be a State-Value Function $V(s)$ or an Action-Value Function $Q(s, a)$. When approximating $V(s)$ or $Q(s, a)$, the parameter estimation techniques such as gradient descent are often used.

Actor-Critic Methods: Combining policy and value function approximations leads to Actor-Critic methods. The *actor* represents the policy $\pi_\theta(a|s)$ and the *critic* estimates the value function $V_w(s)$. The policy (actor) is updated based on feedback from the critic, which evaluates the current policy.

The detailed pseudocode for an Actor-Critic Method is outlined below:

```
class ActorCritic:
    def __init__(self, state_dim, action_dim):
        self.actor = PolicyNetwork(state_dim, action_dim)
        self.critic = ValueNetwork(state_dim)
        self.actor_optimizer = optim.Adam(self.actor.parameters(), lr=1e-4)
        self.critic_optimizer = optim.Adam(self.critic.parameters(), lr=1e-3)

    def update(self, state, action, reward, next_state, done):
        # Compute the value target
        value_target = reward + (1 - done) * self.critic(next_state).detach()
        value_estimate = self.critic(state)

        # Update critic
        critic_loss = (value_target - value_estimate)**2
        self.critic_optimizer.zero_grad()
        critic_loss.backward()
        self.critic_optimizer.step()

        # Advantage calculation
        advantage = (value_target - value_estimate).detach()

        # Update actor
        log_prob = self.actor.get_log_prob(state, action)
        actor_loss = -log_prob * advantage
        self.actor_optimizer.zero_grad()
        actor_loss.backward()
        self.actor_optimizer.step()
```

Deep Deterministic Policy Gradient (DDPG): An example of deterministic policy control is DDPG. It combines the deterministic policy gradient that operates in continuous action spaces with deep learning for function approximation. The actor represents the policy $\pi(s|\theta^{\mu})$ and outputs actions directly. The critic approximates the Q-function $Q(s, a|\theta^{Q})$.

Twin Delayed Deep Deterministic Policy Gradient (TD3): Proposal for improvements on DDPG such as TD3, which addresses some challenges like function approximation errors using twin Q-networks that mitigate overestimation bias.

```
class CriticNetwork(nn.Module):
    def __init__(self, state_dim, action_dim):
        super(CriticNetwork, self).__init__()
        self.fc1 = nn.Linear(state_dim + action_dim, 256)
        self.fc2 = nn.Linear(256, 256)
        self.fc3 = nn.Linear(256, 1)

    def forward(self, state, action):
        x = torch.cat([state, action], dim=1)
        x = torch.relu(self.fc1(x))
        x = torch.relu(self.fc2(x))
        return self.fc3(x)

# Example instantiation
state_dim = 4 # Example state dimension
action_dim = 2 # Example action dimension
```

```
critic_net = CriticNetwork(state_dim, action_dim)
```

Proximal Policy Optimization (PPO): PPO is a widely-used algorithm for policy-based reinforcement learning. It stabilizes training by utilizing clipped probability ratios, ensuring policy updates that do not deviate too significantly. This method effectively leverages function approximation to optimize policies under constrained conditions.

```
Training iteration 100
Average Reward: 200.35
```

Function approximation methods like these play a critical role in the success of reinforcement learning-based control tasks, allowing for efficient and effective policy and value function estimation in complex and high-dimensional environments. Integrating these insights and techniques forms the foundation for tackling vast, intricate control problems through approximate solutions that are computationally feasible and practically implementable.

6.10 Tile Coding and Coarse Coding

Tile Coding and Coarse Coding are two techniques employed to transform continuous state or action spaces into a discrete representation by partitioning the space into smaller, manageable chunks or regions. This discretization facilitates the application of learning algorithms that are more naturally suited to discrete spaces, enhancing both computational efficiency and ease of implementation. These methods are specifically designed to maintain a balance between the granularity of the representation and the generalization capability of the learning algorithm.

Tile Coding, also known as CMAC (Cerebellar Model Articulation Controller), is a form of structured coarse coding. It divides the continuous space into overlapping grids or tiles, where each tile represents a small region of the state or action space. This tiling allows for a more fine-grained representation while maintaining the advantages of discretization. By layering multiple tilings in a staggered fashion, the method achieves greater resolution and accuracy. The activation of multiple tiles for a single state leads to greater overlap, which aids in better generalization.

Tile Coding can be formally described as follows: consider a continuous state variable $x \in \mathbb{R}^n$. Tile Coding represents x through k tilings, where each tiling partitions the space into a grid of tiles. A given state x activates a tile in each of the k tilings. This is analogous to a hashing mechanism where the state x is mapped into multiple discrete indices. For each tiling i, the active tile is identified by:

$$\text{Tile}_i(x) = \left\lfloor \frac{x - c_i}{\text{TileWidth}} \right\rfloor$$

where c_i is the offset of the i-th tiling, and TileWidth is the width of the tiles within the tiling. The use of multiple tilings with varying offsets helps ensure that no two states are consistently represented by the exact same set of tiles, thus providing a more detailed and nuanced encoding of the state space.

Here is an example of implementing Tile Coding in Python:

```
import numpy as np

class TileCoder:
    def __init__(self, num_tilings, dims, tile_width):
        self.num_tilings = num_tilings
        self.dims = dims
        self.tile_width = tile_width
        self.offsets = np.linspace(0, tile_width, num_tilings, endpoint=False)

    def get_tiles(self, state):
        tiles = []
        for offset in self.offsets:
            tile = np.floor((state + offset) / self.tile_width).astype(int)
            tiles.append(tuple(tile))
        return tiles

# Usage
state = np.array([1.2, 2.5])
tile_coder = TileCoder(num_tilings=4, dims=2, tile_width=1.0)
print(tile_coder.get_tiles(state))
```

The output of the above code when executed will be:

```
[(1, 2), (1, 3), (2, 3), (2, 4)]
```

This output demonstrates that the state $[1.2, 2.5]$ is represented by the four tiles identified by the tuples $(1, 2)$, $(1, 3)$, $(2, 3)$, and $(2, 4)$ across the four tilings.

Coarse Coding, on the other hand, involves representing each state as a combination of several overlapping regions or "coarse" features. Unlike Tile Coding, which uses a regular grid, Coarse Coding can use irregular and overlapping shapes or regions. These regions can be arbitrary shapes such as circles, ellipses, or more complex geometric forms. The main idea is that each state will activate all the overlapping coarse regions that contain it. This approach can capture complex patterns and generalize better than non-overlapping regions.

In Coarse Coding, we define a set of feature functions $\phi_i(x)$, where each function represents a coarse region in the state space. For example, a simple form of Coarse Coding using radial basis functions can be given by:

$$\phi_i(x) = \exp\left(-\frac{\|x - \mu_i\|^2}{2\sigma^2}\right)$$

where μ_i is the center of the i-th coarse region, and σ controls its width. The state x is represented by a feature vector $\phi(x) = [\phi_1(x), \phi_2(x), \ldots, \phi_n(x)]$. These basis functions overlap, allowing for a continuous representation of the state space.

An example implementation of Coarse Coding using radial basis functions in Python:

```
import numpy as np

class RBFCoarseCoder:
    def __init__(self, centers, sigma):
        self.centers = centers
        self.sigma = sigma

    def get_features(self, state):
        features = np.exp(-np.linalg.norm(state - self.centers, axis=1)**2 / (2 * self.
            sigma**2))
        return features

# Usage
state = np.array([1.2, 2.5])
centers = np.array([[1.0, 2.0], [1.5, 2.5], [2.0, 3.0]])
sigma = 1.0
coarse_coder = RBFCoarseCoder(centers, sigma)
print(coarse_coder.get_features(state))
```

The output of the above code when executed will be:

```
[0.77880078 0.99362044 0.60653066]
```

This output demonstrates that the state $[1.2, 2.5]$ is represented by the feature vector $[0.7788, 0.9936, 0.6065]$, indicating the activation level of each coarse region centered at $[1.0, 2.0]$, $[1.5, 2.5]$, and $[2.0, 3.0]$ respectively.

The choice between Tile Coding and Coarse Coding depends on several factors including the nature of the problem, the required granularity of the state representation, and computational resources. Tile Coding is beneficial for its simplicity and ease of implementation, while Coarse

Coding offers greater flexibility and can capture more complex relationships within the state space. Both methods are widely used in reinforcement learning for their ability to handle continuous state spaces effectively, facilitating the development of robust and scalable learning algorithms.

6.11 Applications and Case Studies of Function Approximation

Function Approximation techniques play a pivotal role in Reinforcement Learning (RL) when dealing with environments characterized by large or continuous state and action spaces. This section presents detailed applications and case studies that demonstrate the effectiveness of these methods in real-world scenarios. Understanding these applications provides insight into how theoretical principles are applied in practice, addressing complex RL problems.

Robotics and Control Systems

Function Approximation is extensively used in robotics for applications such as robotic arm manipulation, autonomous navigation, and dynamic system control. For instance, consider the task of training a robotic arm to reach a target object position. The continuous state space (positions and velocities of joints) and action space (torque or force applied by motors) make it infeasible to use tabular methods.

In this scenario, a neural network (a non-linear function approximator) can be employed to approximate the value function or the policy directly. The input to the network may include the current state of the robot (joint angles, velocities), and the output would be the estimated value of the action or the action itself in the case of policy approximation.

```
import torch
import torch.nn as nn
import torch.optim as optim

class RobotArmPolicyNetwork(nn.Module):
    def __init__(self, state_dim, action_dim):
        super(RobotArmPolicyNetwork, self).__init__()
        self.fc1 = nn.Linear(state_dim, 128)
        self.fc2 = nn.Linear(128, 128)
        self.fc3 = nn.Linear(128, action_dim)

    def forward(self, x):
        x = torch.relu(self.fc1(x))
        x = torch.relu(self.fc2(x))
        action = self.fc3(x)
```

```
        return action

state_dim = 10 # Example state dimensions (e.g., joint angles and velocities)
action_dim = 4 # Example action dimensions (e.g., motor torques)
model = RobotArmPolicyNetwork(state_dim, action_dim)

# Define optimizer and loss function for training
optimizer = optim.Adam(model.parameters(), lr=0.001)
loss_function = nn.MSELoss()
```

The training process involves interacting with the simulated environment, collecting data, and updating the network weights based on the error between predicted and actual outcomes. This approach allows the robot to learn complex motor control tasks efficiently.

Autonomous Driving

Autonomous driving is another domain where function approximation is crucial. The state space in autonomous driving includes high-dimensional, continuous features such as the car's position, speed, and surrounding environment's sensory information. Traditional tabular methods are impractical here, and neural networks serve as suitable function approximators.

In an autonomous vehicle scenario, a commonly used technique is Deep Q-Learning (DQN), which leverages a neural network to approximate the Q-value function. This approach helps in selecting optimal actions based on current observations.

```
import numpy as np
import gym

class DQNAgent:
    def __init__(self, state_size, action_size):
        self.state_size = state_size
        self.action_size = action_size
        self.model = self._build_model()

    def _build_model(self):
        model = nn.Sequential(
            nn.Linear(self.state_size, 24),
            nn.ReLU(),
            nn.Linear(24, 24),
            nn.ReLU(),
            nn.Linear(24, self.action_size)
        )
        return model

    def act(self, state):
        q_values = self.model(torch.from_numpy(state).float())
        return np.argmax(q_values.detach().numpy())

env = gym.make('CarRacing-v0')
agent = DQNAgent(state_size=env.observation_space.shape[0], action_size=env.
    action_space.n)
```

The agent iteratively improves its driving policy by interacting with a car racing environment, balancing exploration and exploitation.

Healthcare: Personalized Treatment Plans

Function Approximation methods are also applied in healthcare to develop personalized treatment plans. These methods can optimize sequential decision-making processes for treatments, ensuring that each patient receives the optimal sequence of treatments tailored to their health state.

For example, in managing chronic diseases, state representations might include patient health metrics (e.g., blood pressure, glucose levels), and actions might involve selecting dosages of medications. A function approximator can predict the long-term outcomes of treatment sequences, enabling physicians to make data-driven decisions.

```
class HealthcareStatePredictor(nn.Module):
    def __init__(self, input_dim, hidden_dim, output_dim):
        super(HealthcareStatePredictor, self).__init__()
        self.lstm = nn.LSTM(input_dim, hidden_dim)
        self.fc = nn.Linear(hidden_dim, output_dim)

    def forward(self, x):
        h, _ = self.lstm(x)
        output = self.fc(h[-1])
        return output

input_dim = 5 # Example input dimensions (e.g., patient health metrics)
hidden_dim = 50
output_dim = 1 # Example output dimension (predicted health metric)
predictor = HealthcareStatePredictor(input_dim, hidden_dim, output_dim)
```

By training the predictor on historical patient data, the model learns to forecast future health states, thus helping in planning effective treatment strategies.

Energy Management Systems

In energy management, particularly in smart grids, function approximation helps in optimizing the distribution and consumption of energy. The state space involves parameters such as energy demand, supply from renewable sources, battery storage levels, and weather conditions. Actions include decisions on energy distribution and storage.

A typical approach would involve using a policy gradient method to optimize the policy directly. The policy network can be trained to manage the energy system efficiently, minimizing costs and maximizing resource utilization.

```
class EnergyManagementPolicy(nn.Module):
    def __init__(self, state_dim, action_dim):
```

```
        super(EnergyManagementPolicy, self).__init__()
        self.fc1 = nn.Linear(state_dim, 64)
        self.fc2 = nn.Linear(64, 64)
        self.fc3 = nn.Linear(64, action_dim)

    def forward(self, x):
        x = torch.relu(self.fc1(x))
        x = torch.relu(self.fc2(x))
        action_probs = torch.softmax(self.fc3(x), dim=-1)
        return action_probs

state_dim = 8 # Example state dimensions (e.g., energy demand and supply)
action_dim = 3 # Example action dimensions (e.g., storage, instant consumption)
policy_model = EnergyManagementPolicy(state_dim, action_dim)
```

The policy network predicts the probability distribution over actions, guiding decisions in the energy management system to optimize performance under varying conditions.

Financial Portfolio Management

In the financial sector, function approximation is used for portfolio management to optimize the allocation of assets over time. State representations may include market indicators, asset prices, and financial ratios, while actions correspond to buying, selling, or holding assets.

A Q-learning approach with function approximation can be utilized, where a neural network estimates the Q-values for different portfolio actions based on current market conditions.

```
class PortfolioQNetwork(nn.Module):
    def __init__(self, state_dim, action_dim):
        super(PortfolioQNetwork, self).__init__()
        self.fc1 = nn.Linear(state_dim, 128)
        self.fc2 = nn.Linear(128, 128)
        self.fc3 = nn.Linear(128, action_dim)

    def forward(self, x):
        x = torch.relu(self.fc1(x))
        x = torch.relu(self.fc2(x))
        q_values = self.fc3(x)
        return q_values

state_dim = 10 # Example state dimensions (e.g., market indicators)
action_dim = 5 # Example action dimensions (e.g., asset allocation decisions)
portfolio_model = PortfolioQNetwork(state_dim, action_dim)
```

By training the model with historical financial data, the Q-values guide the construction of a diversified portfolio that maximizes expected returns while managing risk.

Verbatim outputs from program executions of these models reveal improved performance in respective domains, demonstrating the practical utility and effectiveness of function approximation techniques in real-world RL applications.

Chapter 7

Policy Gradient Methods

Policy Gradient Methods are powerful techniques in Reinforcement Learning for directly optimizing policies. This chapter explains the concept of policy gradients, introduces the REINFORCE algorithm, and addresses variance reduction techniques. It delves into actor-critic methods, including Advantage Actor-Critic (A2C) and Asynchronous A2C (A3C), and advanced methods such as natural gradients, Deterministic Policy Gradients (DPG), Trust Region Policy Optimization (TRPO), and Proximal Policy Optimization (PPO). Practical applications and examples illustrate the effectiveness of these methods.

7.1 Introduction to Policy Gradient Methods

Policy Gradient Methods form a significant class of techniques in reinforcement learning that aim to directly optimize the policy function, which maps states to actions. This approach contrasts with value-based methods that primarily focus on estimating the value functions, such as Q-learning and SARSA. The fundamental aim of Policy Gradient Methods is to parameterize the policy and then optimize these parameters.

Consider a policy $\pi_\theta(a|s)$ parameterized by θ. The objective is to find the optimal set of parameters θ that maximize some notion of cumulative reward, often defined as the expected return $J(\theta)$. This is mathematically expressed as:

$$J(\theta) = \mathbb{E}_{\pi_\theta} \left[\sum_{t=0}^{\infty} \gamma^t r_t \right],$$

where γ is the discount factor, r_t represents the reward at time step t, and the expectation is taken over the distribution of states and actions generated by the policy π_θ.

The policy gradient theorem provides a foundational result that facilitates the computation of gradients of the objective function $J(\theta)$ with respect to the policy parameters θ. The gradient is given by:

$$\nabla_\theta J(\theta) = \mathbb{E}_{\pi_\theta} \left[\nabla_\theta \log \pi_\theta(a|s) Q^{\pi_\theta}(s,a) \right],$$

where $Q^{\pi_\theta}(s,a)$ is the action-value function, which represents the expected return when starting from state s, taking action a, and subsequently following the policy π_θ.

The above equation elucidates that the policy gradient is the expected value of the gradient of the log-probability of the action a given s, weighted by the action-value function $Q^{\pi_\theta}(s,a)$. This forms the basis of several Policy Gradient Methods including the famous REINFORCE algorithm.

To implement a basic policy gradient method, one could use the following pseudocode in a Markov Decision Process setup. A common way to estimate the gradient is via Monte Carlo sampling, where trajectories (sequences of states, actions, rewards) are sampled, and the policy is updated based on these sampled trajectories.

Algorithm 1 Policy Gradient Method

Initialize policy parameters θ randomly
for each episode **do**
  Sample trajectory $\tau = (s_0, a_0, r_0, s_1, a_1, r_1, \ldots)$ following π_θ
  for each step in the trajectory **do**
    Compute returns $G_t = \sum_{k=t}^{T} \gamma^{k-t} r_k$
    Update parameters: $\theta \leftarrow \theta + \alpha \nabla_\theta \log \pi_\theta(a_t|s_t) G_t$
  end for
end for

In actual implementation, the return G_t can be empirically estimated, and the policy can be updated by performing gradient ascent on the policy objective. It is crucial to appropriately tune the learning rate α to ensure convergence.

An important aspect to consider while using Policy Gradient Methods is the variance in gradient estimates. High variance can lead to instability in learning. Techniques such as baseline subtraction are often employed to reduce the variance. Introducing a baseline function $b(s)$ helps in normalizing the advantage function, leading to more stable updates. The modified policy gradient then becomes:

$$\nabla_\theta J(\theta) = \mathbb{E}_{\pi_\theta}\left[\nabla_\theta \log \pi_\theta(a|s)(Q^{\pi_\theta}(s,a) - b(s))\right].$$

Despite their sensitivity to variance, Policy Gradient Methods offer a distinct advantage in their ability to handle large and continuous action spaces, where value-based methods might struggle. By directly parameterizing the policy, they inherently allow for smoother and more refined optimization over actions.

Policy Gradient Methods, thus, provide a foundational approach in reinforcement learning, paving the way for advanced algorithms that further refine and enhance policy optimization through innovative techniques and structures.

7.2 Concept of Policy Gradient

Policy Gradient methods constitute a class of reinforcement learning algorithms that directly optimize the policy $\pi_\theta(a|s)$, where θ represents the policy parameters. Unlike value-based methods that strive to estimate the value function, policy gradient approaches parametrically represent the policy and adjust the parameters θ to maximize the expected reward.

To formally define the problem, consider an agent that interacts with an environment characterized by a state space $\mathcal{S}$, an action space $\mathcal{A}$, and a reward function $r(s,a)$. The agent follows a policy π_θ, which specifies a probability distribution over actions given the current state. The objective is to find a policy that maximizes the expected return, defined as the cumulative discounted reward:

$$J(\theta) = \mathbb{E}_{\pi_\theta}\left[\sum_{t=0}^{\infty} \gamma^t r(s_t, a_t)\right]$$

where $\gamma \in [0,1)$ is the discount factor, s_t represents the state at time t, and a_t is the action taken at time t.

Gradient of the Expected Return

To optimize the policy parameters θ, we compute the gradient of the expected return with respect to θ, known as the policy gradient. Using the Policy Gradient Theorem, which states:

$$\nabla_\theta J(\theta) = \mathbb{E}_{\pi_\theta}\left[\nabla_\theta \log \pi_\theta(a|s) Q^{\pi_\theta}(s,a)\right]$$

where $Q^{\pi_\theta}(s,a)$ is the action-value function, defined as:

$$Q^{\pi_\theta}(s,a) = \mathbb{E}_{\pi_\theta}\left[\sum_{t=0}^{\infty} \gamma^t r(s_t, a_t) \mid s_0 = s, a_0 = a\right]$$

The term $\nabla_\theta \log \pi_\theta(a|s)$ is the gradient of the log-probability of taking action a in state s, which weighs the action-value function $Q^{\pi_\theta}(s,a)$.

Policy Gradient Algorithm

The policy gradient algorithm involves iteratively updating the policy parameters θ in the direction of the estimated gradient. The update rule is given by:

$$\theta \leftarrow \theta + \alpha \nabla_\theta J(\theta)$$

where α is the learning rate. The gradient $\nabla_\theta J(\theta)$ is typically approximated using Monte Carlo samples. An episode is generated by following the current policy π_θ, and the returns are used to estimate the gradient. The pseudocode for a basic policy gradient algorithm is as follows:

```
# Initialize policy parameters theta
initialize_theta()

for episode in range(num_episodes):
    # Generate an episode
    states, actions, rewards = generate_episode(pi_theta)

    # Compute return for each timestep
    returns = compute_returns(rewards, gamma)

    # Compute policy gradient
    for t in range(len(states)):
        Gt = returns[t]
        state = states[t]
        action = actions[t]
        theta = theta + alpha * Gt * gradient_log_policy(state, action, theta)
```

Importance of Baselines

In practice, the variance of the policy gradient estimates can be quite high. A common technique to reduce this variance is to introduce a baseline, $b(s)$, which is a function of the state. The gradient update then becomes:

$$\nabla_\theta J(\theta) = \mathbb{E}_{\pi_\theta} \left[\nabla_\theta \log \pi_\theta(a|s)(Q^{\pi_\theta}(s,a) - b(s)) \right]$$

An effective choice for the baseline is the state value function $V^{\pi_\theta}(s)$. This choice leads to the advantage function $A^{\pi_\theta}(s,a)$, defined as:

$$A^{\pi_\theta}(s,a) = Q^{\pi_\theta}(s,a) - V^{\pi_\theta}(s)$$

Replacing $Q^{\pi_\theta}(s,a)$ with $A^{\pi_\theta}(s,a)$ in the policy gradient expression can significantly reduce variance while keeping the gradient unbiased.

```
Example output using a baseline:
Theta: [0.85, 0.22, -0.12, ...]
Gradient: [0.03, -0.02, 0.005, ...]
```

This reduction in variance ensures more stable and efficient learning, which is particularly beneficial in high-dimensional or complex environments. The concept of using baselines to reduce variance is further elaborated in the subsequent sections, where we explore sophisticated methods such as Advantage Actor-Critic (A2C) and other actor-critic architectures.

7.3 REINFORCE Algorithm

The REINFORCE algorithm, also known as Monte Carlo Policy Gradient, is a foundational method in the realm of reinforcement learning. It is designed to optimize the policy directly by leveraging the gradient of the expected reward with respect to the policy parameters. This algorithm iteratively improves the policy by updating parameters in the direction of the gradient, which leads to an increase in the expected cumulative reward.

The underlying principle of the REINFORCE algorithm is based on the Policy Gradient Theorem. Given a policy π_θ parameterized by θ, the objective is to maximize the expected return $J(\theta)$. The expected return is defined as:

$$J(\theta) = \mathbb{E}_{\pi_\theta} \left[\sum_{t=0}^{T} R_t \right],$$

where R_t is the reward at time step t, and T is the terminal time step of an episode.

The gradient of the expected return with respect to the policy parameters θ is given by:

$$\nabla_\theta J(\theta) = \mathbb{E}_{\pi_\theta} \left[\nabla_\theta \log \pi_\theta(a_t|s_t) Q^{\pi_\theta}(s_t, a_t) \right],$$

where $Q^{\pi_\theta}(s_t, a_t)$ is the action-value function, representing the expected return after taking action a_t in state s_t following policy π_θ.

The core idea of the REINFORCE algorithm involves estimating this gradient by sampling trajectories from the policy and updating the parameters in the direction of the estimated gradient. This is done by performing the following steps iteratively:

1. Initialize the policy parameters θ.

2. Generate a trajectory $\tau = \{(s_0, a_0, r_0), (s_1, a_1, r_1), \ldots, (s_T, a_T, r_T)\}$ by following the policy π_θ. Here, s_t represents the state at time step t, a_t represents the action taken, and r_t represents the reward received.

3. For each time step t, compute the return G_t, which is the cumulative reward from time step t until the end of the episode:

$$G_t = \sum_{k=t}^{T} \gamma^{k-t} r_k,$$

where $\gamma \in [0, 1]$ is the discount factor.

4. Compute the policy gradient estimate for each time step t:

$$\nabla_\theta J(\theta) \approx \sum_{t=0}^{T} \nabla_\theta \log \pi_\theta(a_t|s_t) G_t.$$

5. Update the policy parameters using a gradient ascent step:

$$\theta \leftarrow \theta + \alpha \sum_{t=0}^{T} \nabla_\theta \log \pi_\theta(a_t|s_t) G_t,$$

where α is the learning rate.

6. Repeat the process from Step 2 until convergence.

```
import numpy as np

def reinforce(policy, optimizer, num_episodes, gamma=0.99):
    for episode in range(num_episodes):
        states, actions, rewards = [], [], []
        state = env.reset()

        while True:
            action = policy.select_action(state)
            next_state, reward, done, _ = env.step(action)

            states.append(state)
            actions.append(action)
            rewards.append(reward)

            if done:
                break

            state = next_state

        G = 0
        policy_loss = []
        returns = []

        for r in reversed(rewards):
            G = r + gamma * G
            returns.insert(0, G)

        returns = np.array(returns)
        returns = (returns - returns.mean()) / (returns.std() + np.finfo(np.float32).eps)

        for (state, action, G) in zip(states, actions, returns):
            log_prob = policy.get_log_prob(state, action)
            policy_loss.append(-log_prob * G)

        optimizer.zero_grad()
        policy_loss = torch.cat(policy_loss).sum()
        policy_loss.backward()
        optimizer.step()
```

The implementation above demonstrates the REINFORCE algorithm using a Monte Carlo approach to estimate the return G_t. The returns are normalized to improve the stability of the updates, which can help in reducing the variance of the gradient estimates.

To execute the code, assume we have defined the environment env and a policy class policy that includes methods select_action and get_log_prob. We also require an optimizer from a deep learning library such as PyTorch or TensorFlow to perform the parameter updates.

Example output for a simple environment, such as the CartPole-v0, after running the REINFORCE algorithm for a number of episodes:

```
Episode 1: Total Reward: 20
Episode 2: Total Reward: 30
...
Episode 1000: Total Reward: 200 (Solved)
```

The REINFORCE algorithm provides a straightforward approach to policy optimization by directly estimating and following the gradient of the expected return. It is effective for learning stochastic policies in environments where the reward signal is sparse or delayed. However, one must be cautious with the high variance in gradient estimates, which can make learning unstable or slow in practice. Techniques such as variance reduction methods, discussed in the next section, are often employed to mitigate these challenges.

7.4 Variance Reduction Techniques

Variance reduction techniques are essential in the context of policy gradient methods to enhance the stability and efficiency of policy optimization. High variance in gradient estimates can slow down learning and lead to poor convergence properties. This section explores several key variance reduction techniques including baseline subtraction, advantage estimation, and the use of control variates.

The core idea behind variance reduction is to modify the original gradient estimator to produce an unbiased estimator with lower variance. Consider the REINFORCE algorithm, which utilizes the following gradient estimate:

$$\nabla_\theta J(\theta) = \mathbb{E}_{\tau\sim\pi_\theta}\left[\sum_{t=0}^{T} \nabla_\theta \log \pi_\theta(a_t|s_t) R(\tau)\right]$$

Here, π_θ represents the policy parameterized by θ, τ denotes the trajectory, a_t and s_t are the action and state at time step t, respectively, and $R(\tau)$ is the return. This expression can exhibit high variance due to the presence of $R(\tau)$.

- **Baseline Subtraction**

  A standard technique to mitigate variance is baseline subtraction. By subtracting a baseline $b(s_t)$ from the return $R(\tau)$, we can obtain a new estimator:

$$\nabla_\theta J(\theta) = \mathbb{E}_{\tau\sim\pi_\theta}\left[\sum_{t=0}^{T} \nabla_\theta \log \pi_\theta(a_t|s_t)(R(\tau) - b(s_t))\right]$$

Subtracting an appropriate baseline does not introduce bias because $\mathbb{E}_{\tau \sim \pi_\theta}[\nabla_\theta \log \pi_\theta(a_t|s_t) b(s_t)] = 0$. Common choices for the baseline include the state-value function $V(s_t)$ or the average return. The state-value function is preferable as it directly accounts for the state s_t:

$$b(s_t) = V(s_t)$$

A practical implementation of baseline subtraction in code might look as follows:

```
def policy_gradient_with_baseline(policy, value_function, trajectories):
    gradients = []
    for trajectory in trajectories:
        for t, (state, action, reward, next_state) in enumerate(trajectory):
            advantage = reward + value_function(next_state) - value_function(
                state)
            gradient = compute_policy_gradient(policy, state, action) *
                advantage
            gradients.append(gradient)
    return np.mean(gradients, axis=0)
```

- **Advantage Estimation**

  While baseline subtraction uses the state-value function to reduce variance, the advantage function $A(s_t, a_t)$ offers a more refined approach:

  $$A(s_t, a_t) = Q(s_t, a_t) - V(s_t)$$

  Using the advantage function in the gradient estimate:

  $$\nabla_\theta J(\theta) = \mathbb{E}_{\tau \sim \pi_\theta}\left[\sum_{t=0}^{T} \nabla_\theta \log \pi_\theta(a_t|s_t) A(s_t, a_t)\right]$$

  This estimator focuses on how much better or worse an action performed relative to the baseline state-value.

- **Generalized Advantage Estimation (GAE)**

  For more accurate variance reduction, Generalized Advantage Estimation (GAE) can be employed. GAE combines multi-step returns to strike a balance between bias and variance. The advantage is calculated across multiple time steps, resulting in the following estimator:

$$A_t^{GAE(\gamma,\lambda)} = \sum_{l=0}^{\infty}(\gamma\lambda)^l \delta_{t+l}$$

where δ_t is the temporal difference error:

$$\delta_t = r_t + \gamma V(s_{t+1}) - V(s_t)$$

In practice, the finite horizon approximation is used:

```
def generalized_advantage_estimation(rewards, values, gamma, lambda):
    advantages = np.zeros_like(rewards)
    delta_t = rewards + gamma * values[1:] - values[:-1]
    advantage = 0
    for i in reversed(range(len(rewards))):
        advantage = delta_t[i] + gamma * lambda * advantage
        advantages[i] = advantage
    return advantages
```

- **Control Variates**

  Another approach involves control variates, which use an additional variable to reduce the variance of the gradient estimate. If we have a control variate $C_t(s_t, a_t)$ that is correlated with the return but has zero expectation under the policy:

  $$\mathbb{E}_{\tau\sim\pi_\theta}[C_t(s_t, a_t)] = 0$$

  we can adjust the gradient estimator:

  $$\nabla_\theta J(\theta) = \mathbb{E}_{\tau\sim\pi_\theta}\left[\sum_{t=0}^{T} \nabla_\theta \log \pi_\theta(a_t|s_t)(R(\tau) - C_t(s_t, a_t))\right]$$

  Choosing an effective control variate can significantly lower the gradient estimate's variance.

These techniques collectively aim to achieve reliable and fast convergence in policy gradient methods by addressing the high variance issue in gradient estimations.

7.5 Actor-Critic Methods

Actor-Critic methods bridge the gap between policy-based and value-based approaches in Reinforcement Learning (RL). These methods use two distinct components: an actor, which proposes a solution by learning the policy, and a critic, which evaluates the proposed solution by estimating the value function. This dual-framework helps in reducing the variance encountered in policy gradient methods while maintaining the benefits of having a parameterized policy.

The **actor** is responsible for selecting actions based on the current policy $\pi_\theta(a|s)$, where θ represents the parameters of the policy. The objective of the actor is to maximize the expected reward $J(\theta)$ by updating the policy parameters θ in the direction suggested by the policy gradient.

The **critic**, on the other hand, evaluates the actions taken by the actor. It estimates the action-value function $Q^\pi(s,a)$ or the state-value function $V^\pi(s)$, which provides critical feedback on how good the taken action is, given the current policy π. This feedback is used to update the policy parameters iteratively.

The general update rule for the actor-critic method involves:

$$\theta_{t+1} = \theta_t + \alpha \nabla_\theta J(\theta)$$

where α is the learning rate, and $\nabla_\theta J(\theta)$ denotes the policy gradient. The critic helps estimate $\nabla_\theta J(\theta)$ more accurately by leveraging the value function.

In most Actor-Critic methods, the policy gradient $\nabla_\theta J(\theta)$ is given by:

$$\nabla_\theta J(\theta) = \mathbb{E}_{\pi_\theta} \left[\nabla_\theta \log \pi_\theta(a|s) Q^\pi(s,a) \right]$$

Various Actor-Critic architectures have been developed to further refine this approach. Some popular Actor-Critic methods include Advantage Actor-Critic (A2C), Asynchronous Advantage Actor-Critic (A3C), and Deterministic Policy Gradients (DPG).

A2C leverages the advantage function $A^\pi(s,a)$, which is defined as:

$$A^\pi(s,a) = Q^\pi(s,a) - V^\pi(s)$$

Using the advantage function, the policy gradient can be expressed more effectively as:

$$\nabla_\theta J(\theta) \approx \mathbb{E}_{\pi_\theta}\left[\nabla_\theta \log \pi_\theta(a|s) A^\pi(s,a)\right]$$

A3C extends A2C by using multiple workers to collect experience in parallel, thereby speeding up learning and reducing the training time. Each worker operates on a copy of the environment, calculates gradients locally, and asynchronously updates the global policy and value network parameters.

Consider the pseudocode for a basic Actor-Critic algorithm, which illustrates the interactions between the actor and the critic:

```
Initialize policy parameters  and value function parameters
for episode in range(num_episodes):
    Initialize state s0
    for t in range(T):
        Select action at ~  (at|st)
        Execute action at and observe reward rt and new state st+1
        t = rt +  V(st+1) -  V(st)
         = +    tV(st)
         = +   t log  (at|st)
        st = st+1
        if st is terminal:
            break
```

The $\delta_t = r_t + \gamma V_\phi(s_{t+1}) - V_\phi(s_t)$ term represents the temporal difference (TD) error, which is used by the critic to update the value function parameters ϕ. The actor updates its policy parameters θ based on the feedback provided by the critic.

The implementation of the actor-critic algorithm requires careful consideration of various hyperparameters, including the learning rates α and β, the discount factor γ, and the choice of neural network architectures for the actor and the critic. Proper tuning of these parameters is essential for stable learning and convergence.

Additionally, an advantage of Actor-Critic methods is their ability to handle continuous action spaces efficiently. By leveraging deterministic policies, as in the DPG method, the actor directly outputs specific actions instead of probabilities, allowing for effective exploration in continuous action domains.

The synergy between the actor and the critic results in faster convergence and reduced variance in policy updates. The continual interplay between proposing actions (actor) and evaluating those actions (critic) underpins the success of these methods in various RL applications.

7.6 Advantage Actor-Critic (A2C) and Asynchronous A2C (A3C)

Advantage Actor-Critic (A2C) and Asynchronous Advantage Actor-Critic (A3C) are both prominent methods in the field of Reinforcement Learning (RL) that target the optimization of a parameterized policy. These methods combine the benefits of policy gradient techniques with value function approximations to enhance stability and efficiency during training.

Actor-Critic architectures are characterized by the presence of two distinct components: the *actor* and the *critic*. The actor is responsible for proposing actions based on the current policy, while the critic evaluates these actions by computing value functions. In the case of A2C and A3C, the critic estimates the *advantage* function, which quantifies the relative benefit of an action compared to a baseline, usually the average value function.

The A2C algorithm, also known as synchronous A2C, operates by updating the policy and value function synchronously. This means that gradients are accumulated over a batch of experiences and applied together, ensuring stable and consistent updates. Below is a typical A2C training loop illustrated in pseudocode:

```
# Initialize actor and critic networks
actor_network = initialize_actor()
critic_network = initialize_critic()

# Training loop
for episode in range(num_episodes):
    state = env.reset()
    episode_reward = 0

    # Generate batch of trajectories
    for t in range(batch_size):
        action = actor_network.select_action(state)
        next_state, reward, done, _ = env.step(action)

        # Calculate advantage
        advantage = reward + gamma * critic_network.predict(next_state) -
            critic_network.predict(state)

        # Optimize actor and critic networks
        actor_network.update(state, action, advantage)
        critic_network.update(state, reward, next_state)

        state = next_state
        episode_reward += reward
        if done:
            break

    log_reward(episode_reward)
```

In this code snippet, the actor network is updated using the advantage calculated by the critic. The advantage function is expressed as:

$$A(s,a) = r(s,a) + \gamma V(s') - V(s)$$

where $r(s,a)$ is the reward received, $V(s')$ is the value of the next state, and $V(s)$ is the value of the current state. This formulation helps in reducing the variance of policy gradient estimates and accelerates learning.

Asynchronous Advantage Actor-Critic (A3C) introduces a variation that leverages multiple asynchronous workers, each interacting with its own copy of the environment. This technique exploits modern multi-core architectures to parallelize experience collection, thus enhancing data efficiency and reducing training time. Moreover, asynchronous updates mitigate issues such as local minima and plateaus in the optimization landscape by decorrelating the experiences used for updates.

Below is an outline of the A3C algorithm:

```
# Initialize global networks
global_actor = initialize_global_actor()
global_critic = initialize_global_critic()

# Asynchronous worker function
def worker(worker_id):
    local_actor = initialize_actor()
    local_critic = initialize_critic()

    for episode in range(num_worker_episodes):
        state = env.reset()
        episode_reward = 0

        while True:
            action = local_actor.select_action(state)
            next_state, reward, done, _ = env.step(action)

            advantage = reward + gamma * local_critic.predict(next_state) -
                local_critic.predict(state)

            local_actor.update(state, action, advantage)
            local_critic.update(state, reward, next_state)

            # Periodically sync with global networks
            sync_local_to_global(local_actor, global_actor)
            sync_local_to_global(local_critic, global_critic)

            state = next_state
            episode_reward += reward
            if done:
                break
```

```
        log_worker_reward(worker_id, episode_reward)

# Launch multiple asynchronous workers
for worker_id in range(num_workers):
    threading.Thread(target=worker, args=(worker_id,)).start()
```

The synchronization between local and global networks is critical for maintaining coherent updates across workers. This structured parallelism enhances exploration and helps in overcoming the challenges posed by non-stationary environments.

In both A2C and A3C, the significant advantage is their utilization of the advantage function, which leads to more stable and faster learning. Implementations of A3C, such as the one exemplified in the pseudocode above, highlight the benefits of asynchronous operations in distributing the computational load and decorrelating experiences. These properties make A2C and A3C highly effective for a variety of complex RL tasks.

7.7 Natural Gradient

The concept of Natural Gradient addresses some of the limitations inherent in traditional gradient descent methods when applied to the optimization of policies in reinforcement learning. The standard gradient descent method adjusts the parameters of a policy using the gradient of the objective function with respect to those parameters. However, this approach might not effectively account for the geometry of the parameter space, leading to inefficient updates and slow convergence.

Natural Gradient methods introduce the notion of a more informed update direction by leveraging the Fisher Information Matrix (FIM). This section will investigate the mathematical foundation of the Natural Gradient, the computation of the Fisher Information Matrix, and the benefits these concepts provide.

Consider a policy parameterized by θ, denoted as $\pi_\theta(a|s)$. When optimizing the expected reward, the gradient of the objective function $J(\theta)$ provides the direction in which θ should be adjusted. However, the Euclidean distance measure used by standard gradient methods may not reflect the underlying structure of the parameter space, leading to inefficient learning.

The Natural Gradient is defined as:

$$\tilde{\nabla}_\theta J(\theta) = F^{-1} \nabla_\theta J(\theta)$$

where F is the Fisher Information Matrix (FIM) described by:

$$F = \mathbb{E}_{s\sim d^{\pi},a\sim\pi_\theta}\left[\nabla_\theta \log \pi_\theta(a|s) \nabla_\theta \log \pi_\theta(a|s)^T\right]$$

Here, d^{π} is the stationary distribution of states under policy π. The FIM encodes information about the sensitivity of the policy to parameter changes and provides a more nuanced notion of distance in the parameter space.

To utilize the Fisher Information Matrix in practice, consider the quadratic approximation of the Kullback-Leibler (KL) divergence between two policies π_θ and $\pi_{\theta+\delta}$. The KL divergence serves as a measure of dissimilarity between the two distributions and is given by:

$$D_{\mathsf{KL}}(\pi_\theta || \pi_{\theta+\delta}) \approx \frac{1}{2}\delta^T F \delta$$

By minimizing this KL divergence, we ensure that the new policy $\pi_{\theta+\delta}$ is not too far from the current policy π_θ, leading to more stable and reliable updates.

Implementing Natural Gradient in practical algorithms involves the inversion of the Fisher Information Matrix, which can be computationally intensive and numerically unstable, especially for high-dimensional parameter spaces. One way to approximate the Natural Gradient without directly inverting the FIM is through iterative methods such as Conjugate Gradient (CG) combined with efficient matrix-vector product computations.

The following pseudocode outlines a simple Natural Gradient ascent algorithm using Conjugate Gradient to avoid direct inversion:

```
def natural_gradient_update(policy, states, actions, advantages):
    # Calculate the policy gradient
    gradient = compute_policy_gradient(policy, states, actions, advantages)

    # Define a function for Fisher Vector Product
    def fisher_vector_product(v):
        # Calculate the product FIM * v
        log_probs = policy.log_prob(states, actions)
        grads = torch.autograd.grad(log_probs, policy.parameters(), grad_outputs=
                log_probs)
        grads = torch.cat([grad.view(-1) for grad in grads])
        fisher_product = torch.matmul(grads, grads.T)
        return fisher_product @ v

    # Use Conjugate Gradient to solve for natural gradient direction
    nat_gradient = conjugate_gradient(fisher_vector_product, gradient)

    return nat_gradient

# Update policy parameters
nat_gradient = natural_gradient_update(policy, states, actions, advantages)
policy.update_parameters(nat_gradient)
```

Here, 'compute_policy_gradient' computes the gradient of the objective function, 'fisher_vector_product' computes the product of the Fisher Information Matrix with a vector, and 'conjugate_gradient' solves the linear system without explicit inversion.

The key advantage of the Natural Gradient approach is its consideration of the curvature of the parameter space, leading to more efficient and effective updates. This often results in faster convergence compared to standard gradient methods, especially in complex, high-dimensional reinforcement learning scenarios.

The mathematical rigor and practical implementation of Natural Gradient methods make them crucial for advancing the capabilities of policy gradient techniques within the broader context of reinforcement learning.

Policy parameters updated using Natural Gradient:
_new = _old + * nat_gradient

7.8 Deterministic Policy Gradients (DPG)

Deterministic Policy Gradient (DPG) algorithms extend the capabilities of policy gradient methods by focusing on deterministic policies. Unlike stochastic policies, which specify a probability distribution over actions, deterministic policies map states directly to specific actions. This approach presents several advantages, such as reduced variance in the gradient estimates and bypassing the need for action sampling during policy training. The DPG framework, introduced by Silver et al., forms the basis for several advanced reinforcement learning algorithms, including Deep Deterministic Policy Gradient (DDPG).

To understand DPG, let us denote the deterministic policy by $\mu_\theta(s)$ where θ represents the policy parameters, and s represents the state. The objective is to maximize the expected return $J(\theta)$, defined as follows:

$$J(\theta) = \mathbb{E}_{s\sim\rho^\mu}[R(s, \mu_\theta(s))],$$

where ρ^μ is the discounted state visitation distribution under policy μ_θ, and $R(s, a)$ represents the expected cumulative reward starting from state s and taking action a.

The key component in DPG is the deterministic policy gradient theorem, which conveniently relates the gradient of the objective function to the expected gradient of the action-value function $Q^\mu(s,a)$:

$$\nabla_\theta J(\theta) = \mathbb{E}_{s\sim\rho^\mu}\left[\nabla_\theta \mu_\theta(s)\nabla_a Q^\mu(s,a)\Big|_{a=\mu_\theta(s)}\right].$$

The training procedure for DPG involves several iterative steps. First, the agent interacts with the environment based on its current policy $\mu_\theta(s)$, collecting transitions of the form (s_t, a_t, r_t, s_{t+1}). These transitions are stored in a replay buffer for efficient sampling during the training phase. Subsequently, the agent updates its policy and value function parameters by leveraging the collected experience.

A typical DPG-based algorithm includes both the policy network $\mu_\theta(s)$ and the critic network $Q^\mu(s,a)$. The critic network evaluates the action-value for state-action pairs, guiding the policy updates to improve decision-making over time. The critic is trained using the Bellman equation as the target for the action-value function. Specifically, the update for the critic network parameters ϕ is performed using the loss function:

$$L(\phi) = \mathbb{E}_{(s_t,a_t,r_t,s_{t+1})\sim\mathcal{D}}\left[(Q_\phi(s_t,a_t) - y_t)^2\right],$$

where the target y_t is given by:

$$y_t = r_t + \gamma Q_{\phi'}(s_{t+1}, \mu_{\theta'}(s_{t+1})).$$

Here, γ is the discount factor, and ϕ' and θ' represent the target networks' parameters, which are periodically updated from the primary network parameters to ensure stable updates.

The policy network $\mu_\theta(s)$ is updated based on the deterministic policy gradient, which requires computing:

$$\nabla_\theta J(\theta) = \mathbb{E}_{s\sim\rho^\mu}\left[\nabla_a Q_\phi(s,a)\Big|_{a=\mu_\theta(s)} \nabla_\theta \mu_\theta(s)\right].$$

Both policy and target networks can leverage neural network architectures to approximate complex functions, enabling the agent to handle high-dimensional state and action spaces.

```
# Initialize parameters theta and phi for policy and value networks
initialize_policy_network(theta)
initialize_critic_network(phi)

# Initialize replay buffer
replay_buffer = ReplayBuffer()

for episode in range(total_episodes):
```

```
state = env.reset()
done = False
while not done:
    # Select action using current policy
    action = policy_network(state, theta)

    # Perform action in the environment
    next_state, reward, done, info = env.step(action)

    # Store transition in replay buffer
    replay_buffer.store(state, action, reward, next_state, done)

    state = next_state

    # Sample a batch of transitions from replay buffer
    batch = replay_buffer.sample(batch_size)

    # Update critic network using the sampled batch
    y_batch = compute_targets(batch, phi, theta, gamma)
    phi_gradient = critic_gradient(batch, y_batch, phi)
    update_critic_network(phi, phi_gradient)

    # Update policy network using the sampled batch
    theta_gradient = policy_gradient(batch, phi, theta)
    update_policy_network(theta, theta_gradient)
```

The replay buffer ensures that the correlation between consecutive updates is minimized, which enhances training stability. The target networks mitigate oscillations and divergence by providing slowly changing targets for the critic updates. The interplay between the actor and critic networks forms the cornerstone of DPG, enabling sophisticated continuous control tasks.

The deterministic policy gradient adapts to various extensions and improvements. One notable advancement is the Deep Deterministic Policy Gradient (DDPG), which introduces additional stabilization measures such as Batch Normalization and parameter noise to address overestimation bias and explore better policies.

The deterministic nature of DPG makes it particularly suitable for environments with continuous action spaces and deterministic dynamics, fulfilling the needs for efficient and scalable policy optimization in complex systems.

7.9 Trust Region Policy Optimization (TRPO)

Trust Region Policy Optimization (TRPO) is an advanced policy gradient method designed to ensure monotonic policy improvement while avoiding large and destabilizing updates. This section explains the principle of trust regions, the derivation and implementation of the TRPO algorithm, and its significance in achieving reliable and robust policy optimization.

TRPO builds upon the policy gradient framework by introducing a constraint to minimize the likelihood of the policy deteriorating after an update. The idea is to restrict the step size in the policy space, ensuring that the new policy remains close to the old one, thus maintaining the stability of learning. The derivation of TRPO starts from the policy improvement theorem, which guarantees improved performance as long as the policy changes are within a trust region.

The theoretical foundation of TRPO involves the Kullback-Leibler (KL) divergence, a measure of how one probability distribution diverges from a second, expected probability distribution. TRPO constrains the KL divergence to a small value to ensure that each policy update does not deviate too much from the previous policy.

The central objective of TRPO can be formulated as:

$$\max_{\theta} \mathbb{E}_{\tau \sim \pi_\theta} \left[\sum_{t=0}^{T} \gamma^t r_t \right] \quad \text{subject to} \quad \mathbb{E}_{s \sim \rho^\pi} \left[D_{KL} \left(\pi_{\theta_{\text{old}}}(\cdot|s) \| \pi_\theta(\cdot|s) \right) \right] \leq \delta$$

Here, θ represents the policy parameters, π_θ denotes the policy parameterized by θ, γ is the discount factor, r_t is the immediate reward at time t, ρ^π is the state distribution under the policy π, D_{KL} is the KL divergence, and δ is a small positive constant defining the trust region.

While the constrained optimization problem is theoretically sound, solving it directly is non-trivial due to the complexity of calculating KL divergence and the expectation. Instead, TRPO uses a linear approximation for the objective and a quadratic approximation for the KL constraint, leading to a more tractable optimization problem.

The approximated optimization problem can be formalized as:

$$\max_{\theta} g^T (\theta - \theta_{\text{old}}) \quad \text{subject to} \quad (\theta - \theta_{\text{old}})^T H (\theta - \theta_{\text{old}}) \leq 2\delta$$

Here, g is the gradient of the expected return with respect to θ, and H is the Hessian matrix of the KL divergence. This quadratic constraint ensures that the policy update remains within the trust region.

Solving this constrained optimization problem requires deriving the step size and direction. The update direction θ_{step} is computed as:

$$\theta_{\text{step}} = \sqrt{\frac{2\delta}{g^T H^{-1} g}} H^{-1} g$$

The final policy parameters are updated using:

$$\theta' = \theta + \alpha \theta_{\text{step}}$$

where α is a step-size parameter typically determined through line search to ensure the KL constraint is satisfied.

The TRPO algorithm can be summarized in the following steps:

- Initialize policy parameters θ.
- Collect a set of trajectories by executing the current policy π_θ.
- Estimate the policy gradient g and the Fisher Information Matrix H.
- Compute the step direction θ_{step}.
- Perform a line search to determine the optimal step size α.
- Update the policy parameters θ using the computed step.

The pseudocode for TRPO is as follows:

```
def trpo_algorithm(env, policy, delta, iterations):
    theta = policy.initialize_params()

    for iter in range(iterations):
        trajectories = collect_trajectories(env, policy, theta)

        g = estimate_policy_gradient(trajectories, policy, theta)
        H = estimate_fisher_information_matrix(trajectories, policy, theta)

        step_dir = np.sqrt(2 * delta / (g.T @ np.linalg.inv(H) @ g)) * np.linalg.inv(H)
            @ g

        alpha = line_search(env, policy, theta, step_dir, delta)

        theta = theta + alpha * step_dir

    return theta
```

In practical implementations, TRPO demonstrates improved stability and reliability in training complex policies, particularly in environments with high-dimensional action spaces. Its main advantage lies in its ability to make large updates in the parameter space without risking the performance collapse that can occur with standard policy gradient methods. This characteristic makes TRPO a valuable tool in the toolkit of reinforcement learning practitioners seeking to train robust and effective policies.

7.10 Proximal Policy Optimization (PPO)

Proximal Policy Optimization (PPO) is an advanced policy gradient method introduced to address the limitations of previous methods like Trust Region Policy Optimization (TRPO). PPO aims to strike a balance between the benefits of first-order optimization techniques and the stability offered by second-order methods, all while maintaining practical ease of implementation.

PPO attempts to maximize a clipped surrogate objective function, which explicitly constrains changes to the policy, thereby reducing the likelihood of catastrophic policy updates. The basic intuition behind PPO is to keep the new policy close to the old policy while still allowing sufficient freedom for improvement.

The objective function in PPO is defined as follows:

$$L^{CLIP}(\theta) = \mathbb{E}_t \left[\text{min}(r_t(\theta)\hat{A}_t, \text{clip}(r_t(\theta), 1-\epsilon, 1+\epsilon)\hat{A}_t)\right]$$

where $r_t(\theta)$ is the probability ratio given by:

$$r_t(\theta) = \frac{\pi_\theta(a_t|s_t)}{\pi_{\theta_{old}}(a_t|s_t)}$$

and $\hat{A}_t$ is the advantage estimate. The clipping parameter ϵ is a small positive number that limits the change in policy. The function clip$(r_t, 1-\epsilon, 1+\epsilon)$ ensures the update does not deviate significantly from the old policy.

To implement PPO, we follow an approach that alternates between sampling data through interaction with the environment and optimizing the policy. Here's a step-by-step overview of the PPO algorithm:

- Initialize policy parameters θ and value function parameters ϕ.
- Repeat for each iteration:

- Collect a set of trajectories by running the policy $\pi_{\theta_{old}}$ in the environment.
- Compute advantage estimates $\hat{A}_t$ using the collected trajectories.
- Optimize the surrogate objective $L^{CLIP}(\theta)$ with multiple epochs of mini-batch gradient descent.
- Update the policy parameters θ using the gradients obtained from the surrogate objective.
- Optionally, update the value function parameters ϕ by minimizing the value loss.

Below is a simplified implementation of the PPO algorithm in Python using PyTorch:

```
import torch
import torch.nn as nn
import torch.optim as optim

class PPOPolicyNetwork(nn.Module):
    def __init__(self, state_dim, action_dim):
        super(PPOPolicyNetwork, self).__init__()
        self.fc1 = nn.Linear(state_dim, 128)
        self.fc2 = nn.Linear(128, 64)
        self.fc3 = nn.Linear(64, action_dim)

    def forward(self, x):
        x = torch.relu(self.fc1(x))
        x = torch.relu(self.fc2(x))
        return torch.softmax(self.fc3(x), dim=-1)

class PPO:
    def __init__(self, state_dim, action_dim, policy_lr=3e-4, clip_param=0.2):
        self.policy_net = PPOPolicyNetwork(state_dim, action_dim)
        self.policy_optim = optim.Adam(self.policy_net.parameters(), lr=policy_lr)
        self.clip_param = clip_param
        self.old_policy_net = PPOPolicyNetwork(state_dim, action_dim)
        self.old_policy_net.load_state_dict(self.policy_net.state_dict())

    def compute_loss(self, states, actions, advantages, log_probs_old):
        log_probs_new = torch.log(self.policy_net(states).gather(1, actions.unsqueeze
            (-1))).squeeze(-1)
        ratio = torch.exp(log_probs_new - log_probs_old)
        surr1 = ratio * advantages
        surr2 = torch.clamp(ratio, 1 - self.clip_param, 1 + self.clip_param) *
            advantages
        return -torch.min(surr1, surr2).mean()

    def update_policy(self, states, actions, advantages, log_probs_old):
        self.policy_optim.zero_grad()
        loss = self.compute_loss(states, actions, advantages, log_probs_old)
        loss.backward()
        self.policy_optim.step()
        self.old_policy_net.load_state_dict(self.policy_net.state_dict())
```

The flexibility and robustness of PPO make it a widely adopted algorithm in both academia and industry for reinforcement learning applications. Its balance of effective policy updates and computational efficiency has demonstrated superior performance across a broad spectrum of tasks, making it a cornerstone for many state-of-the-art RL systems.

The method leverages the simplicity of first-order methods while incorporating mechanisms that safeguard against overly aggressive policy updates, thus enabling stable and reliable learning. It achieves this by utilizing clipped probability ratios to maintain the new and old policies within a constrained proximity, ensuring trust regions without the computational overhead of TRPO's complex conjugate gradient computations. This makes PPO a practical choice for large-scale problems and continuous action spaces.

7.11 Applications and Examples of Policy Gradient Methods

Policy Gradient Methods have been extensively employed across various domains due to their ability to directly optimize the policy. This section explores several practical applications and examples where policy gradient methods have shown remarkable performance.

One notable application of policy gradient methods is in the domain of robotics. Robots require robust and adaptable policies to interact effectively with their environment. Policy gradient methods like Trust Region Policy Optimization (TRPO) and Proximal Policy Optimization (PPO) have been used to train robotic control policies. For instance, in robotic manipulation tasks such as object grasping and manipulation, PPO has demonstrated proficiency in learning stable and efficient policies. Here is an example of training a robotic arm using PPO in Python:

```
import gym
import tensorflow as tf
from stable_baselines3 import PPO

env = gym.make('FetchReach-v1')
model = PPO('MlpPolicy', env, verbose=1)
model.learn(total_timesteps=10000)

obs = env.reset()
for _ in range(1000):
    action, _states = model.predict(obs)
    obs, rewards, done, info = env.step(action)
    env.render()
```

The simulation environment, FetchReach-v1, is from OpenAI's Gym library and represents a simple reach task with a robotic arm. The PPO algorithm is initialized with a multi-layer perceptron (MLP) policy and subsequently trained for 10,000 timesteps. The performance of the trained policy is then visualized, where the policy controls the robotic arm to reach the target locations.

Game playing is another area where policy gradient methods have been successfully applied. Reinforcement learning has achieved human-level performance in various games through methods like Advantage Actor-Critic (A2C) and Asynchronous A2C (A3C). A seminal example is the DeepMind's use of A3C to play Atari games. The asynchronous nature of A3C provides efficient parallel updates, improving both training time and policy performance. Below is an example of employing A3C in training an agent on an Atari game:

```
import gym
import multiprocessing
from stable_baselines3 import A2C

def train_agent():
    env = gym.make('PongNoFrameskip-v4')
    model = A2C('CnnPolicy', env, verbose=1)
    model.learn(total_timesteps=1000000)
    model.save("a2c_atari")

if __name__ == "__main__":
    num_workers = multiprocessing.cpu_count()
    processes = [multiprocessing.Process(target=train_agent) for _ in range(
        num_workers)]

    for p in processes:
        p.start()
    for p in processes:
        p.join()
```

Here, the Atari game PongNoFrameskip-v4 is utilized from OpenAI's Gym, and the A2C algorithm is trained using a convolutional neural network (CNN) policy. The training process demonstrates parallel execution capabilities inherent in actor-critic methods, effectively leveraging multiple processor cores for enhancing training efficiency.

Beyond robotics and gaming, policy gradient methods have found applications in autonomous driving. Self-driving cars must make complex decisions in dynamic environments, necessitating the use of sophisticated RL algorithms. Deterministic Policy Gradients (DPG) and its variant, Deep Deterministic Policy Gradients (DDPG), are often employed for continuous action spaces typical in driving scenarios. These methods efficiently handle the high-dimensional action spaces required for steering, acceleration, and braking controls. The example below highlights the DDPG algorithm in a simulated self-driving environment:

```
import gym
import numpy as np
import matplotlib.pyplot as plt
from stable_baselines3 import DDPG

env = gym.make('CarRacing-v0')
model = DDPG('MlpPolicy', env, verbose=1)
model.learn(total_timesteps=250000)

obs = env.reset()
for _ in range(1000):
    action, _states = model.predict(obs)
    obs, rewards, done, info = env.step(action)
    env.render()
```

The environment CarRacing-v0 from OpenAI's Gym library is targeted by DDPG to develop a policy controlling car dynamics. The model is trained for 250,000 timesteps, and the policy's effectiveness in managing continuous controls is visualized through policy execution.

Financial trading is another field where policy gradient methods have gained traction. Trading agents benefit from nuanced decision-making abilities provided by these methods, optimizing portfolios and executing trades based on learned strategies. Algorithms like A2C and PPO have been applied to predict stock prices and manage trading portfolios autonomously. Here's a simplified example applying PPO for stock trading:

```
import gym
import pandas as pd
from stable_baselines3 import PPO

class StockTradingEnv(gym.Env):
    def __init__(self, data):
        super(StockTradingEnv, self).__init__()
        self.data = data
        self.current_step = 0
        self.action_space = gym.spaces.Box(low=-1, high=1, shape=(1,), dtype=np.
            float32)
        self.observation_space = gym.spaces.Box(low=0, high=np.inf, shape=(6,), dtype
            =np.float32)

    def step(self, action):
        self.current_step += 1
        done = self.current_step >= len(self.data) - 1
        reward = self.data.iloc[self.current_step]['Close'] * action[0]
        obs = self._next_observation()
        return obs, reward, done, {}

    def _next_observation(self):
        frame = np.array([
            self.data.iloc[self.current_step]['Open'],
            self.data.iloc[self.current_step]['High'],
            self.data.iloc[self.current_step]['Low'],
            self.data.iloc[self.current_step]['Close'],
```

```
            self.data.iloc[self.current_step]['Volume'],
            self.current_step,
        ])
        return frame

    def reset(self):
        self.current_step = 0
        return self._next_observation()

data = pd.read_csv('path_to_stock_data.csv')
env = StockTradingEnv(data)
model = PPO('MlpPolicy', env, verbose=1)
model.learn(total_timesteps=10000)
```

This example illustrates a custom environment for stock trading formulated using historical stock prices. The PPO algorithm learns optimal trading strategies by interacting with the environment, iteratively refining its policy to maximize returns.

Policy gradient methods have proven highly effective in areas requiring sequential decision-making and real-world adaptability. These examples underscore the versatility and power of policy gradient methods in solving complex control tasks across diverse applications.

Chapter 8

Deep Reinforcement Learning

Deep Reinforcement Learning leverages deep neural networks to handle high-dimensional state and action spaces, enabling breakthroughs in complex tasks. This chapter covers foundational methods like Deep Q-Networks (DQN) and their improvements, such as Double DQN, Dueling DQN, and Prioritized Experience Replay. It introduces advanced algorithms like Deep Deterministic Policy Gradient (DDPG), Twin Delayed DDPG (TD3), and Soft Actor-Critic (SAC). The chapter also discusses integrating Convolutional and Recurrent Neural Networks with RL, model-based approaches, exploration strategies, and real-world applications.

8.1 Introduction to Deep Reinforcement Learning

Deep Reinforcement Learning (Deep RL) is an innovative area of machine learning that combines reinforcement learning (RL) principles with deep neural networks. This approach has demonstrated remarkable success in solving complex tasks that are intractable for traditional RL methods. The essence of Deep RL lies in its capability to process and learn from high-dimensional sensory inputs, such as images, using the approximative power of deep learning techniques.

In a typical RL framework, an agent interacts with an environment by performing actions, receiving states, and collecting rewards. The goal of the agent is to learn a policy that maximizes the cumulative reward over time. Traditional RL methods struggle with high-dimensional state spaces because they rely on value function approximations or direct policy search methods that become computationally infeasible with increasing state space dimensionality. Deep RL addresses these scalability issues by leveraging deep neural networks to approximate value functions, policies, or even models of the environment.

Figure 8.1: Basic structure of an RL agent interacting with the environment.

The advent of Deep RL started with the groundbreaking work on Deep Q-Networks (DQN) by Mnih et al. (2015), which applied deep convolutional neural networks (CNNs) to directly approximate Q-values from raw pixel inputs. The success of DQN demonstrated that deep neural networks could efficiently approximate complex functions in RL settings, enabling the agent to learn from high-dimensional visual inputs without manual feature engineering.

Formally, a reinforcement learning problem is defined by a Markov Decision Process (MDP), represented as a tuple (S, A, P, R, γ):

- S is the set of states.
- A is the set of actions.
- $P(s'|s, a)$ is the transition probability of moving from state $s \in S$ to state $s' \in S$ by taking action $a \in A$.
- $R(s, a)$ is the reward function, providing the immediate reward received after transitioning from state s to state s' due to action a.
- γ is the discount factor, $0 \leq \gamma \leq 1$, that models the importance of future rewards.

The agent's objective is to learn a policy $\pi(a|s)$ that maximizes the expected cumulative reward (return) starting from an initial state s_0:

$$G_t = \mathbb{E}\left[\sum_{k=0}^{\infty} \gamma^k R(s_{t+k}, a_{t+k}) \middle| s_t = s, a_t = a\right]$$

Deep RL extends this framework by utilizing deep neural networks as function approximators. There are three primary paradigms in deep reinforcement learning:

- **Value-based Methods:** These methods focus on approximating the optimal action-value function $Q^*(s,a)$, which represents the maximum expected return achievable by taking action a in state s and following the optimal policy thereafter. The Q-Network in DQN is an example of a value-based method where deep learning is used to approximate $Q(s,a)$.

- **Policy-based Methods:** These methods directly parameterize and optimize the policy $\pi(a|s;\theta)$ where θ represents the parameters of the neural network. The policy gradient methods, such as REINFORCE, learn the policy by optimizing the expected return using gradient ascent techniques.

- **Actor-Critic Methods:** These methods combine value-based and policy-based approaches. They consist of two components: the actor, which updates the policy $\pi(a|s;\theta)$, and the critic, which evaluates the action-value function $Q(s,a;\phi)$. The actor-critic framework allows for more stable and efficient training compared to purely value-based or policy-based methods.

The architecture of deep neural networks used in Deep RL can vary significantly based on the nature of the input and the task requirements. Convolutional Neural Networks (CNNs) are often utilized for tasks involving image inputs, such as in Atari game environments. For tasks with sequential data, Recurrent Neural Networks (RNNs) or Long Short-Term Memory Networks (LSTMs) are commonly applied. The flexibility in neural network architectures provides Deep RL with the capacity to generalize across diverse applications, from game playing to robotic control and beyond.

```
import torch
import torch.nn as nn
import torch.nn.functional as F

class DQN(nn.Module):
    def __init__(self, input_dim, output_dim):
        super(DQN, self).__init__()
        self.conv1 = nn.Conv2d(input_dim, 32, kernel_size=8, stride=4)
        self.conv2 = nn.Conv2d(32, 64, kernel_size=4, stride=2)
        self.conv3 = nn.Conv2d(64, 64, kernel_size=3, stride=1)
        self.fc1 = nn.Linear(7 * 7 * 64, 512)
        self.fc2 = nn.Linear(512, output_dim)
```

```
def forward(self, x):
    x = F.relu(self.conv1(x))
    x = F.relu(self.conv2(x))
    x = F.relu(self.conv3(x))
    x = x.view(x.size(0), -1)
    x = F.relu(self.fc1(x))
    x = self.fc2(x)
    return x
```

In the above code, we define a simple DQN architecture using the PyTorch library. The network consists of three convolutional layers followed by two fully connected layers. The input to the network comprises image data (e.g., frames from a game), and the output represents the Q-values for each possible action in the given state.

Deep RL methodologies continue to evolve with advancements in neural network architectures and optimization algorithms. By leveraging the representational power of deep learning, Deep RL has opened new horizons in solving high-dimensional and complex RL problems, setting the stage for further breakthroughs in artificial intelligence and machine learning.

8.2 Deep Q-Networks (DQN)

Deep Q-Networks (DQN) represent a significant advancement in the field of Reinforcement Learning (RL), primarily enabling RL methods to scale to problem domains with high-dimensional state spaces. Building on the Q-learning algorithm, DQNs employ deep neural networks to approximate the optimal action-value function, often referred to as the Q-function, which traditionally relies on a lookup table approach.

To understand DQNs, one must first recall the concept of Q-learning. In Q-learning, the agent learns an action-value function $Q(s, a)$, which estimates the expected return of taking action a in state s and thereafter following the optimal policy. Formally, the Q-learning update rule is given by:

$$Q(s_t, a_t) \leftarrow Q(s_t, a_t) + \alpha \left[r_t + \gamma \max_{a'} Q(s_{t+1}, a') - Q(s_t, a_t) \right],$$

where s_t and a_t are the state and action at time t, r_t is the reward received, α is the learning rate, and γ is the discount factor.

In high-dimensional state spaces, it is impractical to maintain and update a Q-value for each state-action pair using a tabular method. DQNs resolve this issue by using a deep neural network to parameterize the Q-function. The DQN algorithm involves training a neural network $Q(s, a; \theta)$ to approximate the Q-values, where θ denotes the parameters of the network.

Training the DQN network involves minimizing the loss function, which measures the discrepancy between the predicted Q-values and the target Q-values. The loss function $L(\theta)$ is typically defined as:

$$L(\theta) = \mathbb{E}_{(s,a,r,s')\sim\mathcal{D}}\left[(y - Q(s, a; \theta))^2\right],$$

where $y = r + \gamma \max_{a'} Q(s', a'; \theta^-)$ is the target Q-value. Here, $\mathcal{D}$ is the experience replay buffer, a memory buffer storing past experiences (s, a, r, s'). The network parameters θ^- represent the target network, which is a separate set of network parameters updated periodically to provide stable targets during training.

DQNs introduce two critical mechanisms to stabilize and improve training: Experience Replay and the Target Network.

- **Experience Replay:** This mechanism involves storing the agent's experiences, denoted as tuples (s, a, r, s'), in a replay buffer. During training, mini-batches of experiences are sampled uniformly from the replay buffer to update the network. This technique breaks the correlation between consecutive samples and leads to more robust training by smoothing over individual updates.
- **Target Network:** In addition to the primary Q-network $Q(s, a; \theta)$, DQN maintains a second target network $Q(s, a; \theta^-)$. The parameters θ^- are periodically updated to match the parameters θ of the primary network. This practice mitigates the issue of unstable targets by keeping the target network fixed for a set number of steps, thus providing more consistent targets for the learning updates.

The overall DQN algorithm can be summarized in the following steps:

1. Initialize replay memory $\mathcal{D}$ to capacity N.
2. Initialize the primary network $Q(s, a; \theta)$ and target network $Q(s, a; \theta^-)$ with random weights.

3. For each episode:
   (a) Initialize the initial state s_0.
   (b) For each time step t:
      i. Select action a_t using an ϵ-greedy policy based on the Q-values $Q(s_t, a; \theta)$.
      ii. Execute action a_t, observe reward r_t and next state s_{t+1}.
      iii. Store transition (s_t, a_t, r_t, s_{t+1}) in replay memory $\mathcal{D}$.
      iv. Sample random mini-batch of transitions (s_j, a_j, r_j, s_{j+1}) from $\mathcal{D}$.
      v. Calculate the target Q-value for each mini-batch transition:

$$y_j = \begin{cases} r_j & \text{if episode terminates at } j + \\ r_j + \gamma \max_{a'} Q(s_{j+1}, a'; \theta^-) & \text{otherwise.} \end{cases}$$

      vi. Perform a gradient descent step on the loss:

$$L(\theta) = \left(y_j - Q(s_j, a_j; \theta)\right)^2 .$$

      vii. Every C steps, update the target network:

$$\theta^- \leftarrow \theta.$$

Implementing DQNs in practice involves several design choices including the architecture of the neural network. Typically, a fully connected feedforward network suffices for simple tasks, while more complex problems benefit from using convolutional layers to handle raw image inputs, as demonstrated in the original DQN paper by Mnih et al. (2015).

Below is an example implementation of a DQN in Python using the PyTorch library:

```
import torch
import torch.nn as nn
import torch.optim as optim
import numpy as np
import random
from collections import deque

class DQNetwork(nn.Module):
    def __init__(self, state_size, action_size, seed):
        super(DQNetwork, self).__init__()
        self.seed = torch.manual_seed(seed)
        self.fc1 = nn.Linear(state_size, 64)
```

```
        self.fc2 = nn.Linear(64, 64)
        self.fc3 = nn.Linear(64, action_size)

    def forward(self, x):
        x = torch.relu(self.fc1(x))
        x = torch.relu(self.fc2(x))
        return self.fc3(x)

class DQNAgent:
    def __init__(self, state_size, action_size, seed):
        self.state_size = state_size
        self.action_size = action_size
        self.seed = random.seed(seed)

        self.qnetwork_local = DQNetwork(state_size, action_size, seed)
        self.qnetwork_target = DQNetwork(state_size, action_size, seed)
        self.optimizer = optim.Adam(self.qnetwork_local.parameters(), lr=0.001)

        self.memory = deque(maxlen=10000)
        self.batch_size = 64
        self.gamma = 0.99
        self.tau = 0.001
        self.update_every = 4
        self.t_step = 0

    def step(self, state, action, reward, next_state, done):
        self.memory.append((state, action, reward, next_state, done))

        self.t_step = (self.t_step + 1) % self.update_every
        if self.t_step == 0:
            if len(self.memory) > self.batch_size:
                experiences = random.sample(self.memory, self.batch_size)
                self.learn(experiences, self.gamma)

    def act(self, state, eps=0.):
        state = torch.from_numpy(state).float().unsqueeze(0)
        self.qnetwork_local.eval()
        with torch.no_grad():
            action_values = self.qnetwork_local(state)
        self.qnetwork_local.train()

        if random.random() > eps:
            return np.argmax(action_values.cpu().data.numpy())
        else:
            return random.choice(np.arange(self.action_size))

    def learn(self, experiences, gamma):
        states, actions, rewards, next_states, dones = zip(*experiences)

        states = torch.from_numpy(np.vstack(states)).float()
        actions = torch.from_numpy(np.vstack(actions)).long()
        rewards = torch.from_numpy(np.vstack(rewards)).float()
        next_states = torch.from_numpy(np.vstack(next_states)).float()
        dones = torch.from_numpy(np.vstack(dones).astype(np.uint8)).float()

        Q_targets_next = self.qnetwork_target(next_states).detach().max(1)[0].
            unsqueeze(1)
        Q_targets = rewards + (gamma * Q_targets_next * (1 - dones))

        Q_expected = self.qnetwork_local(states).gather(1, actions)

        loss = nn.MSELoss()(Q_expected, Q_targets)
```

```
        self.optimizer.zero_grad()
        loss.backward()
        self.optimizer.step()

        self.soft_update(self.qnetwork_local, self.qnetwork_target, self.tau)

    def soft_update(self, local_model, target_model, tau):
        for target_param, local_param in zip(target_model.parameters(), local_model.
            parameters()):
            target_param.data.copy_(tau * local_param.data + (1.0 - tau) *
                target_param.data)
```

The output from training this DQN agent on a simple task, such as the CartPole-v0 environment from OpenAI Gym, looks like this:

```
Episode 100    Average Score: 9.45
Episode 200    Average Score: 50.55
Episode 300    Average Score: 150.25
Episode 400    Average Score: 200.00
```

This implementation encapsulates the core principles of DQN, including the architecture of the network, experience replay, and periodic updates of the target network. Understanding these components is crucial for grasping how DQNs function and their role in advancing the field of deep reinforcement learning.

8.3 Improvements on DQN: Double DQN, Dueling DQN, and Prioritized Experience Replay

Deep Q-Networks (DQN) represent a significant advancement in reinforcement learning by employing deep neural networks to estimate the action-value function. However, DQN faces specific challenges such as overestimation bias and inefficient learning from experience. To address these issues, several improvements have been proposed, namely Double DQN, Dueling DQN, and Prioritized Experience Replay. Each of these methods enhances the original DQN by targeting different aspects of the learning process, ultimately leading to more stable and efficient training.

Double DQN aims to mitigate the overestimation bias present in Q-learning algorithms. Overestimation occurs because the Q-learning algorithm uses the same values both to select and evaluate an action, which can lead to an upward bias. Double DQN decouples the action selection from the action evaluation by using two separate networks. One network is used to determine the best action, and the other network evaluates the Q-value of this action. This approach reduces the overestimation and leads to more accurate value predictions.

To implement Double DQN, a minor modification is made to the target Q-value y during the update step. Instead of using the maximum Q-value as an estimate, Double DQN uses the action chosen by the target network to evaluate the Q-value. The modified Q-value target y is defined as follows:

$$y = r + \gamma Q_{\text{target}}(s', \arg\max_a Q(s', a; \theta_t); \theta_t)$$

where θ are the weights of the network, and θ_t are the weights of the target network. By introducing this decoupling, Double DQN mitigates the overestimation bias.

```
# Double DQN target calculation
import numpy as np

def double_dqn_target(next_state, reward, done, main_network, target_network,
        gamma=0.99):
    best_action = np.argmax(main_network.predict(next_state), axis=1)
    target_q_value = target_network.predict(next_state)[np.arange(len(best_action)),
            best_action]
    return reward + (1 - done) * gamma * target_q_value
```

Dueling DQN, on the other hand, introduces a novel network architecture to separate the representation of state values and advantages for each action. This architecture helps to improve the learning of state values, which can be more informative than individual action advantages in some cases. The Dueling DQN architecture consists of two streams: one stream estimates the state value function $V(s; \theta, \beta)$, and the other stream estimates the action advantages $A(s, a; \theta, \alpha)$. These two streams are then combined to produce the Q-values for each action:

$$Q(s, a; \theta, \alpha, \beta) = V(s; \theta, \beta) + \left(A(s, a; \theta, \alpha) - \frac{1}{|\mathcal{A}|} \sum_{a'} A(s, a'; \theta, \alpha) \right)$$

where θ represents the shared parameters, α and β are the parameters of the advantage and value streams, respectively. The subtraction of the mean advantage ensures that the Q-values are unique.

```
# Dueling DQN architecture
from keras.layers import Input, Dense, Lambda, Subtract
from keras.models import Model
import keras.backend as K
```

```
def dueling_dqn(input_shape, num_actions):
    input = Input(shape=input_shape)
    x = Dense(64, activation='relu')(input)
    x = Dense(64, activation='relu')(x)

    state_value = Dense(1)(x)
    state_value = Lambda(lambda s: K.expand_dims(s[:, 0], -1))(state_value)

    advantages = Dense(num_actions)(x)
    advantages = Lambda(lambda a: a - K.mean(a, axis=-1, keepdims=True))(
        advantages)

    q_values = K.layers.Add()([state_value, advantages])
    model = Model(inputs=input, outputs=q_values)
    return model

input_shape = (4,)
num_actions = 2
dueling_dqn_model = dueling_dqn(input_shape, num_actions)
```

Another critical improvement is Prioritized Experience Replay, which tackles the inefficiency in learning from experience. Traditional experience replay samples experiences uniformly, but in practice, some experiences are more significant for learning than others. Prioritized Experience Replay improves upon this by sampling experiences based on their priority, typically determined by the magnitude of their temporal-difference (TD) error. This ensures that more informative experiences are sampled more frequently.

The priority P of each transition (s, a, r, s', d) can be defined as:

$$P(i) = (|\delta_i| + \epsilon)^{\alpha}$$

where δ_i is the TD error for transition i, ϵ is a small positive constant to ensure that all transitions have a non-zero probability of being sampled, and α is a hyperparameter that controls the degree of prioritization. The probability of sampling transition i is:

$$P(i) = \frac{P(i)^{\alpha}}{\sum_k P(k)^{\alpha}}$$

To ensure the learning updates are unbiased, Importance Sampling (IS) weights are introduced:

$$w_i = \left(\frac{1}{N} \frac{1}{P(i)} \right)^{\beta}$$

where N is the total number of experiences in the replay buffer, and β is an annealing parameter that controls the degree of importance sampling correction.

```
# Prioritized Experience Replay Buffer
import numpy as np

class PrioritizedReplayBuffer:
    def __init__(self, size, alpha):
        self.size = size
        self.alpha = alpha
        self.buffer = []
        self.pos = 0
        self.priorities = np.zeros((size,), dtype=np.float32)

    def add(self, experience, priority):
        max_prio = self.priorities.max() if self.buffer else 1.0
        if len(self.buffer) < self.size:
            self.buffer.append(experience)
        else:
            self.buffer[self.pos] = experience
        self.priorities[self.pos] = max_prio
        self.pos = (self.pos + 1) % self.size

    def sample(self, batch_size, beta=0.4):
        total_priority = self.priorities.sum()
        probs = self.priorities / total_priority
        indices = np.random.choice(len(self.buffer), batch_size, p=probs)
        samples = [self.buffer[idx] for idx in indices]

        total = len(self.buffer)
        weights = (total * probs[indices]) ** (-beta)
        weights /= weights.max()

        return samples, indices, weights

    def update_priorities(self, indices, priorities):
        for idx, prio in zip(indices, priorities):
            self.priorities[idx] = prio ** self.alpha

# Example usage
buffer = PrioritizedReplayBuffer(size=10000, alpha=0.6)
experience = (state, action, reward, next_state, done)
buffer.add(experience, priority=1.0)
samples, indices, weights = buffer.sample(batch_size=32, beta=0.4)
```

By incorporating these three improvements—Double DQN, Dueling DQN, and Prioritized Experience Replay—deep reinforcement learning algorithms can achieve more stable and efficient training, thereby enabling better performance on complex tasks.

8.4 Deep Deterministic Policy Gradient (DDPG)

Deep Deterministic Policy Gradient (DDPG) is a model-free, off-policy algorithm for continuous action spaces that combines the policy gradient method with insights from DQN. The unique attribute of DDPG lies in its ability to extend Q-learning to continuous action spaces, making it particularly useful for applications where action variables need not be discrete.

At its core, DDPG relies on two key neural networks: the actor and the critic. The actor network, denoted by $\mu(s|\theta^{\mu})$, maps states to a specific action deterministically, where θ^{μ} represents the parameters of the actor network. The critic network, represented as $Q(s, a|\theta^{Q})$, evaluates the action selected by the actor in a specific state, yielding a Q-value indicative of the expected future rewards.

The DDPG algorithm, inspired by the Deterministic Policy Gradient (DPG) theorem, computes updates by blending deterministic policies with Q-learning principles. The update rule for the actor and critic networks incorporates experience replay and target networks, leading to stable training.

The workflow of the DDPG algorithm involves the following steps:

1. **Initialize networks:** Set up the actor network $\mu(s|\theta^{\mu})$ and the critic network $Q(s, a|\theta^{Q})$ with random weight initializations. Initialize target networks $\mu'(s|\theta^{\mu'})$ and $Q'(s, a|\theta^{Q'})$ with weights $\theta^{\mu'} \leftarrow \theta^{\mu}$ and $\theta^{Q'} \leftarrow \theta^{Q}$.

2. **Experience replay buffer:** Initialize a replay buffer R, to store state transitions (s_t, a_t, r_t, s_{t+1}). Experience replay breaks correlations by sampling random mini-batches from the buffer to train networks.

3. **Iterative process:** For each episode, follow steps a-e:

   - **Interact and observe:** Select an action $a_t = \mu(s_t|\theta^{\mu}) + \mathcal{N}_t$ using a policy with added noise $\mathcal{N}_t$ (e.g., Ornstein-Uhlenbeck process) for exploration. Observe the reward r_t and next state s_{t+1}.
   - **Store transitions:** Save (s_t, a_t, r_t, s_{t+1}) in the replay buffer R.

- **Sample mini-batches:** Draw random mini-batch $\{(s_i, a_i, r_i, s_{i+1})\}$ from R.
- **Update critic network:** Update the critic by minimizing the loss:

$$L = \frac{1}{N}\sum_i \left(y_i - Q(s_i, a_i|\theta^Q)\right)^2$$

where $y_i = r_i + \gamma Q'(s_{i+1}, \mu'(s_{i+1}|\theta^{\mu'})|\theta^{Q'})$ is the target Q-value. Here, γ denotes the discount factor.

- **Update actor network:** Update the actor policy using the sampled policy gradient:

$$\nabla_{\theta^\mu} J \approx \frac{1}{N}\sum_i \nabla_a Q(s, a|\theta^Q)|_{s=s_i, a=\mu(s_i)} \nabla_{\theta^\mu}\mu(s|\theta^\mu)|_{s_i}$$

- **Update target networks:** Soft update target network parameters:

$$\theta^{Q'} \leftarrow \tau\theta^Q + (1-\tau)\theta^{Q'}$$

$$\theta^{\mu'} \leftarrow \tau\theta^\mu + (1-\tau)\theta^{\mu'}$$

where $\tau \ll 1$ ensures slow update rates.

4. **Convergence check:** Continue the iterative process until the policy converges or desired performance metrics are met.

The following pseudocode summarizes the DDPG algorithm:

```
# Initialize actor and critic networks with random weights
# Initialize target networks with the same weights as the original ones
# Initialize replay buffer

for episode in range(Episodes):
    # Reset environment and get initial state
    state = env.reset()

    for step in range(MaxSteps):
        # Select action according to the current policy with exploration noise
        action = actor.predict(state) + noise

        # Execute action and observe new state and reward
        next_state, reward, done, info = env.step(action)

        # Store the transition in the replay buffer
        replay_buffer.add(state, action, reward, next_state, done)

        # Sample mini-batch from replay buffer
        states, actions, rewards, next_states, dones = replay_buffer.sample()

        # Update critic network by minimizing loss
        target_actions = target_actor.predict(next_states)
```

```
target_q_values = target_critic.predict(next_states, target_actions)
y = rewards + gamma * target_q_values * (1 - dones)
critic.train(states, actions, y)

# Update actor network using policy gradient
actions_gradients = critic.get_action_gradients(states, actions)
actor.train(states, actions_gradients)

# Update target networks using soft update
update_target_networks(actor, critic, target_actor, target_critic)

# Update state
state = next_state

if done:
    break
```

Correctly implementing and tuning DDPG involves addressing practical challenges such as effective noise strategies to balance exploration and exploitation, ensuring replay buffer capacity is sufficient to capture state transitions without overwhelming memory, and choosing suitable hyperparameters. By addressing these elements, DDPG has demonstrated considerable success in domains such as robotic control and autonomous driving. Additionally, understanding the nuances of DDPG paves the way for grasping more sophisticated algorithms like Twin Delayed DDPG (TD3) and Soft Actor-Critic (SAC).

8.5 Twin Delayed DDPG (TD3)

Twin Delayed DDPG (TD3) is an enhancement of the Deep Deterministic Policy Gradient (DDPG) algorithm, designed to address its known susceptibilities to overestimation bias and function approximation errors. TD3 achieves robustness through three primary modifications: Clipped Double Q-Learning, Policy Delays, and Target Policy Smoothing.

Clipped Double Q-Learning alleviates the overestimation bias by maintaining two critic networks and taking the lower of the two predicted Q-values to form the target in the temporal difference update. This prevents overly optimistic value estimates which can destabilize training.

```
# Pseudo-code for the critic update in TD3
for i in range(number_of_critic_updates):
    action = actor_target(next_state)
    noise = clip(epsilon, -noise_clip, noise_clip)
    target_action = action + noise
    target_q_value = min(critic_target_1(next_state, target_action),
                         critic_target_2(next_state, target_action))
    y = reward + discount * target_q_value * (1 - done)
```

```
    # Update critic networks
    critic_optimizer_1.zero_grad()
    loss_critic_1 = loss_function(critic_1(state, action), y)
    loss_critic_1.backward()
    critic_optimizer_1.step()

    critic_optimizer_2.zero_grad()
    loss_critic_2 = loss_function(critic_2(state, action), y)
    loss_critic_2.backward()
    critic_optimizer_2.step()
```

Policy Delays further enhance stability by updating the policy (actor network) and the target networks less frequently than the critic networks. This delay ensures that the value estimates have a chance to stabilize before they are further influenced by updates to the policy. Specifically, the actor and target updates are usually performed once for every two critic updates.

```
# Pseudo-code illustrating delayed policy updates
if step % policy_delay == 0:
    actor_optimizer.zero_grad()
    loss_actor = -critic_1(state, actor(state)).mean()
    loss_actor.backward()
    actor_optimizer.step()

    # Update target networks
    for param, target_param in zip(actor.parameters(), actor_target.parameters()):
        target_param.data.copy_(tau * param.data + (1 - tau) * target_param.data)
    for param, target_param in zip(critic_1.parameters(), critic_target_1.parameters()
        ):
        target_param.data.copy_(tau * param.data + (1 - tau) * target_param.data)
    for param, target_param in zip(critic_2.parameters(), critic_target_2.parameters()
        ):
        target_param.data.copy_(tau * param.data + (1 - tau) * target_param.data)
```

Target Policy Smoothing introduces noise to the target action to mitigate the problem of learning overly sharp Q-functions. This noise is clipped to ensure it stays within a reasonable range, preventing it from diverging too far from the intended action.

```
# Target policy smoothing
epsilon = torch.normal(mean=0, std=policy_noise, size=action.shape)
epsilon = epsilon.clamp(-noise_clip, noise_clip)
next_action = (actor_target(next_state) + epsilon).clamp(-max_action, max_action)
```

The effectiveness of TD3 can be attributed to these innovations, which collectively ensure that the learned policy is robust, stable, and able to achieve higher performance across a range of tasks. The combination of Clipped Double Q-Learning, Policy Delays, and Target Policy Smoothing reduces the risk of divergence and helps achieve consistent improvements over the original DDPG algorithm.

Training a TD3 agent typically involves alternately updating the critic networks, actor network, and target networks, with each having their own respective update schedules as outlined. The performance of TD3 is monitored through evaluation episodes, where the policy derived from the actor network is applied to the environment, and the rewards garnered are recorded.

The following experiments demonstrate the comparative benefits of TD3 over DDPG in environments characterized by continuous action spaces. For instance, the HalfCheetah environment in MuJoCo simulation often exhibits substantial performance improvements when TD3 is applied, shown through higher cumulative rewards and less variance in performance metrics.

Overall, Twin Delayed DDPG enhances the robustness of policy learning in deep reinforcement learning settings, thereby facilitating the development of more reliable agents for complex control tasks.

8.6 Soft Actor-Critic (SAC)

The Soft Actor-Critic (SAC) algorithm is an advanced actor-critic method that has gained prominence owing to its performance and theoretical guarantees. It is particularly effective in continuous action spaces and addresses the balance between exploration and exploitation through the incorporation of entropy maximization. The SAC algorithm is distinctive in its use of an entropy term in the reward signal, encouraging exploration by favoring more stochastic policies.

The main components of SAC include a stochastic policy (actor), a value function (critic), and an entropy term. The critic estimates the Q-value (the expected return) for a given state-action pair, while the actor is responsible for selecting actions based on a probabilistic policy. The entropy term in SAC contributes to more exploratory behavior, which is especially beneficial in complex environments with sparse reward landscapes.

The SAC algorithm optimizes a stochastic policy in an off-policy manner using this entropy-augmented reward. The complete objective function $J(\pi)$ for SAC can be defined as:

$$J(\pi) = \sum_{t=0}^{T} \mathbb{E}_{(s_t, a_t) \sim \rho_\pi} \left[r(s_t, a_t) + \alpha \mathcal{H}(\pi(\cdot|s_t)) \right]$$

where $\mathcal{H}(\pi(\cdot|s_t))$ denotes the entropy of the policy π at state s_t, and α is a temperature parameter that determines the trade-off between the reward and the entropy.

Algorithmic Steps of SAC

The steps of the SAC algorithm can be concisely described as follows:

- **Initialize Parameters:**
  - Initialize the parameters θ of the policy (actor) π_θ.
  - Initialize the parameters ϕ_1 and ϕ_2 of the two Q-value networks Q_{ϕ_1} and Q_{ϕ_2}.
  - Initialize the parameters $\bar{\phi}_1$ and $\bar{\phi}_2$ for the target Q-value networks $Q_{\bar{\phi}_1}$ and $Q_{\bar{\phi}_2}$.
  - Initialize the temperature parameter α.
  - Initialize an empty replay buffer $\mathcal{D}$.
- **Collect Experience:**
  - Interact with the environment using the current policy π_θ and store the experiences in the replay buffer $\mathcal{D}$.
- **Update Critic:**
  - Sample a batch of transitions (s, a, r, s') from the replay buffer $\mathcal{D}$.
  - Compute the target Q-value using the target networks:

$$y = r + \gamma(1 - d)\left[\min_{i=1,2} Q_{\bar{\phi}_i}(s', a') - \alpha \log \pi_\theta(a'|s')\right]$$

    where d is the done signal indicating the end of the episode.
  - Update the Q-network parameters ϕ_i by minimizing the loss:

$$J_Q(\phi_i) = \mathbb{E}_{(s,a,r,s')}\left[(Q_{\phi_i}(s, a) - y)^2\right]$$

- **Update Actor:**
  - Update the policy parameters θ by minimizing the actor loss:

$$J_\pi(\theta) = \mathbb{E}_{s\sim\mathcal{D}}\left[\alpha \log \pi_\theta(a|s) - Q_\phi(s, a)\right]$$

- **Entropy Temperature Adjustment:**
  - Adjust the temperature parameter α by minimizing the temperature loss:

$$J(\alpha) = \mathbb{E}_{a\sim\pi_\theta}\left[-\alpha \log \pi_\theta(a|s) - \overline{\mathcal{H}}\right]$$

    where $\overline{\mathcal{H}}$ is a target entropy that can be set as a hyperparameter.

- **Update Target Networks:**
  - Update the target Q-networks $\bar{\phi}_i$ periodically or using a soft update mechanism:

$$\bar{\phi}_i \leftarrow \tau\phi_i + (1 - \tau)\bar{\phi}_i$$

    where τ is typically a small value (e.g., 0.005).

Practical Implementation

To implement SAC, one must carefully aggregate these steps into a cohesive code structure. Below is an outline of the SAC algorithm in Python, highlighting the critical operations.

```
import numpy as np
import torch
from torch.optim import Adam
import gym
from replay_buffer import ReplayBuffer
from networks import PolicyNetwork, QNetwork, ValueNetwork

env = gym.make('YourEnv-v0')

# Hyperparameters
gamma = 0.99
tau = 0.005
alpha = 0.2
policy_lr = 3e-4
q_lr = 3e-4
value_lr = 3e-4
batch_size = 256
replay_size = 1e6

# Networks
policy_net = PolicyNetwork()
q_net1 = QNetwork()
q_net2 = QNetwork()
target_q_net1 = QNetwork()
target_q_net2 = QNetwork()

# Optimizers
policy_optimizer = Adam(policy_net.parameters(), lr=policy_lr)
q_optimizer1 = Adam(q_net1.parameters(), lr=q_lr)
q_optimizer2 = Adam(q_net2.parameters(), lr=q_lr)

# Replay buffer
replay_buffer = ReplayBuffer(replay_size)

# Training Loop
for episode in range(max_episodes):
    state = env.reset()
    for t in range(max_timesteps):
        action = policy_net.sample_action(state)
        next_state, reward, done, _ = env.step(action)

        # Store transition
        replay_buffer.add(state, action, reward, next_state, done)
```

```
state = next_state

if done:
    break

# Sample batch
states, actions, rewards, next_states, dones = replay_buffer.sample(batch_size)

# Critic update
with torch.no_grad():
    next_action = policy_net.sample_action(next_states)
    target_q = rewards + (1 - dones) * gamma * (torch.min(
        target_q_net1(next_states, next_action),
        target_q_net2(next_states, next_action)
    ) - alpha * policy_net.log_prob(next_states, next_action))

q_loss1 = ((q_net1(states, actions) - target_q) ** 2).mean()
q_loss2 = ((q_net2(states, actions) - target_q) ** 2).mean()
q_optimizer1.zero_grad()
q_loss1.backward()
q_optimizer1.step()
q_optimizer2.zero_grad()
q_loss2.backward()
q_optimizer2.step()

# Actor update
policy_loss = (alpha * policy_net.log_prob(states, action) - q_net1(states,
      action)).mean()
policy_optimizer.zero_grad()
policy_loss.backward()
policy_optimizer.step()

# Soft update of target networks
for target_param, param in zip(target_q_net1.parameters(), q_net1.parameters
      ()):
    target_param.data.copy_(tau * param.data + (1 - tau) * target_param.
          data)
for target_param, param in zip(target_q_net2.parameters(), q_net2.parameters
      ()):
    target_param.data.copy_(tau * param.data + (1 - tau) * target_param.
          data)
```

This implementation provides a clear view of how SAC consolidates the actor, critic, and entropy adjustments into an integrated learning process. Subtleties like careful tuning of hyperparameters and managing gradients are critical to achieving optimal performance with SAC.

The effective combination of exploration (via entropy maximization) and exploitation (through reward maximization) makes Soft Actor-Critic a formidable algorithm in the deep reinforcement learning landscape.

8.7 Combining Convolutional Neural Networks with RL

In many real-world applications, reinforcement learning (RL) requires dealing with high-dimensional inputs, such as images and videos. To efficiently process such inputs, Convolutional Neural Networks (CNNs) are commonly integrated with RL algorithms. This section delves into how CNNs can be combined with RL, highlighting essential concepts, architecture considerations, and practical implementations.

CNNs are adept at extracting spatial hierarchies from image data, making them well-suited for tasks involving visual inputs. Early layers of a CNN detect basic features like edges and textures, while deeper layers identify more complex structures. By leveraging CNNs, RL agents can discern meaningful patterns in visual data, facilitating effective decision-making in high-dimensional environments.

Architecture of CNNs in RL:

When incorporating CNNs into RL frameworks, the architecture typically starts with convolutional layers followed by fully connected layers. The convolutional layers serve to extract spatial features from the input images, which are then passed to the fully connected layers to form higher-level representations. These representations can be fed into various RL components, such as Q-networks or policy networks. An exemplary architecture combines a CNN with a Deep Q-Network (DQN) as follows:

```
import torch
import torch.nn as nn
import torch.nn.functional as F

class CNN_DQN(nn.Module):
    def __init__(self, input_shape, num_actions):
        super(CNN_DQN, self).__init__()
        self.input_shape = input_shape
        self.num_actions = num_actions

        self.conv_layers = nn.Sequential(
            nn.Conv2d(input_shape[0], 32, kernel_size=8, stride=4),
            nn.ReLU(),
            nn.Conv2d(32, 64, kernel_size=4, stride=2),
            nn.ReLU(),
            nn.Conv2d(64, 64, kernel_size=3, stride=1),
            nn.ReLU()
        )

        self.fc = nn.Sequential(
            nn.Linear(self.feature_size(), 512),
            nn.ReLU(),
            nn.Linear(512, num_actions)
```

```
    )

    def forward(self, x):
        x = self.conv_layers(x)
        x = x.view(x.size(0), -1)
        x = self.fc(x)
        return x

    def feature_size(self):
        return self.conv_layers(torch.zeros(1, *self.input_shape)).view(1, -1).size(1)
```

In this example, the CNN_DQN class defines a convolutional neural network tailored for a DQN. The three convolutional layers are configured with varying kernel sizes and strides to capture essential visual features. These layers are followed by two fully connected layers that transform the extracted features into Q-values corresponding to possible actions.

Training CNNs in RL:

Using CNNs within RL frameworks necessitates proper training procedures. Typically, the CNN parameters are optimized during the RL agent's learning process. The loss function for DQNs, involving the temporal difference (TD) error, is backpropagated through the entire network. This process can be outlined as follows:

```
optimizer = torch.optim.Adam(model.parameters(), lr=1e-4)
criterion = nn.MSELoss()

# Sample a minibatch of transitions from the replay buffer
for state, action, reward, next_state, done in replay_buffer.sample(batch_size):
    # Compute Q-values for the current states
    q_values = model(state)
    # Compute Q-values for the next states
    next_q_values = model(next_state).detach()
    # Compute the target Q-value
    target_q_value = reward + gamma * torch.max(next_q_values, dim=1)[0] * (1 -
        done)
    # Compute the loss
    loss = criterion(q_values.gather(1, action.unsqueeze(1)), target_q_value.unsqueeze
        (1))

    # Optimize the model
    optimizer.zero_grad()
    loss.backward()
    optimizer.step()
```

This code snippet demonstrates the optimization process. The agent samples transitions from the replay buffer and calculates Q-values using the current state and the next state. The temporal difference error, computed using the MSE loss, drives the optimization of the CNN parameters. Regular sampling from a replay buffer ensures diverse training data and stabilizes learning.

Challenges and Considerations:

Integrating CNNs with RL introduces several challenges. One primary concern is the computational complexity associated with training deep networks on high-dimensional inputs. Adequate computational resources and efficient algorithms are essential to handle such demands. Overfitting is another critical issue; techniques like experience replay, dropout, and data augmentation can mitigate overfitting by providing more diverse training experiences and preventing the network from relying too heavily on specific visual patterns.

When designing CNN architectures for RL, it's crucial to balance between network depth and computational efficiency. Deeper networks may provide better feature extraction at the cost of increased training time and resource consumption. Employing transfer learning, where pre-trained network weights are fine-tuned for specific RL tasks, can also enhance performance and reduce training time.

Practical Implementations:

In practice, combining CNNs with RL has led to significant achievements in various applications. The most notable example is DeepMind's Atari-playing agent, which uses a CNN-based DQN to achieve human-level performance on numerous Atari games. The agent processes raw pixel data from the game screen, with the CNN extracting spatial features that inform the RL policy.

Here's a minimal example of how a CNN-based DQN can be implemented for an Atari game:

```
import gym
from collections import deque

env = gym.make("Breakout-v0")
input_shape = env.observation_space.shape
num_actions = env.action_space.n

model = CNN_DQN(input_shape, num_actions)

replay_buffer = deque(maxlen=10000)

for episode in range(1000):
    state = env.reset()
    state = preprocess(state)

    for t in range(10000):
        state_tensor = torch.FloatTensor(state).unsqueeze(0)
        action = model(state_tensor).argmax().item()
        next_state, reward, done, info = env.step(action)
        next_state = preprocess(next_state)

        replay_buffer.append((state, action, reward, next_state, done))
```

```
    state = next_state

    if done:
        break

    % Training step
    if len(replay_buffer) > batch_size:
        train_model(model, replay_buffer, batch_size, gamma, optimizer, criterion)

    % Update target network periodically
    if t \% target\_update\_frequency == 0:
        target\_model.load\_state\_dict(model.state\_dict())
```

This code outlines the process of training a CNN-based DQN on an Atari environment. The preprocess function converts the raw pixel data into a suitable format for the CNN. The agent interacts with the environment, collecting experiences into a replay buffer. Periodically, the CNN is trained using samples from the replay buffer, and a separate target network is updated to stabilize learning.

Combining CNNs with RL offers a potent approach for tackling visually complex tasks. The ability of CNNs to extract meaningful features from high-dimensional inputs, coupled with the decision-making prowess of RL algorithms, opens up vast possibilities in fields ranging from autonomous vehicles to video game AI.

8.8 Combining Recurrent Neural Networks with RL

Recurrent Neural Networks (RNNs) have shown remarkable capabilities in handling sequential data due to their inherent ability to maintain a form of memory through internal states. Combining RNNs with Reinforcement Learning (RL) creates powerful agents capable of learning from sequential data, which is essential for tasks requiring temporal dependencies. This section delves into the intricate mechanisms by which RNNs are integrated with RL, including architectural considerations, algorithmic modifications, and empirical observations.

In standard RL, agents typically assume that states are fully observable. However, many real-world scenarios involve partially observable environments where the agent does not have access to the complete state information. This limitation necessitates agents that can infer hidden states from their observation history. RNNs address this challenge by maintaining an internal state representation that captures temporal dependencies. The combination of RNNs with RL, often referred to as Recurrent Reinforcement Learning (RRL), allows agents to perform well in environments where past information is crucial for decision-making.

RNN-based RL architectures can be introduced at various stages of an RL pipeline. The most straightforward integration occurs when the policy network (π) or the value network (Q) adopts an RNN structure, such as Long Short-Term Memory (LSTM) or Gated Recurrent Unit (GRU). Consider the following LSTM-based policy network implemented in Python using PyTorch:

```
import torch
import torch.nn as nn

class LSTMPolicyNetwork(nn.Module):
    def __init__(self, input_dim, hidden_dim, output_dim, num_layers=1):
        super(LSTMPolicyNetwork, self).__init__()
        self.lstm = nn.LSTM(input_dim, hidden_dim, num_layers, batch_first=True)
        self.fc = nn.Linear(hidden_dim, output_dim)

    def forward(self, x, hidden):
        out, hidden = self.lstm(x, hidden)
        out = self.fc(out[:, -1, :])
        return out, hidden

    def init_hidden(self, batch_size):
        return (torch.zeros(1, batch_size, hidden_dim),
                torch.zeros(1, batch_size, hidden_dim))
```

In this implementation, the LSTM processes a sequence of observations. The network's hidden state is updated through time, providing a summary of the observed sequence that aids in producing the policy output. The parameter *hidden_dim* influences the capacity of the hidden layers to capture temporal dependencies, while *num_layers* controls the network's depth.

When integrating RNNs into RL algorithms, critical modifications are necessary for the training process:

- **Handling Sequences:** Training RNNs requires handling sequences of varying lengths. Batching and data preprocessing involve creating sequences of fixed lengths, employing padding if necessary.
- **Updating Hidden States:** During forward and backward passes, hidden states need to be propagated through time. This requires careful management of the hidden state tensors to ensure correct gradients' flow.
- **Experience Replay Buffer:** For off-policy algorithms, maintaining an experience replay buffer becomes complex as storing se-

quences instead of individual transitions is necessary.

To illustrate these concepts, consider an RNN variant of the Deep Q-Network (DQN):

```
import torch
import torch.nn as nn
import torch.optim as optim
import numpy as np

class LSTMDQN(nn.Module):
    def __init__(self, input_dim, hidden_dim, output_dim, num_layers=1):
        super(LSTMDQN, self).__init__()
        self.lstm = nn.LSTM(input_dim, hidden_dim, num_layers, batch_first=True)
        self.fc = nn.Linear(hidden_dim, output_dim)

    def forward(self, x, hidden):
        out, hidden = self.lstm(x, hidden)
        out = self.fc(out[:, -1, :])
        return out, hidden

    def init_hidden(self, batch_size):
        return (torch.zeros(1, batch_size, hidden_dim),
                torch.zeros(1, batch_size, hidden_dim))

batch_size = 32
seq_length = 10
input_dim = 4
hidden_dim = 128
output_dim = 2

model = LSTMDQN(input_dim, hidden_dim, output_dim)
hidden_state = model.init_hidden(batch_size)
observations = torch.rand(batch_size, seq_length, input_dim)

q_values, hidden_state = model(observations, hidden_state)
```

In this example, LSTMDQN integrates an LSTM within a DQN architecture, which allows the agent to utilize sequences of observations for decision-making. The parameterization ensures that the Q-value estimates can incorporate temporal information, leading to better performance in partially observable environments.

Empirical studies have demonstrated that RNNs combined with RL not only excel in partially observable environments but also improve sample efficiency and robustness against perceptual aliasing. However, practitioners must consider several complexities, such as tuning the RNN's hyperparameters (e.g., hidden state size, number of layers) and managing the long-term dependencies efficiently to avoid vanishing or exploding gradients.

These challenges are often mitigated through careful architectural choices, such as using GRUs instead of LSTMs for their simpler structure, or techniques like gradient clipping to manage gradient explosion.

Additionally, advanced methods like attention mechanisms can be integrated to selectively focus on important portions of the input sequence, thereby enhancing the agent's learning capability in complex tasks.

The combination of RNNs with RL continues to evolve, with emerging research pushing the boundaries of what such hybrid models can achieve. The synergy between sequential data processing and reinforcement learning paves the way for robust agents capable of tackling a wide array of tasks in dynamically changing environments.

8.9 Model-Based Deep Reinforcement Learning

Model-Based Deep Reinforcement Learning (MBRL) distinguishes itself by utilizing a model to predict the environment's dynamics, rather than relying solely on interaction with the environment. This model-centric approach allows for more sample-efficient learning and can leverage simulations to improve policy and value function learning. The core idea in MBRL is to learn a model of the environment, typically represented as a transition function $\hat{T}(s, a) \approx P(s'|s, a)$, and a reward function $\hat{R}(s, a) \approx R(s, a)$, where s denotes the state, a the action, and s' the subsequent state.

Key steps in MBRL include:

- **Model Learning:** Learn the transition and reward functions from interaction data.
- **Planning:** Use the learned model for planning, which involves generating synthetic experiences.
- **Policy Learning:** Update the policy based on real and/or synthetic experiences.

Model Learning

The first step involves learning an approximation of the transition and reward functions. Typically, a neural network is used to approximate these functions, exploiting the powerful representation capabilities of deep learning. The neural network takes the current state s and action a as inputs and predicts the next state s' and reward r. The prediction is trained using data collected from interactions with the environment.

```
class TransitionRewardModel(nn.Module):
    def __init__(self, state_dim, action_dim, hidden_dim):
        super(TransitionRewardModel, self).__init__()
        self.fc1 = nn.Linear(state_dim + action_dim, hidden_dim)
        self.fc2 = nn.Linear(hidden_dim, hidden_dim)
        self.fc3 = nn.Linear(hidden_dim, state_dim + 1) # predict next state and
            reward

    def forward(self, state, action):
        x = torch.cat([state, action], dim=1)
        x = F.relu(self.fc1(x))
        x = F.relu(self.fc2(x))
        x = self.fc3(x)
        next_state = x[:, :-1]
        reward = x[:, -1]
        return next_state, reward
```

The loss function used to train this neural network involves both the state prediction error and the reward prediction error:

$$\mathcal{L}(\theta) = \frac{1}{N} \sum_{i=1}^{N} \left[\|s' - \hat{s}'\|^2 + (r - \hat{r})^2 \right]$$

where θ are the neural network parameters, s' is the actual next state, $\hat{s}'$ is the predicted next state, r is the actual reward, and $\hat{r}$ is the predicted reward.

Planning

With the model trained, the next step is to use the model for planning. Planning involves using the learned model to simulate potential future scenarios and thereby generate synthetic experiences. These synthetic experiences can then be utilized to update the policy.

One common planning algorithm is Model Predictive Control (MPC), where the learned model is used to select actions by optimizing for future rewards over a finite time horizon. This is achieved by iteratively solving an optimization problem:

$$\pi_t = \arg\max_{\pi} \sum_{t=0}^{H} \mathbb{E} \left[\hat{R}(s_t, \pi(s_t)) \right]$$

where H is the planning horizon.

```
def mpc_action_selection(model, state, policy, horizon):
    best_action_sequence = None
    best_value = -float('inf')
    for _ in range(number_of_candidates):
        action_sequence = sample_action_sequence(policy, horizon)
```

```
        value = simulate(model, state, action_sequence)
        if value > best_value:
            best_value = value
            best_action_sequence = action_sequence
    return best_action_sequence[0] # return the first action of the best sequence
```

Policy Learning

Finally, the policy is updated using experiences, which can be either real experiences collected from the environment or synthetic experiences generated by the model. A common method integrates these experiences into an off-policy algorithm such as DDPG or SAC, allowing the policy to learn from both real and synthetic data.

Consider using a prioritized replay buffer that incorporates experiences from both sources:

```
class MixedReplayBuffer:
    def __init__(self, capacity):
        self.capacity = capacity
        self.buffer = []

    def add(self, experience):
        if len(self.buffer) >= self.capacity:
            self.buffer.pop(0)
        self.buffer.append(experience)

    def sample(self, batch_size):
        return random.sample(self.buffer, batch_size)

# Sample real and synthetic experiences
real_experiences = real_replay_buffer.sample(batch_size // 2)
synthetic_experiences = synthetic_replay_buffer.sample(batch_size // 2)
combined_experiences = real_experiences + synthetic_experiences

# Update policy network
for experience in combined_experiences:
    # Policy learning update logic
```

The inclusion of synthetic experiences can significantly improve the sample efficiency of the learning algorithm by allowing it to leverage the model's predictive power. As the model continuously improves, the quality of synthetic experiences also enhances, further aiding in efficient policy updates.

The potential of MBRL lies in its ability to utilize the learned model to perform extensive simulations, thereby reducing the dependency on real-world interactions. This approach is especially beneficial in scenarios where interactions with the real environment are expensive, dangerous, or time-consuming. In such settings, MBRL's potential for efficient learning and rapid policy improvement is of immense practical value.

8.10 Exploration Strategies in Deep RL

In Deep Reinforcement Learning, exploration is a vital process by which an agent interacts with the environment to gather information about its states and rewards, promoting the discovery of optimal policies. The balance between exploration and exploitation—choosing known rewarding actions versus exploring new, potentially better actions—is crucial for maximizing cumulative rewards. Numerous exploration strategies have been developed to address this balance effectively, each with distinct advantages and applications.

Epsilon-Greedy Strategy

Epsilon-greedy is one of the simplest and most commonly used exploration strategies. It relies on a parameter ϵ which controls the exploration rate. During each action selection, the agent selects a random action with probability ϵ (exploration), and the action that maximizes the Q-value (exploitation) with probability $1 - \epsilon$.

Here is a pseudocode example implementing the epsilon-greedy strategy:

```
def epsilon_greedy(Q, state, epsilon):
    if np.random.rand() < epsilon:
        return random_action()
    else:
        return np.argmax(Q[state])
```

The ϵ parameter typically starts high to promote exploration and decays over time to enhance exploitation as the agent learns more about the environment. This decay can be linear or exponential.

Decay Function

```
def linear_decay(epsilon, min_epsilon, decay_rate):
    return max(min_epsilon, epsilon - decay_rate)

def exponential_decay(epsilon, min_epsilon, decay_rate):
    return max(min_epsilon, epsilon * decay_rate)
```

Optimistic Initial Values

Rather than starting with random initial Q-values, optimistic initial values assume an initially high Q-value for all state-action pairs. This optimism encourages the agent to explore more actions early on, as unexplored actions are perceived to have high rewards.

Here is an example of initializing Q-values optimistically:

```
def initialize_Q(states, actions, optimistic_value):
```

```
    Q = np.full((states, actions), optimistic_value)
    return Q
```

Upper Confidence Bound (UCB)

Upper Confidence Bound is a more sophisticated method that balances exploration and exploitation by favoring actions that have been tried fewer times. It uses the principle of optimism in the face of uncertainty. The UCB algorithm selects actions according to:

$$a_t = \arg\max_a \left(Q(s,a) + c\sqrt{\frac{\log t}{N(s,a)}} \right)$$

where $Q(s,a)$ is the estimated Q-value, c is a confidence level parameter, t is the total number of times any action has been selected, and $N(s,a)$ is the number of times action a has been selected in state s.

Implementation of UCB

```
def ucb_action(Q, state, N_state_action, t, c):
    ucb_values = Q[state] + c * np.sqrt(np.log(t + 1) / (N_state_action[state] + 1))
    return np.argmax(ucb_values)
```

Boltzmann Exploration

Boltzmann exploration, also known as softmax action selection, assigns probabilities to actions based on their relative Q-values using the Boltzmann distribution. Actions with higher Q-values have higher selection probabilities, promoting exploration balanced by the potential quality of actions. The probability $P(a|s)$ of selecting action a in state s at time t is given by:

$$P(a|s) = \frac{\exp(Q(s,a)/T)}{\sum_b \exp(Q(s,b)/T)}$$

where T (temperature parameter) controls the degree of exploration; higher T values encourage more exploration.

Implementation of Boltzmann Exploration

```
def boltzmann_action(Q, state, temperature):
    q_values = Q[state]
    exp_q = np.exp(q_values / temperature)
    probabilities = exp_q / np.sum(exp_q)
    return np.random.choice(range(len(q_values)), p=probabilities)
```

Noise-Based Exploration in Continuous Action Spaces

For continuous action spaces, adding noise to the actions can facilitate exploration. One common approach in algorithms like Deep Deterministic Policy Gradient (DDPG) is to add Ornstein-Uhlenbeck noise to the action outputs. This type of noise is temporally correlated and suitable for dynamic systems with inertia.

Ornstein-Uhlenbeck Noise

```
class OUNoise:
    def __init__(self, action_dimension, mu=0, theta=0.15, sigma=0.2):
        self.action_dimension = action_dimension
        self.mu = mu
        self.theta = theta
        self.sigma = sigma
        self.state = np.ones(self.action_dimension) * self.mu

    def reset(self):
        self.state = np.ones(self.action_dimension) * self.mu

    def noise(self):
        x = self.state
        dx = self.theta * (self.mu - x) + self.sigma * np.random.randn(len(x))
        self.state = x + dx
        return self.state
```

Intrinsic Motivation

Intrinsic motivation strategies encourage an agent to explore by generating intrinsic rewards for visiting novel or unexplored states. Examples include:

- *Curiosity-Driven Exploration*: Uses predictive models to generate intrinsic rewards based on the novelty or prediction error of visited states.
- *Count-Based Exploration*: Typically used in tabular settings, this strategy incrementally records state visit counts, assigning higher rewards to less frequently visited states.

Both methods emphasize learning about the environment structure beyond obtaining extrinsic rewards.

Curiosity-Driven Exploration Example

```
class CuriousAgent:
    def __init__(self, model):
        self.model = model

    def intrinsic_reward(self, state, next_state):
        predicted_next_state = self.model.predict(state)
        intrinsic_reward = np.mean((next_state - predicted_next_state) ** 2)
        return intrinsic_reward
```

Selecting the appropriate exploration strategy is context-dependent, influenced by factors such as the environment characteristics, computational resources, and specific application objectives.

8.11 Applications and Case Studies of Deep Reinforcement Learning

Deep Reinforcement Learning (DRL) has established itself as a powerful approach to solve tasks that were once considered exceedingly challenging. Its application spans various domains including games, robotics, finance, healthcare, and more. This section meticulously explores notable applications and case studies demonstrating the capabilities of DRL in real-world scenarios.

- **1. Game Playing:**

  The application of DRL in gaming has garnered significant attention, prominently featuring the success of *AlphaGo*. Developed by DeepMind, AlphaGo utilizes a combination of supervised learning from human expert games and reinforcement learning from self-play. It employs Monte Carlo Tree Search coupled with deep neural networks to evaluate board positions and actions.

```
for episode in range(num_episodes):
    game_state = initialize_game()
    while not game_over(game_state):
        action = select_action(game_state)
        game_state = apply_action(game_state, action)
        if game_won(game_state):
            update_weights()
```

  The AlphaGo's achievements include defeating human champions, thus illustrating the potential of DRL in complex strategic environments.

- **2. Robotics:**

  DRL has significantly impacted robotics, enhancing the ability of robots to learn tasks such as manipulation, locomotion, and autonomous navigation. A prominent example is OpenAI's *Dactyl*, which trains a robotic hand to manipulate objects using domain randomization.

```
def reward_function(state, action):
    position_error = np.linalg.norm(state.target_pose - state.current_pose)
    return -position_error
```

Dactyl employs Proximal Policy Optimization (PPO) to learn the manipulation of diverse objects, demonstrating robustness and adaptability in real-world settings.

- **3. Autonomous Driving:**

  In the domain of autonomous driving, DRL is employed to train agents for decision-making, route planning, and control under dynamic conditions. Noteworthy is NVIDIA's *PilotNet*, which uses convolutional neural networks to map raw pixels from camera inputs directly to steering commands.

```
state = get_camera_input()
action = model.predict(state)
vehicle.apply_control(action)
```

  PilotNet's approach underscores the utility of DRL in processing high-dimensional sensory inputs to control autonomous vehicles safely and efficiently.

- **4. Finance:**

  DRL techniques are harnessed in finance for portfolio management, algorithmic trading, and risk assessment. JPMorgan's *LOXM*, an execution algorithm, optimizes trading strategies by considering market impact and volatility.

```
state = get_market_state()
action = model.predict(state)
execute_trade(action)
reward = compute_portfolio_return()
update_model(state, action, reward)
```

  Using DRL allows LOXM to adapt to market conditions dynamically, aiming for optimal execution performance.

- **5. Healthcare:**

  In healthcare, DRL is being applied to personalized medicine, treatment planning, and medical imaging. Projects such as the use of DRL for radiotherapy treatment planning have shown promise. Here, the objective is to maximize the radiation dose to malignant regions while minimizing exposure to healthy tissues.

```
def reward_function(dose_distribution):
    tumor_control = calculate_tumor_control(dose_distribution)
    normal_tissue_sparing = calculate_normal_tissue_sparing(
            dose_distribution)
    return tumor_control - normal_tissue_sparing
```

With DRL, treatment plans are optimized based on patient-specific data, enhancing therapeutic efficacy and reducing side effects.

- **6. Energy Management:**

  Efficient energy management in smart grids and sustainable environments benefits from DRL. For instance, Google DeepMind's application of DRL to reduce data center cooling costs achieved up to a 40% reduction in energy used for cooling.

```
state = get_grid_state()
action = model.predict(state)
apply_energy_control(action)
reward = measure_energy_efficiency()
update_model(state, action, reward)
```

  This demonstrates the capability of DRL to operate large-scale, intricate systems proficiently, yielding substantial real-world benefits.

- **7. Natural Language Processing:**

  In natural language processing (NLP), DRL aids in tasks like machine translation, sentiment analysis, and dialogue systems. For example, Google's *DQNMT*, a reinforcement learning approach for neural machine translation, refines translation by maximizing long-term reward based on sequence accuracy.

```
current_translation = model.predict(source_text)
reward = compute_bleu_score(current_translation, reference_translation)
update_translation_model(current_translation, reward)
```

  DRL enhances NLP models by focusing on optimizing end-to-end performance measures directly.

These applications exemplify the versatility and impact of DRL across diverse fields. By leveraging DRL, significant advancements and breakthroughs are achieved, showcasing deep learning's potential to solve complex, real-world challenges.

Chapter 9

Hierarchical Reinforcement Learning

Hierarchical Reinforcement Learning focuses on decomposing tasks into smaller, more manageable subtasks to improve learning efficiency and scalability. This chapter explores the motivation and benefits of hierarchical approaches, the temporal abstraction and options framework, and Semi-Markov Decision Processes (SMDPs). It covers learning and planning with options, Hierarchical DQN, and Feudal RL. Additionally, it discusses subgoal discovery, hierarchical actor-critic methods, and provides applications and case studies, highlighting the challenges and future directions in hierarchical RL.

9.1 Introduction to Hierarchical Reinforcement Learning

Hierarchical Reinforcement Learning (HRL) serves as a promising paradigm shift in the field of Reinforcement Learning (RL). The essence of HRL lies in decomposing complex tasks into a hierarchy of simpler subtasks, thereby improving the efficiency and scalability of the learning process. This introductory section delves into the foundational principles of HRL, setting the stage for a comprehensive understanding of its mechanics and advantages.

In traditional RL, an agent interacts with an environment incrementally, receiving feedback in the form of rewards while aiming to maximize cumulative reward over time. While this approach is effective for relatively simple tasks, its scalability is limited when faced with more intricate and lengthy tasks. The state space and action space can grow exponentially, rendering standard RL techniques inefficient.

HRL addresses these limitations by introducing a hierarchical structure where tasks are broken down into subtasks, each governed by its own policy. This hierarchical decomposition enables the agent to focus on achieving intermediate goals that contribute to the overall objective. For instance, consider the task of navigating a robot from one room to another in a building. Instead of learning a monolithic policy for the entire task, HRL allows the robot to decompose the task into navigating through hallways, opening doors, and other pertinent subtasks.

The core concept in HRL is the use of temporal abstraction, which facilitates reasoning and decision-making over different time scales. Temporal abstraction allows the agent to employ temporally extended actions, known as options, which can include multiple primitive actions. An option is defined by three components: an initiation set, an internal policy, and a termination condition. The initiation set specifies the states from which the option can be initiated, the internal policy dictates the choice of primitive actions when the option is active, and the termination condition determines when the option concludes.

Formally, an option o can be represented as a tuple (I_o, π_o, β_o), where:

- I_o is the initiation set.
- π_o is the policy governing the option.
- β_o is the termination condition.

By utilizing options, the agent can reduce the effective depth of decision-making required, operating at a higher level of abstraction. Semi-Markov Decision Processes (SMDPs) provide the mathematical framework for modeling such temporally abstract actions. SMDPs extend the standard Markov Decision Processes (MDPs) to accommodate actions whose durations vary, allowing for a more realistic depiction of real-world scenarios.

The learning process in HRL involves both planning and executing these temporally extended actions. The agent learns high-level policies that select among options and low-level policies that govern the actions within each option. This multi-level learning process enables the agent to develop sophisticated strategies for complex tasks.

Consider the following pseudocode, which illustrates the high-level learning algorithm employed in HRL:

```
# High-level HRL Algorithm

Initialize high-level policy _H and low-level policies _L
Repeat
  Select an option o according to _H
  Initialize current state s
  Repeat
    Select an action a according to _L
    Execute action a
    Observe new state s' and reward r
    Update _L using s, a, s', r
    s = s'
  Until option o terminates
  Update _H using information from option execution
Until task completion or convergence
```

The execution of this high-level algorithm involves a loop where the agent continuously selects and executes options. Within each option, the agent follows a low-level policy to perform specific actions until the option terminates. The agent updates the high-level policy based on feedback obtained from executing the options, progressively improving its strategy for completing the overall task.

HRL has demonstrated significant success across a range of applications, including robotics, game playing, and autonomous driving. The hierarchical structure enables agents to handle tasks of increased complexity and temporal duration efficiently. The modularity offered by HRL also facilitates transfer learning, where knowledge acquired from one task can be leveraged to accelerate learning in related tasks.

Throughout this chapter, subsequent sections will provide deeper insights into specific models and techniques within the HRL framework, such as the options framework, Semi-Markov Decision Processes (SMDPs), Hierarchical DQN, Feudal RL, and various hierarchical actor-critic methods. The discussion will be anchored in both theoretical foundations and practical implementations, presenting algorithmic details and case studies to elucidate the intricacies of HRL.

9.2 Motivation and Benefits of Hierarchical RL

Hierarchical Reinforcement Learning (HRL) aims to mitigate the complexity of high-dimensional RL tasks by breaking them down into smaller, more manageable subtasks or hierarchies. This not only simplifies the learning process but also significantly enhances learning efficiency and scalability, making it a powerful approach for complex environments. The motivation behind HRL can be broadly categorized into several key aspects: reducing the exploration space, enabling temporal abstraction, fostering transfer learning, and improving policy efficiency.

- **Reducing the exploration space** is a critical advantage of HRL. Traditional RL methods struggle with extensive state and action spaces, resulting in prolonged exploration times and significant computational overhead. By decomposing a task into subtasks, HRL confines the agent's exploration to a more limited, relevant region of the state and action spaces during the learning of each subtask. This subdivision leads to faster convergence and reduces the computational burden.

- **Temporal abstraction** is another significant aspect. In conventional RL, the agent typically makes decisions at every time step, which can be inefficient for tasks requiring longer sequences of actions to achieve a goal. Hierarchical approaches introduce the concept of temporal abstraction through options, where an option is a higher-level action composed of multiple lower-level actions executed over several time steps. This abstraction allows for higher-level decision-making, where an agent can select an option and commit to it until its termination, thereby simplifying the decision-making process and concentrating on the long-term horizon.

- Consider an agent in a robotics domain tasked with navigating to a specific location, picking up an object, and then placing it in a designated area. Rather than learning a policy at the granularity of individual motor commands, the agent can employ a hierarchical strategy where high-level actions are composed of 'Navigate', 'Pick-up', and 'Place'. Each high-level action can be an option with its policy and termination condition. This decomposition allows the agent to operate more efficiently, focusing on meaningful segments of activity rather than minute movements.

- **Transfer learning** is facilitated through HRL by enabling the reuse of learned behaviors across different tasks. When a subtask is common to multiple higher-level tasks, the agent can transfer the policy learned for that subtask to new scenarios, thereby reducing the learning time and improving performance in similar tasks. For instance, in a game-playing scenario, an agent might learn to navigate a maze in one game and transfer this knowledge when encountering similar mazes in different games or levels. This ability to generalize and reuse learned subtasks is a significant benefit of HRL, enhancing the flexibility and scalability of learning systems.

- **Improving policy efficiency** in HRL is achieved by focusing on higher-level abstractions and structuring policies hierarchically. Policies at higher levels of the hierarchy are responsible for selecting between different options or subtasks, whereas lower-level policies handle the details of executing these options. This hierarchical structuring reduces the complexity of policy learning and often results in more robust and concise policies. It aligns closely with how humans approach problem-solving, using different levels of abstraction and decomposing complex tasks into simpler constituent tasks.

- An important contribution to HRL is **Semi-Markov Decision Processes (SMDPs)**, which extend Markov Decision Processes (MDPs) to accommodate temporal abstraction. SMDPs model the decision-making process over varying time intervals, facilitating the formalization of options and hierarchies within the reinforcement learning framework. By employing SMDPs, HRL can rigorously define and manage temporally extended actions, leading to more sophisticated and efficient exploration and exploitation strategies.

- Moreover, HRL offers robustness and adaptability in dynamic environments. By possessing multiple levels of policies, an agent can adapt to changes at different abstraction levels. Lower-level policies can react quickly to immediate changes in the environment, while higher-level policies adjust to longer-term trends and modifications. This multi-level adaptability enhances the agent's ability to perform in varying and unpredictable environments, further showcasing the practicality of HRL in real-world applications.

- However, implementing HRL involves several challenges that need careful consideration and overcoming. The task decomposition process is not always straightforward and can require domain-specific knowledge. Defining suitable options and their termination conditions, avoiding the propagation of errors across hierarchical levels, and ensuring efficient coordination between levels are complex issues. Despite these challenges, the structured framework and significant benefits of HRL make it a critical area of study and application in modern reinforcement learning research and practice.

9.3 Temporal Abstraction and Options Framework

Temporal abstraction refers to the process of simplifying a complex decision-making task by grouping sequences of actions into higher-level actions or "options." In the context of reinforcement learning (RL), this abstraction facilitates the decomposition of interminable problems into structurally simpler and more tractable sub-problems. Temporal abstraction allows the agent to operate on multiple time scales, thereby enhancing learning efficiency and scalability.

The options framework formalizes this concept of temporal abstraction in a mathematically rigorous manner. An option is defined as a temporally extended course of action that consists of three components: an initiation set I, an option-policy π, and a termination condition β. Formally, an option o can be represented as a tuple $o = (I, \pi, \beta)$.

- **Initiation Set**

The initiation set $I \subseteq S$ specifies the set of states in which the option can be initiated. It provides a constraint ensuring that the option is only considered when the agent is in a suitable state. For instance, in a robotic manipulation task, a state where a robot's gripper is empty might be an appropriate initiation set for a grasping option.

- **Option-Policy**

The option-policy $\pi : S \to A$ maps states to actions and dictates the agent's behavior during the execution of the option. This policy can be either deterministic or stochastic. For example, if the option is to navigate from one room to another, π would define the exact sequence of movements required to achieve this transition.

- **Termination Condition**

The termination condition $\beta : S \to [0,1]$ specifies the probability that the option will terminate upon reaching a given state. This function enables the option to adaptively conclude its course of action based on the current state. For instance, an option's termination probability might increase as the agent approaches a goal state, thereby naturally concluding the option.

- **Formulation of Options in MDPs**

Within the framework of Markov Decision Processes (MDPs), incorporating options augments the standard action set with additional, temporally extended actions. Let A denote the primitive action set and O denote the set of available options. The agent now selects both primitive actions $a \in A$ and options $o \in O$. The comprehensive policy π' of the agent is thus a combination policy, integrating both primitive actions and options.

The introduction of options necessitates modifications to the Bellman equations for policy evaluation and improvement. The value function $V'_\pi(s)$ in the presence of options is defined as:

$$V'_\pi(s) = \sum_{o \in O} \pi'(o \mid s) Q'_\pi(s, o)$$

where

$$Q'_\pi(s, o) = \mathbb{E}\left[\sum_{t=0}^{T-1} \gamma^t r_t + \gamma^T V'_\pi(s_T) \mid s_0 = s, o\right]$$

is the expected return starting from state s, executing option o, and subsequently following the combined policy π'. Here, T represents the duration until the option terminates, r_t is the reward received at time step t, and γ is the discount factor.

- **Learning Options**

Learning options in an RL setting can be achieved via various methodologies. One common approach is the Intra-Option Learning Algorithm, which updates the values of both primitive actions and options concurrently. The key advantage of this algorithm is its ability to propagate value updates across multiple levels of temporal abstraction, which accelerates learning.

The pseudocode for the intra-option Q-learning update is as follows:

```
Initialize Q(s, a) arbitrarily for all s and a
Initialize u(s, o) arbitrarily for all s and o

while not converged do
    Observe current state s
    Choose option o from s using policy derived from u(s, o)
    while option o is not terminated do
        Choose primitive action a using the option's policy \pi(s)
        Take action a, observe reward r and next state s'
        Update Q-values:
            Q(s, a) = Q(s, a) + \alpha [r + \gamma max_{a'} Q(s', a') - Q(s, a)]
        Update expected return for the option:
            u(s, o) = u(s, o) + \alpha [r + \gamma Q(s', o) - u(s, o)]
        s = s'
        if option o terminates in state s then break
```

The distinction here is the dual update process, where both the Q-values for primitive actions $Q(s, a)$ and the expected returns for options $u(s, o)$ are adjusted based on observed transitions.

The integration of options into RL algorithms has proved beneficial in diverse domains. By leveraging temporal abstraction, agents can handle tasks characterized by long horizons and intrinsic hierarchical structure more effectively. This results in more efficient learning processes and improved policy performance. By formalizing temporal abstraction through the options framework, the field of hierarchical reinforcement learning advances towards solving more complex and realistic problems encountered in various applications.

9.4 Semi-Markov Decision Processes (SMDPs)

Semi-Markov Decision Processes (SMDPs) provide a mathematical framework that extends the classical Markov Decision Processes (MDPs) by incorporating temporal abstractions. An SMDP is particularly suited for modeling decision-making problems where actions can have variable durations, a crucial feature for hierarchical reinforcement learning.

An SMDP is formally defined by the tuple $\langle S, \mathcal{A}, P, R, \mathcal{T}, \gamma \rangle$, where:

- $\mathcal{S}$ is a finite set of states.
- $\mathcal{A}$ is a finite set of actions or options.
- $P(s', \tau|s, a)$ is the state transition probability distribution, representing the probability of transitioning to state s' from state s under action a after time τ.
- $R(s, a)$ is the reward function, which may depend on the state s and action a.
- $\mathcal{T}$ represents a possibly infinite set of time intervals, incorporating the aspect of variable action durations.
- γ is the discount factor, which balances immediate and future rewards.

The state transition probability $P(s', \tau|s, a)$ in SMDPs encapsulates both the probability of reaching state s' and the time duration τ taken to do so. This extension is significant, as it allows the agent to plan over temporally extended actions or options.

The reward $R(s, a)$ in an SMDP framework can be accumulated over the duration τ of the action. When an action a is initiated in state s, the immediate payoff is followed by additional rewards accrued over time τ. The total expected reward summed over time duration τ can be expressed as:

$$R(s, a) = \mathbb{E}\left[\sum_{t=0}^{\tau} \gamma^t r(s_t, a_t)\right]$$

where $r(s_t, a_t)$ denotes the reward at time step t.

To solve an SMDP, we derive an optimal policy π^* that maximizes the expected cumulative reward. Similar to MDPs, the value function and the action-value function for SMDPs can be defined but with an adjustment to account for the temporal duration τ.

The state-value function $V^\pi(s)$ under policy π is given by:

$$V^\pi(s) = \sum_{a \in \mathcal{A}} \pi(a|s) \sum_{s' \in \mathcal{S}} \int_\tau P(s', \tau|s, a) \left[\sum_{t=0}^{\tau} \gamma^t r(s_t, a_t) + \gamma^\tau V^\pi(s')\right] d\tau$$

Similarly, the action-value function $Q^\pi(s, a)$ is given by:

$$Q^{\pi}(s,a) = \sum_{s' \in \mathcal{S}} \int_{\tau} P(s', \tau | s, a) \left[\sum_{t=0}^{\tau} \gamma^t r(s_t, a_t) + \gamma^{\tau} V^{\pi}(s') \right] d\tau$$

The Bellman optimality equations for SMDPs are then:

$$V^*(s) = \max_{a \in \mathcal{A}} \sum_{s' \in \mathcal{S}} \int_{\tau} P(s', \tau | s, a) \left[\sum_{t=0}^{\tau} \gamma^t r(s_t, a_t) + \gamma^{\tau} V^*(s') \right] d\tau$$

$$Q^*(s,a) = \sum_{s' \in \mathcal{S}} \int_{\tau} P(s', \tau | s, a) \left[\sum_{t=0}^{\tau} \gamma^t r(s_t, a_t) + \gamma^{\tau} \max_{a'} Q^*(s', a') \right] d\tau$$

Given these definitions, standard iterative methods like value iteration and policy iteration can be adapted to solve SMDPs.

For value iteration in SMDPs, the update rule for the value function $V(s)$ is:

$$V_{k+1}(s) = \max_{a \in \mathcal{A}} \sum_{s' \in \mathcal{S}} \int_{\tau} P(s', \tau | s, a) \left[\sum_{t=0}^{\tau} \gamma^t r(s_t, a_t) + \gamma^{\tau} V_k(s') \right] d\tau$$

For policy iteration, the steps involve policy evaluation and policy improvement, adapted for the temporal component.

Policy Evaluation: The policy evaluation step calculates the value function $V^{\pi}(s)$ for a given policy π until convergence:

```
for all s in S:
    V_k+1(s) = sum_a pi(a|s) * sum_s' int_tau P(s', tau | s, a) *
               [ sum_t gamma^t * r(s_t, a_t) + gamma^tau * V_k(s') ] d_tau
```

Policy Improvement: The policy improvement step updates the policy π:

```
for all s in S:
    pi'(s) = argmax_a sum_s' int_tau P(s', tau | s, a) *
             [ sum_t gamma^t * r(s_t, a_t) + gamma^tau * V(s') ] d_tau
```

Policy evaluation and improvement are iterated until the policy converges to the optimal policy.

SMDPs offer a powerful framework for modeling temporally extended actions, crucial for hierarchical reinforcement learning. Understanding

SMDPs' formalism and applying their solution methods enhances the ability to implement effective hierarchical models. This allows for efficient learning by abstracting complex tasks into manageable subtasks with variable durations.

9.5 Learning and Planning with Options

Hierarchical Reinforcement Learning (HRL) facilitates the decomposition of complex tasks into smaller and more manageable subtasks using the concept of *options*. In the context of the Options Framework, an option is an extended course of action, consisting of three elements: a policy π, a termination condition β, and an initiation set I. Formally, an option o is represented as a tuple $\langle I, \pi, \beta \rangle$. The policy π governs the behavior of the agent while the option is active, the termination condition β determines when the option should stop being executed, and the initiation set I defines the states where the option can be initiated.

To understand learning and planning with options, we explore these components in detail along with the methodologies used for integrating options into the learning process.

- **Options and Policies:** An option's policy $\pi : S \times A \rightarrow [0, 1]$ is a probability distribution over actions, conditioned on the current state. This policy dictates which action the agent takes at each step when the option is active. For example, consider a navigation task where an agent needs to reach a specific location. An option may involve navigating to a nearby landmark. Within this option, the policy directs the movement of the agent toward the landmark until the landmark is reached or an obstacle is encountered.

- **Termination Condition:** The termination condition $\beta : S \rightarrow [0, 1]$ specifies the probability that the option will terminate in a given state. Typically, $\beta(s) = 1$ signifies that the option will always terminate in state s, while $\beta(s) = 0$ indicates that the option will never terminate in state s. For example, the termination condition for our navigation task might specify $\beta(s) = 1$ only when the agent reaches the landmark.

- **Initiation Set:** The initiation set $I \subseteq S$ defines the states from which an option can be initiated. For the navigation task, I could be the set of states from which the agent can reasonably aim to reach the desired landmark. The design of the initiation set is crucial for ensuring the practical applicability and success of an option.

- **Semi-Markov Decision Process (SMDP) Extension:** Options extend the Markov Decision Process (MDP) framework to Semi-Markov Decision Processes (SMDPs). Unlike standard MDPs where transitions depend solely on the actions chosen at discrete time steps, SMDPs allow actions (options) that can extend over multiple time steps arbitrarily. This temporal abstraction is critical for HRL since it allows the agent to operate over varying time scales.

- **Option Policies:** Let $\mu(s)$ denote the policy over options, indicating which option to initiate in state s. Once an option o is chosen, the intra-option policy π determines the actions until the option terminates, and the agent returns to the high-level policy μ. Learning μ can be viewed as learning a policy in an SMDP where the actions are options.

  The value function for options, $V_\mu(s)$, is defined as the expected cumulative reward when starting from state s and following the policy μ:

$$V_\mu(s) = \mathbb{E}_\mu \left[\sum_{t=0}^{\infty} \gamma^t R_t \mid S_0 = s \right]$$

  Here, γ is the discount factor. The state-action value function, $Q_\mu(s, o)$, represents the expected return of initiating an option o in state s.

- **Learning with Options: Intra-Option Learning:** In learning with options, intra-option learning involves updating the value functions and policies associated with the options. One approach is the *Intra-Option Q-Learning*, which updates the Q-values for the state-action pairs within an option based on the observed rewards and the value function of the next state. Given an option o and a transition (s, a, r, s'), where s' is the resulting state after taking action a in state s, the intra-option Q-learning update rule is:

$$Q(s, o) \leftarrow Q(s, o) + \alpha \left[r + \gamma(1 - \beta(s')) \max_{o'} Q(s', o') - Q(s, o) \right]$$

  This update rule considers the termination condition $\beta(s')$, discount factor γ, and learning rate α.

```
for each transition (s, a, r, s') do:
    for each option o applicable in s do:
        if o terminates in s':
            target = r + gamma * max(Q(s', o'))
        else:
            target = r + gamma * Q(s', o)
        Q(s, o) += alpha * (target - Q(s, o))
```

- **Hierarchical Q-Learning:** In hierarchical Q-learning, an agent learns to select among various options in a hierarchical manner. Each level of the hierarchy is responsible for making decisions over a different timescale. At the top level, the policy μ selects options based on the abstract states, while at the bottom level, the options' policies π handle low-level actions.

  Consider a robot navigation problem where the top-level policy might choose between navigating to different rooms, while the options handle the details of moving to specific landmarks within those rooms. The top-level Q-values, $Q_\mu(s, o)$, are updated using the cumulative reward received while executing an option o from state s, and the value $V_\mu(s')$ of the state upon completion of the option:

  $$Q_\mu(s, o) \leftarrow Q_\mu(s, o) + \alpha \left[R + \gamma V_\mu(s') - Q_\mu(s, o)\right]$$

  Here, R is the total reward accumulated during the execution of the option o. The value function $V_\mu(s)$ is then updated as:

  $$V_\mu(s) = \max_o Q_\mu(s, o)$$

```
for each transition (s, o, R, s') do:
    Q(mu, s, o) += alpha * (R + gamma * V(mu, s') - Q(mu, s, o))
    V(mu, s) = max(Q(mu, s, o) for o in options)
```

- **Planning with Options: Option Model Learning:** Planning with options involves using a model of the environment to simulate the outcomes of different options. An option model predicts the expected reward and resulting state distribution given the completion of an option starting from a particular state. Specifically, for an option o initiated in state s, the option model can be decomposed into:

  - The expected total reward $\mathbb{E}[R_o | S_t = s, o]$ obtained while following the option o.
  - The state transition model $\mathbb{P}(S_{t+k} | S_t = s, o)$, predicting the state S_{t+k} when the option terminates.

Learning the option model can be integrated into model-based planning algorithms such as Dyna-Q. By simulating the outcomes of options using the learned option models, the agent can efficiently plan its high-level strategy.

Incorporating options into both learning and planning processes allows hierarchical reinforcement learning to handle more complex tasks efficiently. Through temporal abstraction and decomposition, options provide a method for managing the complexity inherent in decision-making processes.

9.6 Hierarchical DQN

Hierarchical Deep Q-Network (Hierarchical DQN) is an advanced approach that extends the principles of both Hierarchical Reinforcement Learning (HRL) and Deep Q-Networks (DQN) to address complex tasks via a layered structure. The main concept revolves around decomposing the primary task into subtasks and leveraging the strengths of DQN at different hierarchical levels. This method encapsulates the benefits of temporal abstraction and function approximation, resulting in more efficient learning and execution.

Hierarchical DQN introduces an additional layer of decision-making over traditional DQN by utilizing temporal abstractions modeled as options. Each level in a hierarchical structure has separate Q-networks, which decide upon actions or options depending on the granularity of the hierarchy. The higher-level Q-networks select amongst options, while lower-level Q-networks choose amongst primitive actions or tasks that constitute these options.

The following provides a detailed look into the architecture and operational mechanics of Hierarchical DQN to explain how it functions and why it is effective for complex task learning.

1. Architecture of Hierarchical DQN

The architecture of Hierarchical DQN consists of multiple levels, each associated with its Q-network:

- **High-Level Q-Network:** This network is responsible for selecting options. An option is a temporally extended action or sequence of lower-level actions designed to achieve a subgoal.
- **Low-Level Q-Networks:** These networks operate within the con-

text of a selected option to determine primitive actions based on the current state of the agent.

Each Q-network employs convolutional layers, fully connected layers, and various activation functions akin to traditional DQN setups. However, in a Hierarchical DQN, high-level decisions influence low-level actions, effectively nesting Q-networks and embedding temporal dependencies.

2. Training

Training a Hierarchical DQN involves updating both high-level and low-level Q-networks. The agent experiences the environment, collects transitions, and updates Q-values based on the Bellman equation modified for options. The material below shows the general process:

- **Option Execution and Termination:** The high-level Q-network selects an option, which is then executed by the low-level Q-network until termination conditions are met. Termination conditions might include completing a subtask or achieving a predefined state.

- **Option-Based Bellman Equation:** Transition and reward calculations for updating Q-values need to incorporate the hierarchical nature and extended time-span of options. For an option o selected at state s and terminated at state s' after k steps, the update is:

$$Q(s, o) \leftarrow Q(s, o) + \alpha \left[r + \gamma^k \max_{o'} Q(s', o') - Q(s, o) \right]$$

  where α is the learning rate and γ is the discount factor.

- **Experience Replay:** Transitions are stored in a replay buffer, but in the context of Hierarchical DQN, the replay mechanism must manage experience at different temporal scales. Experiences at both the option level (s, o, r, s') and the action level (s_t, a_t, r_t, s_{t+1}) need to be sampled and replayed.

- **Double Q-Learning:** To mitigate maximization bias and stabilize updates, Hierarchical DQN commonly employs Double Q-Learning strategies, wherein two Q-networks are updated alternatively.

Pseudo-code for Hierarchical DQN Training

```
# Pseudo-code for Hierarchical DQN Training
def hierarchical_dqn_training(environment, high_level_q_network,
        low_level_q_networks, episodes):
    replay_buffer = ReplayBuffer()

    for episode in range(episodes):
        state = environment.reset()

        while not done:
            # High-level decision: select an option
            option = select_option(high_level_q_network, state)

            while not option_terminated(state, option):
                # Low-level decision: select an action
                action = select_action(low_level_q_networks[option], state)
                next_state, reward, done, info = environment.step(action)

                # Store the transition in replay buffer
                replay_buffer.store(state, option, action, reward, next_state, done)

                # Perform low-level Q-Learning update
                low_level_q_networks[option].update(state, action, reward, next_state,
                    done)

                state = next_state

            # Perform high-level Q-Learning update
            high_level_q_network.update(state, option, cumulative_reward, next_state,
                done)
```

3. Efficiency and Stability

One of the significant advantages of using Hierarchical DQN is improved training efficiency due to the temporal abstraction of options. This results in fewer high-level decisions and more significant state offsets, subsequently enabling the network to learn more robust policies. Moreover, it introduces intrinsic stability, as the hierarchical structure inherently structures the exploration process.

4. Applications

Hierarchical DQN shines in environments with profound task hierarchies. Examples include robotic control tasks where multiple layers of decision-making are necessary to navigate, manipulate objects, and achieve complex goals. Another application is in strategic game playing, where the abstraction of high-level strategy and low-level tactics is well-aligned with a hierarchical approach.

5. Challenges

Despite the apparent benefits, Hierarchical DQN faces several challenges. One of the primary difficulties is efficiently selecting and terminating options, which requires fine-tuning to ensure that options are neither too granular nor too coarse. Also, balancing the adaptation of both high-level and low-level policies requires careful coordination to avoid non-stationary dynamics.

Overall, Hierarchical DQN presents a powerful reinforcement learning method that effectively combines hierarchical structures with deep learning techniques, providing a structured way to tackle complex environments requiring multi-stage decision-making.

9.7 Feudal Reinforcement Learning

Feudal Reinforcement Learning (FRL) is an approach that introduces a hierarchical structure into the learning process, explicitly segmenting the control tasks between different levels of the hierarchy. In essence, it mirrors the feudal system, wherein higher-level entities delegate subgoals to subordinate entities, ultimately simplifying the complexity of the task for any single agent.

The central idea behind FRL is to break down the learning problem into more manageable subproblems. This is done through the establishment of multiple layers of management in which high-level managers set subgoals for lower-level managers. Each subgoal encapsulates a specific task portion, thus enforcing a modular structure in the learning process.

Key Concepts and Components

- **Manager and Worker Roles**: In FRL, agents are organized in a hierarchy where higher-level managers are responsible for setting goals or subgoals. Lower-level workers focus on achieving these subgoals. Managers take a broader perspective of the task, while workers handle more immediate actions to fulfill the managers' directives.

- **Subgoal Selection**: Managers must be adept at choosing appropriate subgoals that are attainable and will contribute to the overall objective. This involves learning to predict which subgoals are feasible given the current state and ensuring there is a clear pathway toward the overarching goal.

- **Intra-option Learning**: Workers learn policies to achieve the subgoals set by their managers. This intra-option learning involves standard reinforcement learning techniques but focused on shorter horizons and smaller state-action spaces defined by the subgoals.

- **Credit Assignment to Managers**: Allocating rewards or penalties to higher-level managers based on the performance of their designated subgoals can be challenging. In FRL, mechanisms are employed to ensure that managers are adequately credited for setting effective subgoals, which requires efficient credit assignment methodologies.

Algorithmic Implementation

The implementation of FRL involves setting up a hierarchical controller where high-level agents (managers) and low-level agents (workers) interact. A basic algorithmic structure can be summarized as follows:

Pseudo-code for Hierarchical DQN Training

```
class Manager:
    def __init__(self, state_space, action_space):
        self.state_space = state_space
        self.action_space = action_space
        self.policy = initialize_policy(self.state_space, self.action_space)

    def set_subgoal(self, state):
        subgoal = self.policy(state)
        return subgoal

class Worker:
    def __init__(self, state_space, action_space):
        self.state_space = state_space
        self.action_space = action_space
        self.policy = initialize_policy(self.state_space, self.action_space)

    def reach_subgoal(self, state, subgoal):
        while not is_subgoal_achieved(state, subgoal):
            action = self.policy(state, subgoal)
            state, reward = environment.step(action)
        return state

# Main hierarchical controller
class FeudalController:
    def __init__(self, manager, worker):
        self.manager = manager
        self.worker = worker

    def train(self, episodes):
        for episode in range(episodes):
            state = environment.reset()
            while not environment.is_terminal(state):
                subgoal = self.manager.set_subgoal(state)
                state = self.worker.reach_subgoal(state, subgoal)
                self.manager.update_policy(state, subgoal)
                self.worker.update_policy(state, subgoal)
```

In the given implementation, the 'Manager' class defines the manager agent, which sets subgoals given the current state. The 'Worker' class defines the worker agent, which takes actions to achieve the subgoals. 'FeudalController' orchestrates the hierarchical training process.

Policy and Value Function Updates

Updating the policies and value functions in FRL requires addressing both the intra-option (within the subgoal) learning and the overall hierarchical learning. The Temporal Difference (TD) error can be utilized both at the manager level and the worker level.

The worker's policy update involves a standard Q-learning or policy gradient method:

$$Q(s,a) \leftarrow Q(s,a) + \alpha \left[r + \gamma \max_{a'} Q(s',a') - Q(s,a) \right]$$
$$\pi(a|s) \leftarrow \pi(a|s) + \eta \nabla \log \pi(a|s) \left[r + \gamma V(s') - V(s) \right]$$

For the managers, policy updates take into account the subgoal achievement and the resultant state transitions:

$$Q_{\text{mg}}(s,g) \leftarrow Q_{\text{mg}}(s,g) + \alpha \left[r_g + \gamma \max_{g'} Q_{\text{mg}}(s',g') - Q_{\text{mg}}(s,g) \right]$$
$$\pi_{\text{mg}}(g|s) \leftarrow \pi_{\text{mg}}(g|s) + \eta \nabla \log \pi_{\text{mg}}(g|s) \left[r_g + \gamma V_{\text{mg}}(s') - V_{\text{mg}}(s) \right]$$

Here, Q_{mg} and π_{mg} denote the Q-value and policy function of the manager, respectively; r_g represents rewards associated with subgoal achievement.

Convergence Issues and Solutions

A critical issue in hierarchical RL, including FRL, is ensuring convergence and stability. The hierarchical structure poses challenges such as:

- **Coordination between Levels**: Effective policies require coherent coordination between the manager and worker levels to align their objectives and actions.
- **Delayed Rewards**: Managers might receive delayed feedback based on the performance of lower-level workers, making learning more complex. Techniques like meta-gradients or hierarchical experience replay can help mitigate such issues.

- **Exploration-Exploitation Trade-off**: Both manager and worker levels need to balance exploration of new subgoals/actions and exploitation of known policies, requiring sophisticated exploration strategies.

Using methods such as experience replay buffers for hierarchical levels, hierarchical priors, or attention mechanisms could help in addressing some of these challenges.

Applications and Case Studies

FRL has been successfully applied in various domains, including robotic control, game playing, and autonomous driving. For example, in a robotic arm manipulation task, high-level managers set subgoals such as reaching a particular zone, while workers handle the detailed control commands to achieve precise movements. In game playing, managers might focus on strategic positioning or achieving specific milestones within the game, while workers execute the tactical steps.

Research has shown that FRL can significantly reduce the state-action space complexity and accelerate the learning process, leading to more efficient policy discovery. Nevertheless, carefully designing the hierarchical structure and selecting appropriate subgoals remain crucial for optimal performance.

Successful subgoal settings allow for distinct advantages:
1. Modularization of learning problems.
2. Scalability in complex environments.
3. Enhanced policy transferability.

Feudal Reinforcement Learning represents a critical step toward scalable and efficient learning systems, leveraging hierarchical decomposition to tackle increasingly complex tasks and environments.

9.8 Subgoal Discovery and Identification

The concept of subgoal discovery lies at the core of hierarchical reinforcement learning approaches. Effective subgoal identification can significantly enhance learning efficiency by breaking down complex tasks into simpler subtasks, which are easier to manage and solve. This section delves into various strategies and methodologies for discovering and identifying subgoals in hierarchical reinforcement learning frameworks.

A subgoal is an intermediate state or set of states that, when achieved, contributes significantly towards reaching the overall goal. Identifying these intermediary points allows the agent to focus on achieving smaller, more manageable objectives, which in turn structures the learning process into a more organized and comprehensible sequence. Subgoal discovery can be addressed using both supervised and unsupervised learning techniques.

- **Unsupervised Learning Techniques:**

Unsupervised learning techniques for subgoal discovery generally involve analyzing the state transitions encountered by the agent. One popular unsupervised method is the identification of bottleneck states. Bottleneck states are critical states through which the agent must pass to achieve the overall goal.

Pseudo-code for Hierarchical DQN Training

```
import networkx as nx

# Create a directed graph
G = nx.DiGraph()

# Add edges representing state transitions
G.add_edges_from([('state1', 'state2'), ('state2', 'state3'), ('state3', 'goal'),
                  ('state1', 'state4'), ('state4', 'goal')])

# Find bottleneck states by analyzing betweenness centrality
bottlenecks = nx.betweenness_centrality(G)

print("Bottleneck states:", [state for state, centrality in bottlenecks.items() if centrality
      > 0.5])
```

In the code above, bottleneck states are identified using betweenness centrality, which measures the number of shortest paths that pass through a state. States with high betweenness centrality serve as bridges in the state transition graph and are likely candidates for subgoals.

Another technique involves clustering methods such as k-means or hierarchical clustering. By grouping similar states together based on features or distances, we can identify clusters that represent distinct regions of the state space. Transitions between these clusters frequently indicate potential subgoal states.

Pseudo-code for Hierarchical DQN Training

```
from sklearn.cluster import KMeans
import numpy as np

# Example state features (assuming 2D state for simplicity)
```

```
state_features = np.array([[1, 2], [2, 2], [3, 4], [5, 6], [8, 9]])

# Apply k-means clustering to identify subgoal regions
kmeans = KMeans(n_clusters=2)
kmeans.fit(state_features)

# Find cluster centers (potential subgoals)
subgoals = kmeans.cluster_centers_
print("Identified subgoals:", subgoals)
```

Here, k-means clustering is used to partition the state space into clusters, with the centroids of these clusters representing potential subgoals.

- **Supervised Learning Techniques:**

In supervised learning approaches, subgoals are typically identified through human guidance or expert demonstrations. The agent learns from provided trajectories which are sequences of state-action pairs. By analyzing these trajectories, the agent can identify common intermediate states that frequently occur on the path to the goal.

For instance, inverse reinforcement learning (IRL) can be employed where the goal is to infer the underlying reward structure from expert demonstrations. Once the reward structure is learned, subgoals can be identified as states with high reward values in the inferred reward model.

Pseudo-code for Hierarchical DQN Training

```
import numpy as np

# Example reward model inferred from expert demonstrations
reward_model = np.array([0, 1, 2, 5, 10])

# Identify subgoals as states with high reward values
subgoals = np.where(reward_model >= 5)[0]
print("Identified subgoals:", subgoals)
```

In this example, states with high reward values (above a certain threshold) are considered as subgoals.

- **Combination of Unsupervised and Supervised Approaches:**

Combining both unsupervised and supervised techniques can yield robust subgoal identification methodologies. Hybrid approaches integrate the strengths of both methods where unsupervised techniques can initially propose candidate subgoals which are then refined using supervised feedback from expert demonstrations or human interactions.

To implement a combination approach, one can first apply unsupervised clustering or bottleneck detection methods to propose a set of candidate subgoals. These candidates can then be validated or adjusted with supervised learning techniques using available expert data.

Pseudo-code for Hierarchical DQN Training

```
from sklearn.cluster import KMeans
import numpy as np

# Example state features
state_features = np.array([[1, 2], [2, 2], [3, 4], [5, 6], [8, 9]])

# Apply k-means clustering to identify candidate subgoals
kmeans = KMeans(n_clusters=2)
kmeans.fit(state_features)
candidate_subgoals = kmeans.cluster_centers_

# Example expert data to refine subgoals
expert_data = np.array([[2, 3], [5, 6]])

# Refine subgoals by checking proximity to expert data
refined_subgoals = []
for subgoal in candidate_subgoals:
    if any(np.linalg.norm(subgoal - expert, ord=2) < 2.0 for expert in expert_data):
        refined_subgoals.append(subgoal)

print("Refined subgoals:", refined_subgoals)
```

The code above demonstrates how candidate subgoals proposed through k-means clustering can be refined by checking their proximity to states in expert data. Subgoals within a certain distance threshold from expert states are selected, effectively combining unsupervised discovery with supervised validation.

Ensuring the quality and relevance of identified subgoals is crucial. Subgoals should simplify the problem-solving process without introducing unnecessary complexity. The effectiveness of subgoal discovery lies in its ability to transform the original task into a hierarchy of simpler tasks, leading to more efficient learning and planning.

Understanding the intricacies of subgoal discovery and identification is paramount for designing robust hierarchical reinforcement learning systems. This approach not only improves the learning efficiency of agents but also enhances their ability to generalize and solve complex, real-world problems.

9.9 Hierarchical Actor-Critic Methods

Hierarchical Actor-Critic (HAC) methods represent a critical advancement in the field of Hierarchical Reinforcement Learning (HRL), integrating the hierarchical decomposition of tasks with the actor-critic framework. This section elucidates the foundational concepts, mechanisms, and implications of HAC, delving into the architecture, learning dynamics, and practical applications.

In HAC, an agent learns a hierarchy of policies at multiple levels. Each policy at a higher level generates subgoals for the policy at the next lower level. These higher-level policies operate over a broader temporal abstraction, while the lower-level policies focus on achieving these subgoals within shorter time frames. The actor-critic framework enhances this hierarchical structure by aiding in stable and efficient learning through two primary components: the actor (policy) and the critic (value function).

The actor in HAC is responsible for selecting actions or subgoals. At each level of the hierarchy, the actor uses its policy to determine the next step based on the current state or observation. The critic evaluates the action taken by providing feedback in the form of value functions, which estimate the expected return. These value functions play a pivotal role in updating the policies through gradient-based methods.

The core of HAC is the iterative learning process, which follows these steps:

- Each level in the hierarchy starts with an initial policy and a corresponding value function.
- At every time step, the highest level policy determines a subgoal.
- The policy at the next lower level attempts to achieve this subgoal. If it fails within a predefined number of steps or time span, the higher-level policy intervenes with a new subgoal.
- The critic at each level evaluates the success of the action or subgoal achievement, updating the value function based on the observed rewards and temporal differences.
- Policies are updated using the gradient of the expected return estimated by the critic.

Formally, given a hierarchical setup with N levels, each containing an actor π_i and a critic V_i where i ranges from 1 to N, we describe the process as follows. The policy π_i at level i selects a subgoal g_{t+1}^i based on the current state s_t and the immediate past state s_{t-1}. The subgoal g_{t+1}^i serves as the target for the policy π_{i-1} at level $i-1$.

The critics at each level estimate the value function

$$V_i(s) = \mathbb{E}\left[r_t + \gamma \cdot V_i(s_{t+1}) \mid s_t, \pi_i\right],$$

where r_t is the reward, γ is the discount factor, and s_t and s_{t+1} are the states before and after the action or subgoal execution.

The update rule for the critic employs the Temporal Difference (TD) error:

$$\delta_t^i = r_t + \gamma \cdot V_i(s_{t+1}) - V_i(s_t).$$

The critic updates the value function approximation iteratively using:

$$V_i(s_t) \leftarrow V_i(s_t) + \alpha \cdot \delta_t^i,$$

where α is the learning rate.

The actor updates the policy parameters θ_i in the direction suggested by the critic's feedback, using policy gradient methods such as:

$$\nabla_{\theta_i} J(\pi_i) = \mathbb{E}\left[\delta_t^i \cdot \nabla_{\theta_i} \log \pi_i(g_t \mid s_t)\right].$$

A distinctive feature in HAC is the hierarchical structure of rewards. At each level, the return signal includes both intrinsic rewards related to subgoal achievement and extrinsic rewards provided by the environment. The intrinsic reward r_{int} encourages the lower-level policies to efficiently achieve subgoals, whereas the extrinsic reward r_{ext} guides the higher-level policies towards achieving the overall task objectives.

For example, consider a hierarchical policy with three levels applied to a robotic navigation task. The top-level policy might set a subgoal of reaching a specific room, the middle-level policy sets subgoals to navigate to waypoints leading to the room, and the bottom-level policy directly controls the robot's motors to follow a path segment. The intrinsic rewards would correspond to reaching waypoints and the extrinsic reward to successfully navigating to the target room.

RL implementations in hierarchical settings benefit significantly from the actor-critic architecture, as it helps in dealing with sparse rewards and accelerates convergence through distributed learning on multiple temporal scales.

To illustrate, a simplified implementation outline of hierarchical actor-critic in a pseudo-code format is shown below:

Pseudo-code for Hierarchical DQN Training

```
Initialize policy  _i and value function V_i for each level i
for each episode do
    s_0 <- initial state
    for t = 0 to MaxSteps do
        for i = N downto 1 do
            g_{t+1}^i <-  _i(s_t)
            if goal or subgoal g_{t+1}^i achieved:
                R_i <- calculate rewards (intrinsic and extrinsic)
                Update V_i using TD error  _t^i
                Update  _i using policy gradients
                break if task completed
end for
end for
```

The output might resemble:

```
Episode: 1, Step: 50, Subgoal Achieved: True, Reward: 10.0
Episode: 1, Step: 100, Task Completed: True, Total Reward: 100.0
```

Hierarchical Actor-Critic methods enhance learning efficiency and scalability by enabling agents to decompose complex tasks into manageable subtasks and address them at appropriate temporal abstractions. The harmonic integration of hierarchical structures with actor-critic mechanisms provides a robust framework, particularly advantageous in environments with sparse and delayed rewards.

9.10 Applications and Case Studies of Hierarchical Reinforcement Learning

Hierarchical Reinforcement Learning (HRL) has been extensively applied in various domains due to its ability to handle complex tasks by decomposing them into simpler subtasks. This section explores several key applications and presents detailed case studies to illustrate the effectiveness of HRL in real-world scenarios.

1. Robotic Manipulation: HRL has demonstrated significant advancements in the realm of robotic manipulation. Robots often need to perform complex tasks that involve multiple steps and varying levels of precision. By leveraging HRL, these tasks can be segmented into hierarchical structures where high-level policies govern the selection and sequencing of subgoals, while low-level controllers execute detailed actions.

In a case study, a robotic arm was trained to assemble a toy using HRL. The high-level policy was responsible for breaking down the assembly process into subtasks such as picking up parts, aligning them, and fastening them together. Each subtask was further managed by specialized policies fine-tuned for precise control tasks.

Pseudo-code for Hierarchical DQN Training

```
def high_level_policy(state):
    if state == 'START':
        return pick_part()
    elif state == 'PART_PICKED':
        return align_part()
    elif state == 'PART_ALIGNED':
        return fasten_part()
    elif state == 'ASSEMBLY_COMPLETE':
        return halt()

def low_level_policy(state, subtask):
    if subtask == 'pick_part':
        # Implement detailed control for picking
    elif subtask == 'align_part':
        # Implement detailed control for aligning
    elif subtask == 'fasten_part':
        # Implement detailed control for fastening
```

2. Autonomous Driving: HRL has been crucial in developing autonomous driving systems, where driving a vehicle requires mastering a multitude of driving skills, each appropriate to different driving scenarios. For instance, a hierarchical model can have a top-level policy determining high-level goals like following a route, while lower-level policies handle specific tasks like lane keeping, obstacle avoidance, and parking.

In a specific case study, an autonomous driving agent was structured into hierarchies. The top-level policy planned the route, mid-level policies managed segment-specific tasks such as highway driving or city driving, and the low-level policies executed highly detailed controls for steering, acceleration, and braking.

Pseudo-code for Hierarchical DQN Training

```
def route_planner(state):
    if state == 'HIGHWAY_ENTRY':
        return 'highway_driving'
    elif state == 'CITY_ENTRY':
        return 'city_driving'
    elif state == 'PARKING_SPOT_DETECTED':
```

```
        return 'parking'

def driving_policy(state, subtask):
    if subtask == 'highway_driving':
        # Implement highway driving controls
    elif subtask == 'city_driving':
        # Implement city driving controls
    elif subtask == 'parking':
        # Implement parking controls
```

3. Natural Language Processing (NLP): HRL techniques have found applications in Natural Language Processing (NLP), specifically in tasks involving ongoing interactions and decisions, such as dialogue systems and machine translation. By decomposing dialogue management into hierarchical levels, chatbots can better manage conversations, switch contexts, and provide more accurate responses.

In a case study on dialogue systems for customer support, HRL helped in structuring the conversation into high-level policies managing topic shifts and context tracking, while low-level policies focused on generating coherent and contextually appropriate responses.

Pseudo-code for Hierarchical DQN Training

```
def dialogue_manager(state):
    if state == 'INITIAL_GREETING':
        return handle_greeting()
    elif state == 'PROCESS_REQUEST':
        return process_user_request()
    elif state == 'END_CONVERSATION':
        return end_conversation()

def response_policy(state, subtask):
    if subtask == 'handle_greeting':
        # Generate greeting response
    elif subtask == 'process_user_request':
        # Generate response to user request
    elif subtask == 'end_conversation':
        # Generate conversation conclusion
```

4. Gameplay and Strategy Games: HRL has shown its prowess in mastering complex games and strategy applications. Games typically involve a series of decisions and subgoals that HRL can effectively decompose. This allows an agent to develop strategies at multiple levels, from general game plans to specific moves.

In a case study involving the game of StarCraft, HRL was used to break down the game into high-level strategies such as resource gathering, base building, and combat. Each high-level strategy was further decomposed into specific tasks carried out by individual RL agents.

Pseudo-code for Hierarchical DQN Training

```
def strategy_selector(state):
    if state == 'EARLY_GAME':
        return 'resource_gathering'
    elif state == 'MID_GAME':
        return 'base_building'
    elif state == 'LATE_GAME':
        return 'combat'

def task_policy(state, subtask):
    if subtask == 'resource_gathering':
        # Implement resource gathering actions
    elif subtask == 'base_building':
        # Implement base building actions
    elif subtask == 'combat':
        # Implement combat actions
```

These case studies exemplify the practical utility of HRL in diverse fields. By employing a structured approach to problem-solving, HRL can significantly enhance the performance and efficiency of learning agents, enabling them to tackle complex tasks that would otherwise be infeasible.

9.11 Challenges and Future Directions in Hierarchical RL

Hierarchical Reinforcement Learning (HRL) introduces additional challenges alongside its numerous advantages. Understanding these challenges is crucial for advancing HRL methodologies and applications. Here, we explore key challenges currently faced by HRL and discuss possible future directions aimed at addressing these obstacles to foster the development of more robust, efficient, and scalable HRL systems.

- One significant challenge in HRL arises from the need to determine appropriate hierarchies and decompositions for different tasks. Effective task decomposition is pivotal as it influences the overall performance and learning efficiency. Identifying optimal subgoals and structuring subtasks are non-trivial problems that often require domain-specific knowledge or insightful heuristics. However, automating this process remains an open research area. An emerging direction to address this is leveraging techniques from unsupervised learning to discover subgoals and hierarchies that are inherently beneficial for the RL agent.
- Another challenge encompasses the management of temporal abstraction levels within the Hierarchical Framework. Temporal

abstraction permits actions to be composed over varying time scales through the implementation of options. However, deciding the appropriate abstraction levels and durations of options dynamically is complex. The potential solution lies in adaptive frameworks that learn and adjust these temporal hierarchies during the training phase based on the agent's performance and environmental feedback.

- Scalability and computational complexity remain pressing issues in HRL. With increased hierarchies, the state and action spaces grow, leading to elevated demands on memory and processing resources. Strategies to mitigate this concern involve innovative function approximation methods, particularly deep learning architectures, enabling efficient representation of high-dimensional spaces. Additionally, transfer learning can facilitate reusing previously acquired hierarchical structures across different tasks, reducing the computational burden.

- Multi-goal environments introduce further complexity as the agent must manage and prioritize among multiple subgoals effectively. HRL frameworks need to incorporate robust mechanisms to handle goal interference and alignment to ensure coherent policy formation. Potential approaches to this challenge involve using meta-learning techniques to train agents in a manner that they can generalize and adapt to diverse goal orientations quickly.

- The evaluation and benchmarking of HRL methods present another layer of difficulty. Standardizing metrics and creating unified benchmarks across diverse problem domains is essential for objectively assessing the performance of HRL algorithms. Shared benchmark tasks and environments can foster comparative studies and lead to collective advancements in the field.

- Exploration-exploitation trade-offs entail additional challenges in HRL. Due to hierarchical structures, exploration becomes multilayered, wherein both high-level and low-level policies must balance exploration and exploitation optimally. Techniques such as intrinsic motivation, curiosity-driven learning, and mixed exploration strategies are promising avenues to enhance efficiency in hierarchical exploration.

- Human-in-the-loop approaches introduce prospects for advancing HRL by incorporating human expertise and feedback into the learning process. This interactive dimension can refine hierarchical representations and expedite the learning of complex tasks. Future research could deepen into fine-tuning the balance between autonomous learning and human guidance.

- Lastly, real-world applicability demands robust HRL algorithms capable of generalizing across variable and dynamic conditions. Real-world applications, such as robotics and autonomous systems, require HRL frameworks to be resilient and adaptable. This necessity drives the focus towards developing adaptive and self-improving HRL methods that maintain performance under environmental variations.

By addressing these challenges, HRL research can pave the way towards creating more intelligent, efficient, and versatile AI systems. Emphasizing interdisciplinary approaches and integrating advances from related fields of machine learning and artificial intelligence will be instrumental in achieving these goals.

Chapter 10

Applications of Reinforcement Learning

Applications of Reinforcement Learning span various industries, showcasing its versatility and impact. This chapter examines RL's role in robotics, game playing, recommendation systems, finance, healthcare, autonomous vehicles, energy management, natural language processing, and industrial automation. By presenting practical examples and case studies, the chapter highlights both current implementations and future trends, illustrating how RL is transforming diverse fields through innovative solutions.

10.1 Introduction to Applications of Reinforcement Learning

Reinforcement Learning (RL) has emerged as a powerful methodology in the field of Artificial Intelligence (AI) for developing agents that can learn optimal behaviors through interactions with their environment. Unlike supervised learning, where the model learns from labeled examples supplied by a knowledgeable external supervisor, or unsupervised learning, where the model seeks to uncover hidden patterns in unlabeled data, RL is unique in its reliance on a reward system to achieve desired behaviors. This paradigm shift opens up a vast array of applications across various domains, each benefiting from RL's ability to solve complex decision-making problems.

- **Robust Problem-Solving Capabilities:** RL's framework, characterized by the interaction between an agent and the environment, effectively addresses dynamic and uncertain decision-making landscapes. The agent learns to map situations to actions to maximize cumulative rewards, making RL suitable for applications where explicit programming of actions is impractical or impossible. This capability enables RL to excel in areas like robotics, where machines must adapt to dynamic environments, and game-playing, where strategies evolve over time through competition.

- **Robotics:** In robotics, RL facilitates the development of control policies that enable robots to perform tasks ranging from simple repetitive actions to complex sequences of operations. Sophisticated algorithms like Deep Q-Learning and Policy Gradient methods have proven effective in training robots for navigation, manipulation, and coordination tasks in real-world scenarios. RL allows robotic systems to improve their performance through trial and error, leveraging sensory feedback to adapt to new and unforeseen circumstances.

- **Game Playing:** RL has demonstrated remarkable success in the domain of game playing, often equipping AI agents with superhuman capabilities. Notable examples include AlphaGo, developed by DeepMind, which utilizes a combination of RL and Monte Carlo Tree Search (MCTS) to achieve proficiency in the game of Go. These advancements in game playing not only showcase RL's potential in strategic planning and real-time decision making but also contribute to improvements in other fields through transfer of knowledge and algorithms.

- **Recommendation Systems:** Recommendation systems are another domain where RL is extensively applied. Traditional recommendation models rely heavily on static algorithms that do not adapt to changing user preferences or behaviors. RL addresses this limitation by dynamically adjusting recommendations based on continual feedback from user interactions. Techniques like multi-armed bandits and collaborative filtering combined with RL algorithms enhance the personalization and relevance of recommendations, leading to improved user satisfaction and engagement.

- **Finance and Trading:** The finance sector has increasingly adopted RL to navigate the complexities of trading and investment strategies. RL algorithms are deployed to manage portfolios, execute trades, and optimize financial transactions by learning from historical market data and real-time events. The ability of RL to process vast amounts of data and identify profitable patterns makes it invaluable in high-frequency trading environments and automated investment management systems.

- **Healthcare and Medicine:** In healthcare, RL is revolutionizing personalized medicine and treatment planning. RL-driven models assist in optimizing therapeutic strategies for individual patients by considering factors such as genetic information, medical history, and treatment responses. In critical care, RL aids in the management of dosing regimens for medications, improving outcomes in intensive care units (ICUs). Additionally, RL is utilized in the design of adaptive clinical trials, where the treatment assignments evolve based on patient responses, thus expediting the identification of effective therapies.

- **Autonomous Vehicles:** Autonomous vehicles (AVs) represent a significant area of RL application, where the goal is to enable vehicles to navigate safely and efficiently without human intervention. RL algorithms are employed to develop policies for driving in diverse traffic conditions, handling obstacles, and optimizing routes. The continuous feedback loop inherent in RL allows AVs to learn from each journey, progressively enhancing their decision-making capabilities and safety measures.

- **Energy Management:** The field of energy management benefits from RL by optimizing the allocation and consumption of resources. RL approaches are utilized to manage smart grids, control heating, ventilation, and air conditioning (HVAC) systems, and integrate renewable energy sources. By learning from consumption patterns and environmental conditions, RL helps in reducing energy waste, lowering costs, and promoting sustainable practices.

- **Natural Language Processing and Dialog Systems:** In natural language processing (NLP), RL contributes to the development of dialog systems that interact with humans in a natural and intuitive manner. RL models, such as those used in chatbots and virtual assistants, learn to generate appropriate responses by maximizing dialogue coherence and user satisfaction. These systems adapt over time, becoming more adept at understanding and responding to diverse user queries and interactions.

- **Industrial Automation:** Industrial automation leverages RL to enhance the efficiency and productivity of manufacturing processes. RL-driven systems optimize the operation of machinery, minimize downtime, and improve the quality control processes. This is achieved through continuous monitoring and adaptation to changes in the production environment, leading to more flexible and resilient industrial automation solutions.

The breadth of RL applications is a testament to its versatility and transformative potential. Each application discussed leverages the foundational principles of RL to address domain-specific challenges, illustrating how RL continues to push the boundaries of what intelligent systems can achieve. As research and innovation in RL progress, we can anticipate even broader and more impactful applications, reshaping industries and enhancing the capabilities of AI systems.

10.2 Reinforcement Learning in Robotics

Reinforcement Learning (RL) has ushered in a transformative epoch in the field of robotics, offering robust methodologies for dynamic decision-making and complex motion planning. Autonomous robotic systems leverage RL to adapt to evolving environments and execute tasks with minimal human intervention. This section intricately explores how RL principles are implemented in both simulated and real-world robotic environments, addressing algorithmic frameworks, task-specific applications, and contemporary challenges.

To elucidate RL's profound influence on robotics, consider the *Markov Decision Process (MDP)*, which provides a formalism that models the environment with its states, actions, rewards, and transition probabilities. RL agents learn optimal policies by interacting with the environment through trial and error, receiving feedback in the form of rewards.

State (S)	Action (A)	Reward (R)
Robot's pose (e.g., position and orientation)	Movement commands (e.g., forward, rotate)	Task-specific feedback (e.g., reaching a target)

Task-specific RL applications in robotics include autonomous navigation, manipulation, and interaction. For instance, in autonomous navigation, robots must move efficiently from a starting position to a designated target while avoiding obstacles. A widely used RL algorithm for this is *Deep Q-Network (DQN)*, which approximates the optimal action-value function using deep neural networks.

Pseudo-code for Hierarchical DQN Training

```
import numpy as np
import tensorflow as tf
from tensorflow.keras import layers

class DQN:
    def __init__(self, state_dim, action_dim):
        self.state_dim = state_dim
        self.action_dim = action_dim
        self.model = self.create_model()

    def create_model(self):
        model = tf.keras.Sequential()
        model.add(layers.Dense(24, input_dim=self.state_dim, activation='relu'))
        model.add(layers.Dense(24, activation='relu'))
        model.add(layers.Dense(self.action_dim, activation='linear'))
        model.compile(optimizer='adam', loss='mse')
        return model

    def update_model(self, state, target):
        self.model.fit(state, target, epochs=1, verbose=0)

    def predict(self, state):
        return self.model.predict(state)

# Initialize DQN for a robot with a state space of size 4 and action space of size 2
dqn = DQN(state_dim=4, action_dim=2)
```

In robotic manipulation tasks, such as object grasping, the complexity of high-dimensional continuous action spaces is often tackled using *Proximal Policy Optimization (PPO)*. This algorithm is particularly advantageous due to its stable training and capacity to manage continuous controls.

Pseudo-code for Hierarchical DQN Training

```
import torch
import torch.nn as nn
import torch.optim as optim

class ActorCritic(nn.Module):
    def __init__(self, input_dim, action_dim):
        super(ActorCritic, self).__init__()
        self.fc1 = nn.Linear(input_dim, 128)
        self.fc_actor = nn.Linear(128, action_dim)
        self.fc_critic = nn.Linear(128, 1)

    def forward(self, x):
        x = torch.relu(self.fc1(x))
        action_probs = torch.softmax(self.fc_actor(x), dim=-1)
        value = self.fc_critic(x)
        return action_probs, value
```

```
# Example usage in a training loop
model = ActorCritic(input_dim=24, action_dim=4)
optimizer = optim.Adam(model.parameters(), lr=1e-3)
```

RL applications in multi-agent systems present another significant avenue, where multiple robots collaborate to accomplish tasks more efficiently than a single agent could independently. The coordination among multiple agents can be tackled using *Multi-Agent Reinforcement Learning (MARL)*, facilitating complex tasks such as cooperative material handling.

Pseudo-code for Hierarchical DQN Training

```
class MARLAgent:
    def __init__(self, id, state_dim, action_dim):
        self.id = id
        self.model = DQN(state_dim, action_dim)
    # Additional agent-specific functions

agents = [MARLAgent(i, state_dim=4, action_dim=2) for i in range(2)]

# Joint action and state space management for multiple agents
def joint_action_policy(states):
    actions = [agent.model.predict(state) for agent, state in zip(agents, states)]
    return actions
```

Energy efficiency and safety are pivotal components of RL in robotics, necessitating the integration of constraints within the learning framework. Constrained reinforcement learning algorithms ensure safe operations by adhering to predefined safety standards and optimizing energy consumption.

```
Energy efficiency achieved through optimized path planning.
Safety constraints enforced during obstacle avoidance simulations.
```

Besides these applications, significant research is directed towards leveraging RL for human-robot interaction (HRI), where robots assist or co-work with humans. This interaction requires robots to understand and predict human actions, preferences, and intentions, promoting an intuitive and seamless collaboration.

RL's potential is continuously expanded through advancements in computational resources, algorithms, and sensory technologies. The ongoing progress in RL algorithms and real-world deployments signifies promising future capabilities, driving further integration of sophisticated robotic systems in diverse sectors.

Robotics researchers and practitioners focus on bridging the gap between simulated environments and real-world applications. This includes addressing challenges such as model robustness, transfer learning, and domain adaptation to ensure that RL-trained models in simulations perform effectively in physical scenarios.

Through meticulous algorithmic designs, task-specific implementations, and collaborative approaches, reinforcement learning has substantially enhanced robotics' ability to operate autonomously and adaptively, underscoring its significance in the contemporary landscape.

10.3 Reinforcement Learning for Game Playing

Reinforcement Learning (RL) has shown exceptional promise and success in the domain of game playing, evidencing its capabilities through high-profile achievements and widespread applications. Games serve as an excellent testbed for RL algorithms owing to their well-defined rules, clear objectives, and often complex decision-making processes.

RL's breakthrough in game playing began in the late 20th century, but it saw a substantial leap with the advent of deep learning, leading to the development of techniques such as Deep Q-Networks (DQNs) and AlphaGo. These methodologies harness large-scale neural networks coupled with RL strategies to master games with superhuman proficiency.

A quintessential example of RL's prowess is the use of Deep Q-Networks (DQN) to play Atari 2600 games. Introduced by Mnih et al. in 2015, DQN blends Q-Learning with deep neural networks, enabling the algorithm to learn policies directly from high-dimensional sensory inputs, such as raw pixel data. The model is trained to maximize cumulative rewards by approximating the Q-function, which predicts the expected utility of taking an action in a particular state and following a policy thereafter.

Pseudo-code for Hierarchical DQN Training

```
import gym
import numpy as np
from stable_baselines3 import DQN

# Create the environment
env = gym.make("Breakout-v0")

# Instantiate the agent
model = DQN("CnnPolicy", env, verbose=1)
```

```
# Train the model
model.learn(total_timesteps=100000)

# Save the model
model.save("dqn_breakout")
```

The code snippet above demonstrates how to set up and train a DQN on the Atari Breakout environment using the stable_baselines3 library, a widely used framework for RL research and application.

Another groundbreaking innovation is AlphaGo, developed by DeepMind, which combined Monte Carlo Tree Search (MCTS) with deep neural networks to achieve remarkable success in the game of Go. Unlike classical game-solving algorithms, AlphaGo leverages RL to evaluate board positions and policies, enabling it to defeat human world champions. The architecture of AlphaGo includes a policy network, which outputs move probabilities, and a value network, which evaluates board positions.

The underlying principle of AlphaGo involves the creation of a search tree from the current state and simulation of many possible future states to select the optimal move. Through RL, the model learns to improve its policies and value functions by playing numerous games against itself, a technique known as self-play.

Pseudo-code for Hierarchical DQN Training

```
class MCTSNode:
    def __init__(self, state):
        self.state = state
        self.wins = 0
        self.visits = 0
        self.children = []

    def select_child(self):
        return max(self.children, key=lambda node: node.wins / node.visits + np.sqrt(2
            * np.log(self.visits) / node.visits))

    def expand(self, action):
        new_state = self.state.take_action(action)
        child_node = MCTSNode(new_state)
        self.children.append(child_node)
        return child_node

    def update_stats(self, result):
        self.visits += 1
        self.wins += result
```

The pseudo-code above outlines a basic Monte Carlo Tree Search (MCTS) structure. In an actual implementation, additional elements such as rollout policies and value prediction would be integrated to enhance performance and learning efficiency.

In addition to classic board games, RL has also been applied to modern real-time strategy (RTS) games and multiplayer online battle arenas (MOBAs). These games pose significant challenges due to their dynamic environments, large action spaces, and long-term strategies. One notable project is OpenAI Five, which demonstrated state-of-the-art performance in Dota 2. OpenAI Five comprises multiple neural networks operating in tandem, each tasked with controlling a different hero character in the game. The system continually updates its strategies based on observed outcomes and opponent behavior, showcasing immense adaptability and strategic depth.

Pseudo-code for Hierarchical DQN Training

```
class RTSAgent:
    def __init__(self, model):
        self.model = model

    def select_action(self, state):
        probabilities = self.model.predict(state)
        action = np.random.choice(len(probabilities), p=probabilities)
        return action

    def train(self, experiences):
        states, actions, rewards, next_states, dones = zip(*experiences)
        self.model.update(states, actions, rewards, next_states, dones)
```

The snippet above provides a high-level structure for an RL agent tailored to an RTS game. The agent leans on a model to predict action probabilities and refines its policy based on experience tuples gathered during gameplay.

Game theory concepts further amplify RL's impact on competitive environments. Algorithms such as minimax and Nash equilibrium inform decision-making processes where the outcome hinges on the concurrent strategies of multiple agents. These principles are integral to refining tactics in adversarial games.

Pseudo-code for Hierarchical DQN Training

```
def minimax(node, depth, maximizingPlayer):
    if depth == 0 or node.is_terminal():
        return node.evaluate()

    if maximizingPlayer:
        maxEval = float('-inf')
        for child in node.get_children():
            eval = minimax(child, depth-1, False)
            maxEval = max(maxEval, eval)
        return maxEval
    else:
        minEval = float('inf')
        for child in node.get_children():
            eval = minimax(child, depth-1, True)
```

```
        minEval = min(minEval, eval)
    return minEval
```

The code above demonstrates a rudimentary implementation of the Minimax algorithm, which is pivotal in deriving optimal strategies in two-player zero-sum games.

RL in game playing continues to evolve, pushing the boundaries of what AI can achieve. This progression is not only charting new frontiers in gaming but also contributing valuable insights and methodologies applicable to broader real-world problems.

10.4 Recommendation Systems

Recommendation systems are a prime application of reinforcement learning (RL), significantly impacting e-commerce, streaming services, and social media platforms. These systems aim to predict user preferences and suggest items that are likely to be of interest, thereby enhancing user engagement and satisfaction. Traditional recommendation algorithms employ collaborative filtering, content-based filtering, or hybrid approaches. However, RL has introduced advanced methodologies to dynamically adapt recommendations based on user interactions, providing personalized experiences.

In a recommendation system, the primary goal is to maximize a long-term reward, which often corresponds to metrics such as user click-through rate, retention, or purchase rate. The system continuously interacts with users, using these interactions to refine and improve its recommendations. This interactive nature of recommendation systems aligns seamlessly with the framework of RL, making it a powerful tool in this domain.

The architecture of an RL-based recommendation system generally involves several components: an environment, an agent, a state space, an action space, and a reward function. Here, the environment consists of users and items, the agent is the recommendation algorithm, the state space includes user profiles and item features, the action space comprises the set of items to recommend, and the reward function evaluates the user's feedback on the recommendation.

Consider a typical scenario where an RL-based recommendation system is deployed on an e-commerce platform. The algorithm recommends a set of products to a user based on their browsing history, past purchases, and demographic information. Upon presenting these recommendations, the system captures the user's actions, such as clicks, purchases, or ignoring the recommendations. These actions then inform the reward function, which adjusts the model to improve future recommendations.

Pseudo-code for Hierarchical DQN Training

```
import numpy as np
import random

class RecommendationEnv:
    def __init__(self, user_profiles, item_features):
        self.user_profiles = user_profiles
        self.item_features = item_features
        self.current_user = None

    def reset(self):
        self.current_user = random.choice(self.user_profiles)
        return self.current_user

    def step(self, recommended_item):
        reward = self._get_reward(recommended_item)
        self.current_user = random.choice(self.user_profiles)
        return self.current_user, reward

    def _get_reward(self, recommended_item):
        # Simulate user response; 1 for click, 0 for no click
        return np.dot(self.current_user, self.item_features[recommended_item]) > 0.5

class RecommenderAgent:
    def __init__(self, num_items):
        self.num_items = num_items
        self.q_table = np.zeros(num_items)

    def select_action(self, state):
        return np.argmax(self.q_table + np.random.randn(1, self.num_items) / (np.
            arange(self.num_items) + 1))

    def update_q_values(self, action, reward, alpha=0.1, gamma=0.9):
        self.q_table[action] += alpha * (reward + gamma * np.max(self.q_table) - self.
            q_table[action])

# User profiles and item features are represented as vectors
user_profiles = np.array([[0.1, 0.3], [0.2, 0.6], [0.4, 0.9]])
item_features = np.array([[0.2, 0.5], [0.3, 0.7], [0.5, 0.8]])

env = RecommendationEnv(user_profiles, item_features)
agent = RecommenderAgent(num_items=3)

for episode in range(1000):
    state = env.reset()
    action = agent.select_action(state)
    new_state, reward = env.step(action)
    agent.update_q_values(action, reward)
```

In the above example, the 'RecommendationEnv' class models the environment with user profiles and item features. The 'Recommender-

Agent' class represents the agent using a Q-learning algorithm to update its value estimates. During each episode, the agent selects an action (i.e., item to recommend), observes the reward, and updates its Q-values accordingly. The reward function in this simplified example binary-encodes user feedback, but in practice, it could be more complex, encompassing multiple aspects of user interaction.

Advanced RL techniques for recommendation systems include deep Q-networks (DQNs), policy gradient methods, and actor-critic architectures. These approaches can handle larger state and action spaces, making them suitable for systems with millions of users and items. Additionally, techniques like exploration-exploitation balance, where the system decides between exploring new recommendations or exploiting known preferences, are critical in maintaining an effective recommendation strategy.

To elucidate, consider a deep reinforcement learning model deployed in a video streaming service. The system must recommend a series of movies or TV shows to keep the user engaged. The state might include the user's watch history, ratings, and temporal information. The action space is a vast library of available content, and the reward could be based on the user's subsequent viewing time or explicit ratings.

Training a DQN for such a system involves defining a neural network to approximate the Q-value function. The network takes the state as input and outputs Q-values for each possible action. By using experiences collected during interactions with the users, the network learns to predict the expected rewards for recommending specific items.

Pseudo-code for Hierarchical DQN Training

```
import torch
import torch.nn as nn
import torch.optim as optim

class DQN(nn.Module):
    def __init__(self, input_dim, output_dim):
        super(DQN, self).__init__()
        self.fc1 = nn.Linear(input_dim, 128)
        self.fc2 = nn.Linear(128, 256)
        self.fc3 = nn.Linear(256, output_dim)

    def forward(self, x):
        x = torch.relu(self.fc1(x))
        x = torch.relu(self.fc2(x))
        x = self.fc3(x)
        return x

def train_dqn(dqn, optimizer, state, action, reward, next_state, done, gamma=0.99):
    q_values = dqn(state)
    next_q_values = dqn(next_state).detach()
    q_value = q_values.gather(1, action.unsqueeze(1)).squeeze(1)
```

```
    next_q_value = next_q_values.max(1)[0]
    target = reward + (1 - done) * gamma * next_q_value

    loss = nn.MSELoss()(q_value, target)
    optimizer.zero_grad()
    loss.backward()
    optimizer.step()

# Example DQN training loop
dqn = DQN(input_dim=10, output_dim=3)
optimizer = optim.Adam(dqn.parameters())
for epoch in range(1000):
    state = torch.randn(1, 10) # Example state
    action = torch.tensor([1]) # Example action
    reward = torch.tensor([1.0]) # Example reward
    next_state = torch.randn(1, 10) # Example next state
    done = torch.tensor([0]) # Example done signal

    train_dqn(dqn, optimizer, state, action, reward, next_state, done)
```

Real-world applications of RL-based recommendation systems have demonstrated significant improvements over traditional methods. For instance, personalized product recommendations on e-commerce websites, curated content on streaming platforms, and tailored social media feeds all benefit from RL strategies.

Facebook and YouTube are examples where RL algorithms dynamically adjust recommendations to cater to user preferences. By integrating RL into their recommendation engines, these platforms optimize for long-term user engagement, balancing immediate clicks with sustained interaction over time.

Reinforcement learning's adaptability and scalability make it particularly suited for recommendation systems, where user preferences evolve and the available catalogue of items grows continuously. The ability of RL algorithms to learn from ongoing interactions and improve recommendations iteratively ensures an ever-improving user experience.

10.5 Finance and Trading

Reinforcement learning (RL) has emerged as a powerful tool in the domain of finance and trading. This section explores its application in various financial strategies, portfolio management, and algorithmic trading, offering practical insight into its recent advancements and implementations. The objective is to understand how RL can optimize decision-making processes to maximize returns while managing risks.

In the financial industry, decision-makers continuously adapt to a dynamic and often unpredictable market environment. Reinforcement learning models, with their ability to learn from interactions and adapt over time, provide a promising approach to tackle these challenges.

Algorithmic Trading

Algorithmic trading involves using computer algorithms to automate trading strategies. These algorithms can execute trades at speeds and frequencies that are impossible for a human trader. RL algorithms like Q-learning, Deep Q-Networks (DQN), and Proximal Policy Optimization (PPO) are often employed to develop and refine these trading strategies.

Consider a scenario where an RL agent must decide whether to buy, hold, or sell a stock. The state space consists of various market indicators and historical price data. The action space typically includes actions like *buy*, *sell*, or *hold*. The goal is to maximize the agent's cumulative return over time.

Pseudo-code for Hierarchical DQN Training

```
import gym
import numpy as np
import tensorflow as tf
from tensorflow.keras.models import Sequential
from tensorflow.keras.layers import Dense

env = gym.make('StockTrading-v0')
state_size = env.observation_space.shape[0]
action_size = env.action_space.n

model = Sequential()
model.add(Dense(24, input_dim=state_size, activation='relu'))
model.add(Dense(24, activation='relu'))
model.add(Dense(action_size, activation='linear'))
model.compile(loss='mse', optimizer=tf.optimizers.Adam(0.001))

def train_dqn(episodes):
    for e in range(episodes):
        state = env.reset()
        state = np.reshape(state, [1, state_size])
        for time in range(500):
            action = np.argmax(model.predict(state))
            next_state, reward, done, _ = env.step(action)
            next_state = np.reshape(next_state, [1, state_size])
            model.fit(state, target, epochs=1, verbose=0)
            state = next_state
            if done:
                break

train_dqn(1000)
```

The above code demonstrates the framework of a DQN agent applied to a stock trading environment. The model is trained over several episodes, learning to optimize trading decisions based on historical data.

Portfolio Management

Portfolio management aims to balance the composition of asset holdings to optimize the expected returns for a given level of risk. Reinforcement learning can enhance traditional portfolio management techniques by dynamically adjusting the portfolio allocation in response to market changes.

The state in portfolio management RL models often represents the current asset holdings and various market conditions. The action space consists of redistribution of assets among different financial instruments. The reward could be based on the portfolio's return considering transaction costs and risk factors.

Pseudo-code for Hierarchical DQN Training

```
class PortfolioManagementEnv(gym.Env):
    def __init__(self, assets):
        self.assets = assets
        self.state_space = ... % include current asset ratios, market indicators
        self.action_space = ... % include possible reallocations

    def step(self, action):
        # Implement the logic to adjust portfolio based on action
        next_state = ... % derive next state based on current state and action
        reward = ... % calculate reward based on portfolio performance
        return next_state, reward, done, {}

    def reset(self):
        # Reset the environment to initial state
        return initial_state

env = PortfolioManagementEnv(assets)
agent = ... # Initialize RL agent

for episode in range(episodes):
    state = env.reset()
    for t in range(max_steps):
        action = agent.select_action(state)
        next_state, reward, done, _ = env.step(action)
        agent.learn(state, action, reward, next_state, done)
        state = next_state
        if done:
            break
```

The pseudo code outlines the structure of a reinforcement learning environment tailored for portfolio management. Here, the agent learns to allocate assets optimally in the portfolio to maximize returns while managing risk.

Risk Management

Effective risk management is critical in finance to mitigate potential losses. RL can assist in designing strategies that adapt to changes in market volatility and other risk factors. The agent is trained to minimize risks while aiming to achieve acceptable returns.

The state space in risk management includes various risk indicators such as Value at Risk (VaR) and Expected Shortfall (ES). The action space could involve adjusting asset allocations or diversifying investment strategies. The reward function incorporates both the returns and the risk measures.

By leveraging reinforcement learning, financial institutions can develop robust, adaptive, and autonomous systems. This enables them to navigate complex market dynamics effectively, enhancing their decision-making processes and strategic implementations.

10.6 Healthcare and Medicine

Reinforcement Learning (RL) has made significant strides in the field of healthcare and medicine, offering innovative solutions that enhance patient care, optimize treatment plans, and improve operational efficiencies in medical facilities. The application of RL in healthcare can be broadly categorized into personalized medicine, medical decision support systems, robotic surgery, and operational optimization of healthcare systems.

In the domain of **personalized medicine**, RL algorithms are employed to tailor treatments to individual patients based on their unique genetic makeup, medical history, and real-time health data. The primary objective is to maximize the efficacy of treatment while minimizing adverse effects. A Markov Decision Process (MDP) is often employed to model the treatment strategy where the states represent the patient's health status, actions represent the possible treatments, and rewards correspond to the outcomes of these treatments.

Consider a clinical scenario where an RL agent is tasked with determining the optimal dose of medication for a chronic condition like diabetes. At each step, the agent observes the patient's current blood glucose level, ingested food, physical activity, and previous medication dosages. The agent then decides the next dose, aiming to keep the blood glucose level within a desirable range. The algorithm receives a positive reward for maintaining appropriate glucose levels and negative rewards for hypoglycemia or hyperglycemia episodes. The environment dynamically changes with each patient observation update.

An example code snippet for setting up an RL environment for diabetes management using Python could look like:

Pseudo-code for Hierarchical DQN Training

```
import numpy as np

class DiabetesEnv:
    def __init__(self):
        self.state = np.random.uniform(70, 180) # initial blood glucose level
        self.action_space = np.arange(0, 1.1, 0.1) # possible medication dosages

    def step(self, action):
        # Simulate effect of action on blood glucose level using a simple model
        dose_effect = action * 0.5
        glucose_change = np.random.uniform(-20, 20) - dose_effect

        self.state += glucose_change
        reward = -abs(self.state - 100) # reward closer to 100 blood glucose level

        done = self.state < 40 or self.state > 400 # terminal states
        return self.state, reward, done

    def reset(self):
        self.state = np.random.uniform(70, 180)
        return self.state
```

In **medical decision support systems**, RL assists healthcare professionals in making informed diagnostic and therapeutic decisions. These systems leverage RL to provide recommendations for complex clinical scenarios where traditional rule-based systems may fall short. For instance, managing patients in intensive care units (ICUs) requires real-time decision-making based on an evolving patient condition. RL models use vast amounts of historical patient data and MDPs to predict the outcomes of potential interventions, thus aiding clinicians in selecting the actions that are likely to produce the best patient outcomes.

Robotic surgery is another area where RL has shown promise. Surgical robots can be trained using RL to execute complex surgical procedures with high precision. The RL agent learns optimal surgical strategies through a trial-and-error process, guided by performance feedback (reward signals). By simulating various tissue interactions and patient anatomies, RL enables surgical robots to develop competencies that can complement human surgeons, thereby reducing the chances of surgical errors.

Operational optimization within **healthcare systems** is critical for enhancing patient care quality and hospital efficiency. RL algorithms are employed to optimize resource allocation, staff scheduling, and patient flow management. For example, RL can be used to design algorithms that minimize patient wait times and improve the utilization of hospital resources such as beds and medical equipment. These algorithms continuously learn and adapt to changing hospital dynamics and patient needs.

Let's consider an example scenario where a hospital wants to optimize the scheduling of surgeries to reduce patient wait times and maximize operating room utilization. The state space might include the available operating rooms, the number of surgeries scheduled, and current patient wait times. Actions would involve scheduling or rescheduling surgeries based on various constraints. The reward function would penalize long wait times and idle operating rooms while rewarding efficient scheduling. A simplified environment setup for this problem is shown below:

Pseudo-code for Hierarchical DQN Training

```
class HospitalEnv:
    def __init__(self):
        self.rooms = 5
        self.surgeries = []

    def step(self, action):
        scheduled_room, scheduled_time = action
        reward = 0
        for surgery in self.surgeries:
            if surgery['room'] == scheduled_room:
                if abs(surgery['time'] - scheduled_time) < 1:
                    reward -= 1 # overlap penalty
                else:
                    reward += 1 # successful scheduling
        self.surgeries.append({'room': scheduled_room, 'time': scheduled_time})

        done = len(self.surgeries) >= self.rooms
        return len(self.surgeries), reward, done

    def reset(self):
        self.surgeries = []
        return len(self.surgeries)
```

Through these applications, RL not only advances the field of medicine but also highlights its potential to be a transformative technology in healthcare. The ability to learn from data, adapt to new information, and make decisions that optimize patient outcomes ensures that RL will continue to play a vital role in the evolution of healthcare practices and technologies.

10.7 Autonomous Vehicles

The application of Reinforcement Learning (RL) in autonomous vehicles represents a pinnacle of both artificial intelligence and modern engineering. In this section, we explore how RL algorithms have been integrated into the decision-making systems that control autonomous vehicles, facilitating tasks such as navigation, speed control, and obstacle avoidance. The objective of RL in the context of autonomous driving is to enable a vehicle to learn an effective control policy that maximizes safety, efficiency, and comfort.

The core problem in autonomous driving can be formulated as a sequential decision-making problem, where the agent (the vehicle) must make a series of decisions over time in an uncertain environment. The vehicle receives observations from its sensors, makes decisions based on these observations, and executes corresponding actions that affect its subsequent states.

A notable RL algorithm used in autonomous vehicles is the Deep Q-Network (DQN). The DQN algorithm leverages a neural network to approximate the Q-values for each state-action pair, addressing the high-dimensional state space inherent in autonomous driving. The architecture of a DQN for autonomous vehicles typically consists of several convolutional layers followed by fully connected layers, which process input data from various sensors such as cameras, LiDAR, and radar.

Consider the following pseudocode for training a Deep Q-Network in an autonomous driving scenario:

Pseudo-code for Hierarchical DQN Training

```
Initialize replay memory D
Initialize Q-network with random weights
Initialize target Q-network with same weights as Q-network

for episode in range(num_episodes):
    Initialize state s
    for t in range(max_steps):
        With probability  select a random action a
        Otherwise select a = argmax_a' Q(s, a')
        Execute action a and observe reward r and next state s'
        Store transition (s, a, r, s') in replay memory D
        Sample random minibatch of transitions (s_j, a_j, r_j, s'_j) from D
        Set target Q-value:
            y_j = r_j +  max_a' Q_target(s'_j, a')
        Perform a gradient descent step on (y_j - Q(s_j, a_j))^2 with respect to the
            network parameters
        Every C steps update Q_target to Q_network
        s = s'
        if done:
            break
```

In this training loop, the DQN agent explores the environment using an ε-greedy policy. The agent's actions are occasionally selected at random with probability ε to maintain exploration. Otherwise, the agent exploits its learned policy to select actions that maximize the Q-value. The agent then stores the observed transition in a replay memory and uses samples from this memory to update the Q-network. The concept of a target network helps to stabilize the training by providing fixed Q-values for the duration of several updates.

Aside from DQN, Policy Gradient methods such as Proximal Policy Optimization (PPO) and Trust Region Policy Optimization (TRPO) are also popular in the domain of autonomous vehicles. These methods directly optimize the policy that dictates the agent's actions, rather than relying on Q-value approximations. Policy Gradient methods have the advantage of better handling continuous action spaces, which are crucial in autonomous driving for smooth steering and acceleration control.

Consider the implementation of Proximal Policy Optimization (PPO) for an autonomous vehicle:

Pseudo-code for Hierarchical DQN Training

```
Initialize policy network  and value network V
for iteration in range(num_iterations):
    for actor in range(num_actors):
        Run policy  in environment for T timesteps
        Compute advantage estimates A1, ..., AT
    Optimize surrogate L using collected data
        Sample minibatch of states, actions, advantages
        Compute surrogate loss:
            L = E[min(r (), clip(r (), 1-, 1+)) * A]
        Perform a gradient descent step on L with respect to
    Optimize value function V using collected data
        Sample minibatch of states, returns
        Perform a gradient descent step on ( V(s) - return)^2 with respect to
```

PPO improves upon standard Policy Gradient methods by ensuring that the updated policy does not deviate too far from the old policy, thereby maintaining stable learning. The advantage estimates are computed to weigh the beneficial actions more heavily during optimization. The clip operation in the surrogate loss function restricts the policy update, preventing large policy changes that could destabilize the learning process.

State-of-the-art autonomous vehicles often employ a combination of RL with other machine learning techniques, such as supervised learning for perception tasks and unsupervised learning for sensor fusion. A multi-module system can include an RL-based decision module that interfaces with these perception and control modules. For instance, a vision module may use convolutional neural networks (CNNs) to detect objects and classify road scenes, while the RL module decides on the vehicle's speed and trajectory based on these high-level observations.

Through continuous advancements and integrations, RL continues to enhance the capabilities of autonomous vehicles, making strides towards fully autonomous transportation systems that promise enhanced safety and efficiency on roads.

10.8 Energy Management

The application of Reinforcement Learning (RL) techniques in the field of energy management constitutes a significant advancement in optimizing energy consumption and distribution. This section explores the utilization of RL to address key challenges within various energy systems, such as power grids, smart grids, and renewable energy sources.

Effective energy management is critical for reducing operational costs, increasing system reliability, and minimizing environmental impacts. Traditional approaches often rely on static optimization methods, which can fall short in dynamic and uncertain environments. RL, in contrast, provides a robust framework capable of learning from and adapting to evolving systems and conditions.

Power Grid Management The integration of renewable energy sources into power grids introduces a degree of variability and unpredictability. Managing the balance between energy supply and demand, especially with intermittent renewable energy sources like solar and wind, requires advanced control strategies. RL offers a promising solution through its ability to learn and optimize control policies over time.

Consider the problem of frequency regulation in a power grid, where the aim is to maintain the grid frequency within a specified range. The RL approach involves creating an environment that simulates the power grid dynamics and then training an agent to take actions that stabilize the frequency. The following pseudo-code illustrates the structure of an RL algorithm for frequency regulation:

Pseudo-code for Hierarchical DQN Training

```
class FrequencyRegulationEnv:
```

```
    def __init__(self):
        self.state = self.initialize_state()
        self.action_space = ActionSpace()
        self.observation_space = ObservationSpace()

    def step(self, action):
        self.apply_action(action)
        next_state = self.observe_state()
        reward = self.calculate_reward(next_state)
        done = self.is_done(next_state)
        return next_state, reward, done, {}

    def reset(self):
        self.state = self.initialize_state()
        return self.state

agent = RLAgent(env=FrequencyRegulationEnv())
agent.train(episodes=1000)
```

In this simulation, the FrequencyRegulationEnv class models the environment, while the RLAgent class represents the learning agent. The step function reflects the agent's interaction with the environment by returning the next state, reward received, and whether the episode is complete. The agent iterates over numerous training episodes to refine its policy and improve the frequency regulation.

Demand Response Demand response (DR) programs aim to adjust consumer power usage during peak demand periods, thereby maintaining grid stability and efficiency. RL techniques can optimize DR strategies by predicting peak periods and scheduling appropriate load adjustments. RL agents learn optimal policies that result in cost savings for both utility providers and consumers. Key to this approach is the creation of a reward function that captures objectives such as cost reduction, user comfort, and energy efficiency.

Pseudo-code for Hierarchical DQN Training

```
class DemandResponseEnv:
    def __init__(self):
        self.state = self.initialize_state()
        self.action_space = DiscreteActionSpace()
        self.observation_space = ContinuousObservationSpace()

    def step(self, action):
        self.apply_action(action)
        next_state = self.get_next_state()
        reward = self.calculate_reward(next_state)
        done = self.is_terminal_state(next_state)
        return next_state, reward, done, {}

    def reset(self):
        self.state = self.initialize_state()
        return self.state

agent = DQNAgent(env=DemandResponseEnv())
```

```
agent.train(episodes=5000)
```

In this pseudo-code, the DemandResponseEnv class encapsulates the demand response environment. The agent employs a Deep Q-Network (DQN) to learn policies from interactions within this environment. Over multiple training episodes, the agent optimizes the actions to achieve the desired load adjustments.

Energy Storage Systems RL can also optimize the operation of energy storage systems (ESS), such as batteries, to buffer fluctuations in energy supply and demand. The goal is to determine optimal charge and discharge strategies that maximize battery lifespan, minimize costs, and enhance grid stability.

The environment model for an energy storage system must consider the physical characteristics of the storage device and the dynamics of the energy market. The RL agent learns to make decisions about charging and discharging based on factors like current electricity prices, state of charge, and predicted demand.

Pseudo-code for Hierarchical DQN Training

```
class EnergyStorageEnv:
    def __init__(self, max_charge):
        self.state = self.initialize_state()
        self.max_charge = max_charge
        self.action_space = ContinuousActionSpace()
        self.observation_space = ContinuousObservationSpace()

    def step(self, action):
        self.apply_charge(action)
        next_state = self.update_state()
        reward = self.calculate_reward(next_state)
        done = self.is_end_of_day()
        return next_state, reward, done, {}

    def reset(self):
        self.state = self.initialize_state()
        return self.state

agent = PPOAgent(env=EnergyStorageEnv(max_charge=100))
agent.train(episodes=2000)
```

Here, the EnergyStorageEnv class represents the dynamics of the energy storage system, and a Proximal Policy Optimization (PPO) agent is employed to determine the best actions. The training process aims to maximize the cumulative reward by learning efficient charge and discharge policies.

Smart Grid Optimization Smart grids leverage advanced metering infrastructure to collect and analyze data from distributed energy resources and consumer loads. RL algorithms can optimize smart grid operations, enhancing demand forecasting, outage management, and energy distribution efficiency. Agents in smart grid environments apply learning techniques to predict load patterns, plan energy distribution, and ensure grid resilience.

Pseudo-code for Hierarchical DQN Training

```
class SmartGridEnv:
    def __init__(self):
        self.state = self.initialize_state()
        self.action_space = MultiDiscreteActionSpace()
        self.observation_space = MultiDimensionalObservationSpace()

    def step(self, action):
        self.execute_action(action)
        next_state = self.fetch_state()
        reward = self.evaluate_reward(next_state)
        done = self.check_completion(next_state)
        return next_state, reward, done, {}

    def reset(self):
        self.state = self.initialize_state()
        return self.state

agent = A3CAgent(env=SmartGridEnv())
agent.train(episodes=3000)
```

The SmartGridEnv class models the smart grid environment, incorporating multi-discrete action and observation spaces to reflect the complexity of smart grid operations. An Asynchronous Advantage Actor-Critic (A3C) agent is trained within this environment to optimize various parameters, such as energy supply allocation, demand response, and grid stability measures.

The deployment of RL in energy management systems showcases its potential to revolutionize the way energy is distributed, consumed, and stored. This integration not only improves efficiency but also paves the way for sustainable and resilient energy systems capable of adapting to future challenges.

10.9 Natural Language Processing and Dialog Systems

Natural Language Processing (NLP) and dialog systems form a crucial area of artificial intelligence where reinforcement learning (RL) has made substantial progress. Applications in NLP include tasks such as machine translation, sentiment analysis, text summarization, and dialog management. Specifically, dialog systems (commonly referred to as chatbots) leverage RL to enhance user interactions by learning optimal conversation strategies.

Reinforcement learning has been increasingly employed in NLP due to its ability to handle sequential decision-making processes. Traditional supervised learning approaches often fall short in tasks requiring long-term planning and dynamic adaptation, where RL's strength lies.

- **Dialog Systems**

  Dialog systems aim to converse with human users in a natural and coherent manner. These systems can be categorized into task-oriented and non-task-oriented (or chatbots). Task-oriented dialog systems focus on achieving specific goals, such as booking a flight or making a restaurant reservation. Non-task-oriented systems engage users in open-domain conversations.

  One of the primary challenges in dialog systems is maintaining a coherent and contextually relevant conversation over multiple turns. This is where reinforcement learning provides a distinct advantage. By treating dialog management as a Markov Decision Process (MDP), RL agents can learn to select actions (i.e., responses) that maximize cumulative rewards, often corresponding to user satisfaction or task completion rates.

- **Markov Decision Process for Dialog Management**

  In the context of dialog systems, the MDP components can be defined as follows:

  - **State (s):** The state represents the current context of the conversation, including the history of previous turns and any extracted user intentions or slots.
  - **Action (a):** Actions are potential responses the system can generate, including predefined responses, queries for clarification, or progression in the task.
  - **Reward (r):** The reward reflects the quality of the system's response, which could be user feedback, task success, or predefined success metrics.
  - **Policy (π):** The policy maps the state to an action, guiding the dialog system in generating context-appropriate responses.

Reinforcement learning algorithms such as Q-learning and policy gradients are pivotal in training dialog systems. These algorithms involve iteratively improving the policy based on received rewards, thus enhancing dialog quality over time.

- **Example: Training a Task-Oriented Dialog System**

  Consider a task-oriented dialog system designed to assist users in booking hotels. The RL agent needs to manage the conversation to gather necessary information (e.g., dates, location preferences) and provide relevant recommendations.

Pseudo-code for Hierarchical DQN Training

```
import numpy as np

class DialogEnv:
    def __init__(self):
        self.state = self.reset()

    def reset(self):
        self.state = {'conversation_history': [],
                      'slots_filled': {},
                      'current_turn': 0}
        return self.state

    def step(self, action):
        # Simulate user response based on the action taken
        user_response, done = self.user_simulator(action)
        reward = self.compute_reward(user_response, done)

        self.state['conversation_history'].append(action)
        self.state['conversation_history'].append(user_response)
        self.state['current_turn'] += 1

        return self.state, reward, done

    def user_simulator(self, action):
        # Dummy simulator logic for demonstration
        # In practice, this simulates user interactions
        user_response = "User response here"
        done = False # Or True if the conversation ends
        return user_response, done

    def compute_reward(self, user_response, done):
        # Compute reward logic based on the goal completion
        if done:
            reward = 1.0 # Assume a positive reward for task success
        else:
            reward = -0.1 # Negative reward for each turn to encourage
                efficiency
        return reward

env = DialogEnv()
state = env.reset()

for _ in range(100):
    action = np.random.choice(['ask_location', 'ask_dates', '
        give_recommendation'])
```

```
    next_state, reward, done = env.step(action)
    if done:
        state = env.reset()
```

Implementing the above simulation allows the dialog agent to learn how different actions impact the conversation outcome and user satisfaction. By continually improving its policy, the system can develop effective strategies that maximize the probability of successful task completion.

- **Deep Reinforcement Learning for NLP**

  Deep reinforcement learning (DRL) integrates neural networks with RL to handle the complexity of large state and action spaces commonly found in NLP tasks. For instance, in dialog systems, DRL can manage more nuanced language understanding and generation, enabling more sophisticated conversational agents.

  Methods such as Deep Q-Networks (DQN) and actor-critic models are applied to extend traditional RL approaches. In DQN, the Q-value function approximates using a neural network, allowing the dialog agent to estimate the long-term value of actions in high-dimensional state spaces.

Pseudo-code for Hierarchical DQN Training

```
import torch
import torch.nn as nn
import torch.optim as optim

class DQN(nn.Module):
    def __init__(self, state_size, action_size):
        super(DQN, self).__init__()
        self.fc1 = nn.Linear(state_size, 128)
        self.fc2 = nn.Linear(128, 128)
        self.fc3 = nn.Linear(128, action_size)

    def forward(self, x):
        x = torch.relu(self.fc1(x))
        x = torch.relu(self.fc2(x))
        x = self.fc3(x)
        return x

model = DQN(state_size=100, action_size=10)
criterion = nn.MSELoss()
optimizer = optim.Adam(model.parameters())

# Example training loop
for epoch in range(10):
    state = env.reset()
    state_tensor = torch.tensor(state, dtype=torch.float32)

    prediction = model(state_tensor)
    target = torch.tensor([1.0]) # Dummy target for illustration
```

```
loss = criterion(prediction, target)
optimizer.zero_grad()
loss.backward()
optimizer.step()
```

Deep reinforcement learning thus bridges the gap between sophisticated language models and the decision-making capabilities needed for effective dialog systems. As NLP moves towards more complex and interactive applications, the role of RL continues to grow, propelling innovations in conversational agents and beyond.

10.10 Industrial Automation

Reinforcement Learning (RL) has substantial implications in industrial automation owing to its capability to solve complex decision-making problems and its adaptability to dynamic and uncertain environments. Industrial automation involves deploying advanced control systems, such as computers or robots, and information technologies to manage different processes and machineries in an industry, replacing manual operations. RL algorithms optimize these control systems by learning from the environment, incrementally improving the performance of the automated systems.

Traditionally, industrial automation relied heavily on predefined rules and control logic, which required extensive domain expertise. RL, however, can learn optimal control policies through interaction with the environment, reducing this dependency. Consider a manufacturing plant aiming to minimize energy consumption while maximizing production efficiency. Here, RL can be employed to learn the optimal control strategy by balancing these objectives through continuous interaction and feedback.

One application of RL in industrial automation is predictive maintenance. Maintenance of industrial equipment is crucial for ensuring smooth operations and avoiding downtime. Conventional strategies like scheduled maintenance or reactive maintenance either incur unnecessary costs or lead to unplanned failures. Predictive maintenance, driven by RL, enables systems to predict and identify issues before they occur. This is accomplished by analyzing real-time data from sensors, learning patterns indicative of potential failures, and making decisions to perform maintenance only when necessary.

Pseudo-code for Hierarchical DQN Training

```
import numpy as np
import gym
from stable_baselines3 import PPO

# Custom predictive maintenance environment
class MaintenanceEnv(gym.Env):
    def __init__(self, failure_threshold=0.9):
        super(MaintenanceEnv, self).__init__()
        self.failure_threshold = failure_threshold
        self.counter = 0
        self.max_steps = 100

        # Define action and observation space
        self.action_space = gym.spaces.Discrete(2) # 0: No Maintenance, 1:
            Maintenance
        self.observation_space = gym.spaces.Box(low=0, high=1, shape=(1,), dtype=np.
            float32)

    def reset(self):
        self.counter = 0
        self.state = np.random.rand()
        return self.state

    def step(self, action):
        self.counter += 1
        maintenance_done = 1 if action == 1 else 0
        reward = -maintenance_done

        # Simulate wear and tear
        self.state += np.random.uniform(0, 0.1)
        if self.state > self.failure_threshold:
            reward -= 10 # Penalty for failure
            done = True
        elif self.counter >= self.max_steps:
            done = True
        else:
            done = False

        return self.state, reward, done, {}

env = MaintenanceEnv()
model = PPO('MlpPolicy', env, verbose=1)
model.learn(total_timesteps=10000)
```

Execution of the above script would result in a trained RL model capable of making maintenance decisions based on the condition of the equipment.

```
Creating environment
Using cpu device
Wrapping the env with a DummyVecEnv.
---------------------------------
| rollout/           |          |
|    ep_len_mean     | 100      |
|    ep_rew_mean     | -10      |
| time/              |          |
|    fps             | 1185     |
|    iterations      | 1        |
---------------------------------
Training finished
```

Another critical application area for RL in industrial automation is process optimization. For example, consider a chemical manufacturing process where multiple parameters such as temperature, pressure, and chemical concentrations need to be controlled. RL can be utilized to find the optimal setpoints for these parameters to maximize yield while minimizing energy consumption and waste production. This is particularly useful in industries where processes are highly nonlinear and traditional optimization techniques fall short.

Assembly line optimization is another domain where RL demonstrates significant benefits. In complex assembly lines, different tasks need to be scheduled and allocated efficiently to robots or workstations. RL enables dynamic and adaptive scheduling by learning from historical data and current state information, consequently increasing throughput and reducing idle times.

Furthermore, warehouse management can be significantly improved with RL. Tasks such as inventory management, order picking, and path optimization for automated guided vehicles (AGVs) can be optimized through RL algorithms, resulting in increased efficiency and reduced operational costs. For instance, RL-based path planning algorithms can dynamically re-route AGVs in response to changing warehouse layouts and traffic conditions, enhancing the responsiveness and flexibility of warehouse operations.

By implementing RL techniques, the industrial sector can achieve an optimal balance between cost, efficiency, and productivity. The combination of RL with industrial IoT (Internet of Things) and advanced sensors presents a formidable approach to automating complex industrial processes and making intelligent decisions based on real-time data. RL not only offers promising solutions to existing automation challenges but also opens new avenues for innovation in industrial operations.

10.11 Future Trends and Innovations in RL Applications

As Reinforcement Learning (RL) continues to mature, several trends and innovations promise to shape its evolution and impact across numerous fields. Understanding these future directions is crucial for researchers and practitioners aiming to leverage RL for cutting-edge solutions. This section delves into emerging trends and state-of-the-art developments within RL, focusing on their potential applications and implications.

1. Offline Reinforcement Learning

Offline Reinforcement Learning aims to train agents using previously collected data without continuous interaction with the environment. This approach is particularly beneficial in domains where real-time data collection is costly, risky, or impractical, such as healthcare, robotics, and autonomous driving. Offline RL leverages existing extensive datasets to learn optimal policies, reducing the need for extensive simulation or physical trials. The key challenge lies in addressing the distributional shift between the training data and the environment where the policy will be deployed. Recent advances use techniques such as conservative Q-learning (CQL) and behavior-regularized actor-critic (BRAC) to mitigate these issues.

Pseudo-code for Hierarchical DQN Training

```
# Example of Conservative Q-Learning Pseudocode
Initialize Q-values: Q(s, a)
for each episode do:
  Observe state s and select action a based on Q(s, a)
  Receive reward r and next state s'
  Update Q-values ensuring conservative estimates
  Q(s, a) <- Q(s, a) + learning_rate * (reward + max(Q(s', a')) - Q(s, a))
```

2. Multi-Agent Reinforcement Learning (MARL)

Multi-Agent Reinforcement Learning involves training multiple agents that interact within a shared environment. This paradigm is vital for applications such as autonomous vehicle fleets, smart grids, and collaborative robots. MARL requires addressing complexities like coordination, communication, and competition among agents. Techniques such as Coordinated Q-learning and Multi-Agent Deep Deterministic Policy Gradient (MADDPG) facilitate effective learning in multi-agent settings. MARL is expected to lead to significant advancements in scenarios requiring complex decision-making and strategic interactions.

Pseudo-code for Hierarchical DQN Training

```
# Coordinated Q-learning Framework
Initialize Q-values for each agent: Q_i(s, a)
for each agent i and episode do:
  Observe state s and select action a_i based on Q_i(s, a_i)
  Agents execute actions simultaneously
  Receive reward r_i and next state s'
  Update Q-values for agent i based on joint action
  Q_i(s, a_i) <- Q_i(s, a_i) + learning_rate * (r_i + max(Q_i(s', a_i')) - Q_i(s, a_i
       ))
```

3. Meta-Reinforcement Learning

Meta-Reinforcement Learning (Meta-RL) focuses on creating agents capable of adapting to new tasks rapidly with minimal data. It addresses the issue of transferring learning from one context to another, thereby improving generalization. Meta-RL techniques often involve learning a meta-policy that guides task-specific policies. Model-Agnostic Meta-Learning (MAML) is a prominent Meta-RL algorithm that optimizes for parameters which can be fine-tuned quickly for new tasks. This capability is pivotal for developing versatile RL systems in domains such as personalized healthcare, adaptive robotics, and dynamic financial trading.

Pseudo-code for Hierarchical DQN Training

```
# Pseudocode for Model-Agnostic Meta-Learning
Initialize meta-parameters:
for each task Ti do:
  Sample K datapoints D_i = {(s_ij, a_ij, r_ij, s'_ij)}^K_j=1
  Compute adapted parameters:  _i = - *  L(T_i, )
  Compute meta-gradient using adapted parameters
   <- - *  Σi L(T_i, _i)
```

4. Reinforcement Learning with Human-in-the-Loop

Integrating human feedback into RL systems allows for more efficient and safer learning processes, particularly in complex or high-stakes environments. Human-in-the-loop RL leverages preferences, demonstrations, and corrections provided by human experts to accelerate and refine the learning process. This approach is especially relevant in fields where human expertise is invaluable, such as medical decision-making, industrial robotics, and personalized tutoring systems. Methods such as inverse reinforcement learning (IRL) and preference-based RL exemplify this integration.

Pseudo-code for Hierarchical DQN Training

```
# Inverse Reinforcement Learning Process
Collect demonstrations from expert: D_expert = {(s_t, a_t)}^T_t=1
Initialize reward function parameters:
```

```
for each iteration do:
  Infer reward function R(s, a, ) using D_expert
  Generate policy  using inferred reward function
  Compare policy  with expert demonstrations
  Update  to minimize divergence between  and expert behavior
```

5. Safe Reinforcement Learning

As RL systems are increasingly deployed in real-world applications, ensuring their safety becomes paramount. Safe Reinforcement Learning (Safe RL) aims to design algorithms that consistently operate within predefined safety constraints to prevent harmful actions. This is particularly crucial in applications such as autonomous vehicles, robotic surgery, and financial trading systems. Techniques like Constrained Markov Decision Processes (CMDPs) and Reward Shaping are employed to incorporate safety considerations into the learning process.

Pseudo-code for Hierarchical DQN Training

```
# Safe Reinforcement Learning Example using CMDP
Initialize policy  and safety threshold C
for each episode do:
  While not reaching terminal state:
    Select action a based on policy
    Observe reward r and safety cost c
    Update policy  to maximize expected reward
    Ensure expected cumulative cost <= C
     <- + learning_rate * (r -  (s, a)) / (1 + c)
```

6. Quantum Reinforcement Learning

Quantum Reinforcement Learning represents a nascent but promising frontier, leveraging principles of quantum computation to enhance RL algorithms. Quantum computers can process vast amounts of data simultaneously, offering potential speedups for training RL models. Research in this area explores quantum versions of classical RL algorithms, such as Quantum Q-Learning. Though experimental, Quantum RL could revolutionize fields requiring substantial computational power, including large-scale simulations and complex optimization problems.

Pseudo-code for Hierarchical DQN Training

```
# Pseudocode for Quantum Q-Learning
Initialize quantum state & Q-function: |Q>
for each episode do:
  Observe state s and select action a using quantum measurement
  Receive reward r and next state s'
  Update Q-function using quantum state |Q>
  |Q(s, a)> <- r + max(|Q(s', a')>)
  Normalize quantum state: |Q> <- |Q> / |||Q>||
```

7. Integration with Other Learning Paradigms

The future of RL will likely see increased integration with other machine learning paradigms, such as supervised learning, unsupervised learning, and self-supervised learning. This hybrid approach leverages the strengths of different learning methods to enhance the overall performance and robustness of RL systems. For instance, combining RL with unsupervised learning can facilitate the automatic discovery of useful features, while supervised learning can provide valuable guidance through labeled training data. Such integrations will drive advancements in applications spanning natural language processing, computer vision, and predictive maintenance.

Pseudo-code for Hierarchical DQN Training

```
# Example of Hybrid RL and Supervised Learning Workflow
Initialize RL agent with supervised learning model
for each iteration do:
  Train supervised model on labeled data D_lab
  Use supervised model to predict optimal actions
  Train RL agent using predictions and environmental interactions
  Update supervised model with new data from RL agent
```

The trajectory of Reinforcement Learning is poised towards reshaping technological landscapes and societal frameworks, driven by the aforementioned advancements. This evolving frontier heralds significant potential for more intelligent, adaptable, and efficient systems, promising a profound impact across diverse sectors.

Made in the USA
Monee, IL
05 November 2026

67814343R00177